The Correctional Officer

A Practical Guide

Gary F. Cornelius

Carolina Academic Press
Durham, North Carolina

Copyright © 2001
Gary F. Cornelius
All rights reserved.

ISBN 0-89089-700-X
LCCN 99-068952

Carolina Academic Press
700 Kent Street
Durham, North Carolina 27701
Telephone: (919) 489-7486
Fax: (919) 493-5668
email: cap@cap-press.com
www.cap-press.com

Printed in the United States of America.

This book is for the correctional workers—the men and women who put their lives on the line everyday to work in our nation's correctional facilities—and by doing a good job, you keep all of us safe. May this book be a valuable tool in your endeavors.

A special dedication is for my wife, Nancy, and my children— Gary Jr., and Amber Beth. Once again, thanks for putting up with me and showing me your love and support.

Contents

Acknowledgments

The following people were helpful in the preparation of this book. The author wishes to thank:

Clarke-Frederick-Winchester Regional Adult Detention Center: Superintendent Fred Hildebrand, Lt. Patty Barr, and staff.

Alexandria (Va.) Office of the Sheriff

Manatee County Sheriff's Office, Charles B. Wells, Sheriff, special thanks to Lt. Jim Conway

Maryland House of Correction: Lt. Martin Ice

Albany County Correctional Facility: Ed Szostak, Superintendent

The following organizations were gracious enough to permit excerpts from their works:

The American Correctional Association: Gabriella Daley and Alice Fins

The American Jail Association: Steve Ingley and Ken Kerle

Photo Credits

Maryland Department of Corrections: pp. 22, 29, 128, 133, 145, 146, 149, 188, 216. Photos courtesy of Lt. Martin Ice.

Clarke-Frederick-Winchester Regional Adult Detention Center: pp. 25, 26, 27, 34, 86, 96, 99, 115, 129, 131, 134, 143, 178, 193, 197. Photos taken by author.

Manatee County (Florida) Sheriff's Office: pp. 31, 62, 65, 67, 194, 195, 206, 212, 214. Photos courtesy of Lt. Jim Conway.

Albany County (New York) Correctional Facility: pp. 144, 147, 190, 192. Photos by Al Roland, Senior Identification Officer. Courtesy of Ed Szostak, Superintendent.

Introduction

Correctional officer...When most people hear the words, they think of a person or jail guard—patrolling the cellblocks, hallways, and walls of our nation's correctional institutions.

The job of today's correctional officer is a demanding one. The days of an officer simply being a "watchdog" or custodian of inmates are long gone. Also, the philosophy of merely warehousing inmates in overcrowded institutions has changed. Revolutionary techniques such as direct supervision, home detention and alternative sanctions are being used.

Recent public opinion has resulted in mandatory sentencing, "three strikes and you're out," and the abolition of parole in many states. These changes, plus research that indicates that inmates now are more violent than in the past, have made an impact on the job of a correctional officer. Today's officers need all the knowledge and job skills possible in order to perform effectively *and* safely.

This book, while concise, will present relevant "hands on" information that officers can use in order to provide security for the correctional institution and to safely deal with inmates.

The book's target audience is the men and women who work daily in our nation's jails, prisons, and community corrections facilities. This book is designed as a training aid for entry level and in-service training with the following goals:

- to be a training resource for agency training and staff instructors;
- to assist in recruit and in-service training;
- to provide insight into the history, philosophy, and evolution of past and present correctional systems;
- to be an instructional guide to correctional officer job skills;
- to provide information to the officer concerning the social/economical/educational characteristics of inmates;
- to give information to the officer on positive traits and characteristics needed to maintain a successful career in corrections; and
- to give insight into the future of corrections and the necessary skills which will be needed.

Chapter 1

Overview of Present Day Corrections in the U.S.

Most people in the public sector, when they hear the term *corrections,* think of a large walled prison or county jail with bars, guards, and keys. In reality, corrections includes all government agencies (such as police, judiciary, treatment programs, probation and parole, etc.), facilities (such as prisons, jails, community corrections centers, juvenile detention facilities), programs, procedures, personnel, and techniques involving the investigation, intake, custody, confinement, supervision, or treatment of adult offenders [or inmates], delinquent juveniles, or status offenders. [Allen & Simonsen, 1995]

In examining this definition more closely, corrections involves simply dealing with criminals after arrest by the police and while being adjudicated by the judicial system. Dealing with these criminals—called inmates after incarceration—means keeping them confined in order to protect the correctional staff, the public, and the inmates themselves from harm or escape.

The term *correctional staff* means all of the workers in a correctional facility: the officers who are responsible for security and confinement, the medical officers who tend to inmate health problems, the counselors who classify inmates into housing areas, etc. These staff roles will be discussed in detail later.

One of corrections' main goals, which involves the staff described above, is to answer these two questions. [Allen & Simonsen, 1995]:

- Who are the offenders or inmates?
- What should we [the correctional system] do with them?

According to Allen & Simonsen in their work *Corrections in America, 7th Edition,* the current state of corrections is based on three correctional ideologies. They define the term *correctional ideology* as a "body of ideas and practices that pertain to the treatment of offenders." [Allen & Simonsen, 1995]

By understanding these three philosophies, correctional officers will better understand the various purposes of different correctional institutions and programs. Also, belief and commitment to these philosophies

3

have resulted in various levels of funding for different types of programs and the construction of correctional facilities.

The correctional ideologies are:

1. The Punishment Ideology

This philosophy holds that the offender or criminal is an enemy of society. This adversarial approach further states that these lawbreakers deserve severe punishment, which includes banishment, death, or incarceration for long periods of time, or forever, such as in the case of life without parole.

The punishment philosophy has its roots in early society where vengeance and retaliation was an underlying theme in early punishments and prisons (*see* Chapter 4). According to researcher Heinrich Oppenheimer, retaliation fulfills a religious mission to punish the criminal. He also says that punishment re-establishes a sense of harmony as well as the washing away of guilt through suffering. [Allen & Simonsen, 1995]

In a similar view, Ledger Wood advocates that punishment can achieve social benefits by applying a specific form and degree of punishment to a particular type of offender who has been carefully studied. The punishment is deemed to be the most appropriate. [Allen & Simonsen, 1995]

An example of this in recent years is the repeat offender—the career criminal. Many states now have adopted "three strikes and you're out" laws—which place the third-time felon in prison for life with no chance of parole.

The punishment ideology, as pleasing to some and conservative, has several "root" cores. They are:

Retribution: In other words, society should get even with the criminal; he or she should get his or her "just desserts." Some advocates of the death penalty use retribution in their rationale. Opponents believe that offenders should not suffer merely for the sake of suffering. The concept of retribution has fostered ideas such as public executions and electroshock instead of imprisonment.

For example, a recent *Time Magazine* poll found that 74% of Americans favor the death penalty for offenders convicted of serious crimes while only 20% oppose it. [Pooley, *Time*, 6/16/97]

When Michael Fay, an American, was due to be punished by caning (lashes on the buttocks), a $2,220.00 fine and four months imprisonment for vandalism in Singapore, a *Newsweek* poll found that 38% of Americans *approved* the caning, 52% did not. [Elliott, *Newsweek*, 4/18/94]

A Virginia newspaper columnist advocated in 1994 that pedophiles should be locked up together and be allowed to molest each other. [Lynch, *Fairfax Journal*, 9/19/94]

Deterrence: Punishment advocates believe that punishment can have a deterrent effect on criminal behavior—either on the specific offender or generally on a group of offenders who are thinking about committing crimes. In order for crime to be deterred by punishment, the punishment (sentence) must be swift and visible to people in the community. It also must be very closely linked to the crime so potential offenders can relate the offense to the punishment. Finally, once the offender has served his sentence, he must be allowed to return to his prior place in society without the label or "stigma" of being an "ex-con"—once the sentence is served, it's done.

Views on whether severe punishment deters crime are split. For example, a 1997 *Time Magazine* poll found that 45% of Americans believe capital punishment deters crime; 52% do not. [Pooley, *Time*, 6/16/97]

Not all issues of deterrence involve serious crimes, such as murder. In 1995, the Transportation Safety Board recommended touch crackdowns on repeat drunk drivers. These crackdowns included certain license revocations and confiscating vehicles. [Phillips, *Washington Post*, 3/11/95]

In 1994, Virginia eliminated parole and lengthened sentences. Offenders convicted of murder, robbery and burglary under this plan do 125% to 500% more prison time. [Cauchon, *USA Today*, 9/30/94]

Incapacitation: Advocates of the punishment ideology feel that in certain cases, there is no real hope for rehabilitation and the best solution is to temporarily or permanently remove the offender from society, thus hindering and crippling their criminal activities. Allen & Simonsen (1995) refer to this criminal isolation theory as the theory of disablement—using the death penalty, long sentences, or mutilation (in some countries) as ways to keep the criminal out of circulation. A recent trend among supporters of this ideology is the "selective incapacitation" view. Researchers such as Miller and Greenwood advocate putting only violent and repeat offenders in prison.

The best example of society incapacitating criminals are the "three strikes and you're out" laws which target repeat offenders and "truth in sentencing." The *three strikes* laws aim to increase prison sentences or penalties for a second offense and mandate life without parole for a third offense. "Three strikes" is very popular among the public and is supposedly geared to take violent criminals off the streets.

In some cases, offenders have faced 25 years to life for third offenses which seem trivial when compared to other more violent crimes. For example, an unemployed offender with two "strikes" (crimes involving small amounts of money and heroin addiction) got a third "strike" for stealing chuck steaks when his mother's Social Security check failed to arrive. The value of the meat? $5.62. [Donziger, Ed., 1996]

California passed one of the strictest "three strikes" laws. Studies have shown that many offenders sentenced under "three strikes" are not the targeted violent offenders. In 1994, 70% of all filed second and third strike cases in California were termed "non-violent or non-serious offenders. (*Report of the National Criminal Justice Commission*, 1996).

The cost of "three strikes" is prohibitive. A study by the Rand Corporation found that the new "three strikes" laws will cost *$4.5 and $6.5 billion annually* to operate due to keeping inmates locked up longer. [Donziger, Ed., 1996; Greenwood, *et al.*]

Truth in sentencing requires an inmate to serve his or her entire sentence without the early release of parole. Like three strikes, this approach is pleasing to the public, but expensive.

2. The Treatment Ideology

With this view, the offender is viewed as one whose criminal behavior is viewed as somewhat "sick." (Allen & Simonsen, 1995) Having a treatment view of the inmate does not mean that his or her criminal behavior is due to some medical illness; it means that the criminals must realize their criminal behavior and take concrete steps to deal with it and improve their lives. For example, a person having a drinking problem that has resulted in a driving while intoxicated arrest or an assault on his wife, in jail, he may be referred to an alcohol treatment program.

Fox and Stinchcombe in 1994 defined treatment in correctional institutions as involving "all of the programs and services that bring socializing influences to bear on the inmate." Programs such as Alcoholics Anonymous (AA), Narcotics Anonymous (NA), Adult Education, religious programs, and job training programs are operating in our jails and prisons, employing counselors and teachers, plus utilizing the energies of thousands of volunteers.

The treatment ideology has four doctrines:

(1) *The Quaker Doctrine*: Religion influences this doctrine, offenders are urged to put religion into their lives.

(2) *The Educational Doctrine* supports the usage of educational, vocational, and occupational skills programs in order to give the inmate basic skills to survive *legally* on the outside.

(3) *The Medical Model* holds that the individual offender has problems that must be diagnosed. A treatment plan must be devised and implemented.

(4) *Reintegration* means that in order for the offender to effectively deal with problems, resources in the community must be utilized such as self-help groups (AA or NA), adult education programs, etc.

[Allen & Simonsen, 1995]

All four of these doctrines can be found in our nation's correctional facilities.

Many jails and prisons have chaplains with inmates who need spiritual guidance, as well as performing religious services. The Good News Jail and Prison Ministry, based in Northern Virginia, trains and places chaplains in correctional facilities in the United States as well as four foreign countries. [Davis, 1994]

Many jails and prisons provide educational services to inmates by operating General Equivalency Diplomas (GED) programs, as well as classes in reading, writing, etc.

In the Alexandria, Virginia, Adult Detention Center, the Sober Living Unit (SLU) is an intensive program that uses the Twelve Step cure to substance abuse developed by Alcoholics Anonymous. The SLU program started in 1990 with the support of Sheriff James H. Dunning. At that time, research revealed that 95% of SLU inmates had been previously incarcerated and 80% had never had *any* prior treatment. [Mclain, 1990] Many jails and prisons conduct programs to identify and treat inmate problems, particularly in substance abuse and mental health.

3. Prevention Ideology

Prevention ideology simply means using programs and methods in order to give youths a positive rather than a negative direction in life. The goal is to *prevent* the potential offender from entering a life of crime.

Prevention programs can be formal and structured such as a vocational training programs (keyboarding, office skills, auto repair, etc.) and educational programs or informal programs. Informal means may use inmate volunteers to talk to young people about the dangers of drug use and criminal behavior. A police officer may speak to school age children about staying crime free and out of trouble.

Prevention is also frequently combined with treatment, especially in community corrections. A work release program may start an offender in an in-house substance abuse program and require him to go to an AA or NA group in his community when authorized to go out into the community. The idea is to *treat* the problem and by referring the offender to a community program, *prevent* a recurrence of crime.

While punishment is important when dealing with violent, repeat offenders, treatment and prevention are critical when dealing with the majority of inmates in our nation's jails and prisons.

Bernard Gauzer, in the August 13, 1995, issue of *Parade Magazine*, wrote the following facts concerning state prison inmates: 45% of inmates have been in prison *three or more* times previously, 19% have been in six or more times, and almost 7% have been in *eleven or more* times! At the time of arrest, 46.5% of jail inmates were on bail, probation, parole, or another type of status in the criminal justice system. More than 75% of jail inmates had prior sentences for incarceration or probation. [Cornelius, 1996]

Correctional officers must realize that most inmates in their care are very familiar with the correctional system and are used to "doing time."

Thus, corrections has different philosophies or opinions on the care and management of offenders. Add to this the public's concerns abut crimes and high rates of repeat offenders, the discipline of corrections developed functions which embody the three philosophies: [Champion, 1990]

(1) retribution
(2) deterrence or prevention
(3) incapacitation or isolation
(4) rehabilitation
(5) reintegration
(6) control

While the first five have been discussed, some researchers feels that control involves the monitoring and surveillance of offenders on probation and parole. However, control is a very important function of the correctional officer—controls of inmate movement, behavior, and accountability as we will see in Chapter 9.

Summary

Corrections is the discipline that involves all of government agencies and staff that deal with the treatment and confinement of inmates. This discipline consists of three philosophies—punishment, treatment, and prevention. The punishment philosophy believes that the offender is society's enemy and must be held responsible and pay dearly while the treatment and prevention philosophies deal with treating the inmates' problems and preventing criminal behavior from recurring.

"Three strikes" and truth in sentencing laws apparently are the trends as we approach the end of the 1990's and the new millennium. The cost of these methods may be high.

Treatment includes several different doctrines, but their one goal is to help inmates stay out of prison. While many treatment programs are innovative, such as the Sober Living Unit, corrections components will remain balanced between punishment and treatment.

Review Questions

1. What are the philosophies of the punishment, treatment and prevention ideologies?

2. Define the "three strikes and you're out" concept.

3. Explain the four doctrines of the treatment philosophy.

4. What are the six functions of corrections?

Terms/Concepts

Corrections

Correctional ideology

Punishment ideology

Treatment ideology

Prevention ideology

Quaker doctrine

Educational doctrine

Correctional staff

Medical model

Reintegration

Retribution

Deterrence

Incapacitation

"Three strikes" laws

"Truth in sentencing"

References

Allen, Harry, and Clifford Simonsen, *Corrections in America, An Introduction*, 7th Ed., Prentice Hall. Englewood Cliffs, NJ, 1995.

Cauchon, Dennis, "Virginia Jumps on Get-Tough Train with No-Parole Plan," *USA Today*, 9/30/94, p. 9A.

Champion, Dean J., *Corrections in the United States: A Contemporary Perspective*, Prentice Hall, Englewood Cliffs, NJ, 1990.

Cornelius, Gary, *Jails in America: An Overview of Issues*, American Correctional Association, Lanham, MD 1996.

Davis, Patricia, "A Narc Angel Makes a Turn," *Washington Post*, 4/28/94, Va. 1, Va. 3.

Donziger, Steven R. (Ed.), *The Real War on Crime: The Report of the National Criminal Justice Commission*, Harper Perennial, NY, 1996.

Elliott, Michael, "Crime & Punishment: The Caning Debate: Should America Be More Like Singapore?" *Newsweek*, 4/18/94, pp. 18-23, Vol. CXX, No. 16.

Fox, Vernon & Jeanne Stinchcombe, *Introduction to Corrections*, 4th Ed., Englewood Cliffs, Prentice Hall, 1994.

Garzer, Bernard, "Life Behind Bars," *Parade Magazine*, 8/13/95, pp. 4-7.

Greenwood, Peter, *et al.*, "Three Strikes and You're Out—Estimated Benefits and Costs of California's New Mandatory Sentencing Law," Santa Monica, Cal., The Rand Corporation, 1994.

Greenwood, Peter, *Selective Incapacitation* (Santa Monica, Cal., Rand Corp.), 1983.

Johnson, Elmer H., *Crime, Correction, and Society* (Homewood, Ill., Dorsey Press, 1974), p. 173 (Information: Oppenheimer, Wood).

Lynch, Don, "Lock up all the pedophiles together and let them molest each other," *Fairfax Journal*, 9/19/94, p. A4.

Mclain, Buzz, "Program Sobers Prisoners' Lives," *Fairfax Journal*, 8/31/90, p. A3.

Miller, Stuart, Simon Dinitz, and John Conrad, *Careers of the Violent* (Lexington, Mass., Lexington Books), 1982.

Phillips, Don, "Panel Urges Toughening of Drunk Driver Laws," *Washington Post*, 3/11/95, p. A12.

Pooley, Eric, "Death or Life?" *Time*, 6/16/97, pp. 31-36, Vol. 149, No. 24.

Chapter 2

Types of Correctional Facilities

Most people in the public, when they hear the word "corrections" think of the local jail or prison or what the media—television and motion pictures—portray. While this view is simplistic, the truth is that correctional facilities come in different varieties.

The most common facilities for adult corrections are in order of usage:

- lockup
- jail
- prison

Other types of correctional facilities are:

- community corrections centers
- juvenile detention centers
- boot camps

Lockup: A lockup is a temporary holding facility, often the offender's first step in being incarcerated. Lockups are generally operated by the local police or sheriff's office and are located in police headquarters, station houses, or a designated area of the jail building. The functions of a lockup are: [Cornelius, 1996]

- to hold arrestees for no more than forty-eight hours, excluding weekends and holidays. Arrestees are held until they are taken before a magistrate, a judge, or are released through personal recognizance or bonding.
- to hold inebriated arrestees until they sober up or "dry out."
- to hold juveniles detained by the police until their parents can be contacted or placement in a juvenile detention center or shelter can be arranged.

There are more than 15,000 lockups across the United States. Generally, lockups are operated by the police or sheriff's departments—the agencies whose members arrest the offenders. Lockups are similar to jails in several respects—they confine people, the staff is responsible for the health and safety of the prisoner, and many problems that jail officers have to deal with may be displayed in lockups. These problems may include aggressive behavior, effects of substance abuse, suicidal behavior, or mental illness. It is imperative that lockup officers, like jail officers, be trained in these areas.

Lockup officers must also be trained in the fundamentals of corrections security. Prisoners brought into a lockup must be carefully searched, observed and restrained if necessary. Releases from a lockup must be legal and proper. Lockup prisoners must not be allowed to escape. Although lockups are temporary holding facilities, prisoners' property must be properly confiscated, inventoried, documented, and stored.

Catastrophic incidents do happen in lockups. One of the most serious incidents is suicide. For example, in 1985, a 38-year-old man arrested for driving while intoxicated hung himself at a Maryland State Police barracks lockup. [*Washington Post*, 6/2/85] The offender hung himself *one* hour after being placed in the lockup by pulling an electrical cord from the ceiling of the holding cell, wrapped it around his neck, and jumped off a bunk to the floor. Escapes, suicides, and assaults can happen at a lockup just as in a jail or prison. Wherever people are held against their will, incidents such as these can occur.

Jail: The next major type of correctional facility is the jail. Prisoners who do not get released from the lockup are transported to the local jail of the jurisdiction in which they were arrested. For many offenders, incarceration in the local jail means experiencing what it means to be locked up for the first time.

A jail is a confinement facility for adult offenders and it may hold juveniles under certain conditions. A jail is usually funded, administered, and operated by a local law enforcement agency, such as a county department of corrections or sheriff's office.

The local jail has eight main functions. They are: [Cornelius, 1996]

- detain offenders who have been arrested and are awaiting trial called "pre-trial detainees;" these offenders are awaiting their first court appearance, a bail or bond amount to be set, their own trials, or release on their own personal recognizance, or PR.
- hold offenders who have been sentenced by the courts to short sentences, usually a year or less, for a misdemeanor or non-violent felony.
- hold convicted prisoners awaiting transfer to state or federal prisons.
- hold mentally disordered inmates who are awaiting transfer to state mental facilities. Jails may also hold substance abusers awaiting placement in substance abuse facilities.
- under certain conditions, hold juvenile offenders, i.e., per court order or because there are no juvenile facilities available.

- confine parole and probation violators until their hearings.
- confine federal prisoners until they are taken into the custody of United States Marshals.
- hold inmates who are charged in other jurisdictions. These outstanding warrants are called *detainers*.

The jurisdiction for which arrestees and inmates a jail is responsible may be a city, county or several counties. Counties who pool their funding and resources operate *regional jails*. These facilities are responsible for the arrestees in the contributing counties.

Jails are known by a variety of names—adult detention center, detention center, correctional facility, county prison, workhouse, or house of corrections. Six states—Delaware, Alaska, Hawaii, Rhode Island, Vermont, and Connecticut administer combined jail/prison systems. [Cornelius, 1996]

Characteristics of Local Jails

One of the fundamental purposes of the jail is to maintain offenders in custody—offenders whose freedom has been taken away by either arrest or conviction from the courts. Inmates are not to be submitted to dirty, inhumane living conditions, brutality, physical/sexual assault, etc. [Fox and Stinchcombe, 1994]

Jails are more restrictive than prisons. Where prisons confine inmates for long periods of time and allow inmates more freedom of movement in the facility, jails confine inmates for a shorter time and as a rule, place more restrictions on inmate movement.

The development of correctional facilities will be discussed in Chapter 5. The following is a summary of the status of jails in the United States:

Number: From 1983 to 1993, the total number of United States jails has remained relatively constant. In 1983, United States jails numbered 3,338; in 1988, 3,316; and in 1993, 3,304. [BJS, 1995] The different figures mean that old jails are being closed down and some jurisdictions are consolidating facilities into regional systems. [Cornelius, 1996] Regionally, the South has the largest number of jails, 1,591; the Northeast the lowest, 228. [BJS, 1995] By state, not including the District of Columbia, Alaska has five jails (lowest) and the largest number was Texas with 267. [BJS, 1995]

Population: In 1998, the total rated capacity (or capacity facilities were designed for) was 612,780 inmates, or 92% of rated capacity occupied. [Bureau of Justice Statistics Sourcebook, 1996] In 1998, 593,808 adults were incarcerated in jails [average daily population] resulting in 97% of capacity being occupied [Bureau of Justice Statistics Sourcebook, 1998]. Jail population is hovering around a half million people.

Adults in Jail
[Average daily population]

1992	441,889
1993	466,155
1994	479,757
1995	509,828
1996	515,432
1997	556,586

[Sourcebook of Criminal Justice Statistics, 1998]

Types: Due to the nature of our political system, there are individual local government agencies: sheriff's offices, county correctional departments, etc., who have influenced the types of jails that have developed in this country. Some jails are the old-fashioned linear design, some indirect supervision, and some are moving towards the direct supervision style of inmate management.

When discussing jails, it is important to note that a significant number are old. In 1990, in research done by Fox and Stinchcombe, over 700 jails were over 50 years old—and 140 of those were 100 years old or more! In 1993, the American Jail Association surveyed 3,272 jails and found that 177 facilities were under new construction and 350 new facilities were being planned. [Cornelius, 1996]

Prisons

The second type of facility that comes to mind upon hearing the word "corrections" is the *prison*.

Quite simply, a prison is defined as a correctional facility that houses convicted offenders under long sentences, usually over one year. Prisons receive funding from state governments and the federal government. The term "prison" is often interchangeably used with the term "penitentiary."

Prisons hold inmates serving long terms. Characteristics of prisons are high custody levels, solitary confinement for high risk dangerous inmates, and single cell occupancy when possible. However, where a jail may restrict inmate movement and have more cellblocks, prisons allow inmates more freedom of movement—in dormitories, exercise yards, etc., and a more flexible routine.

Number: There are 957 state prison facilities in the United States. [Fox and Stinchcombe, 1994] North Dakota only has one, New York has 57. The United States Bureau of Prisons has 80 institutions, bringing the total to 1,037. This is far below in comparison to the 3,000 plus local jail facilities in the United States. Prisons are part of state and federal correctional "systems." These systems administer about 250 state facilities not considered prisons—pre-release centers, work release centers, training centers, halfway houses, etc.

The United States military also maintains correctional facilities. The total number of facilities is 33. The United States Army has 12, the Marine Corps 5 and the United States Navy 16. The only military long-term confinement facility is the United States Disciplinary Barracks at Fort Leavenworth, Kansas. Inmates in these institutions have been convicted of crimes in civilian jurisdictions or violations of the United States Code of Military Conduct. The primary goal of military corrections is the restoration of the inmate to active duty, wherever possible. [Fox and Stinchcombe, 1994, *Sourcebook of Criminal Justice Statistics*, 1995]

Population: At the end of 1998, 1,825,000 prisoners were held in federal and state adult correctional facilities. State prisons were operating at 113% capacity; federal prisons were at 127% capacity. The increase in 1996 was at the rate of 1,151 more inmates per week! Female prisoners in 1998 increased 6.5%, compared to 4.7% increase for males. The ten jurisdictions having the highest prison populations at year end 1996 were (in descending order): California, Texas, Federal, New York, Florida, Ohio, Michigan, Illinois, Georgia and Pennsylvania. [BJS, 1999]

The number of prisons are growing: according to a United States Department of Justice report, 213 federal and state prisons with over 280,000 beds were built from 1990-1995. [ACA, 1997]

Type: While the typical image of a prison is a large, walled institution with towers, razor wire, drab buildings, and a large main "yard," prisons actually vary in scope and design, depending on the type of inmates housed, custody levels which are appropriate, and capacity needed. The development of the modern prison will be explored in Chapter 5. At this point, it is important to note that in the 20th century, prison design and type have ranged from the island maximum security federal prison of Alcatraz to the medium security "campus" designs. This modern type of prison has single rooms and dormitories for inmates, not the traditional "cell." [Allen and Simonsen, 1998]

Community Corrections Facilities

The third type of adult correctional facility involves community corrections. Simply defined, the term "community corrections" means programs that deal with offenders in the community, such as work release, home/electronic detention, diversion, pre-trial release, community service, restitution or fine options. [Cornelius, 1996] Community corrections centers include pre-release centers, halfway houses, and day reporting centers. Inmates (or offenders, residents, or clients) work and attend rehabilitative programs in the community, after approval by the sentencing court or correctional agency for release. Community corrections centers are minimum security and trust is placed on the offender to follow the rules and return each day to the Center. The development of community corrections facilities will be discussed in Chapter 5. The purpose of community corrections centers (CCC's) is to provide the offender with a way back to the community with the tools to handle problems and to live crime free. All three jurisdictions—federal, state and local—have made use of this philosophy by instituting various types of these facilities. The exact number of these facilities is not known, but in 1996, 41,055 inmates were placed in work release programs in thirty-two agencies; in twenty agencies, 35,315 were placed in halfway houses. [Camp & Camp, 1997]

Security Levels

As previously stated, many prisons and jails are assigned for security or levels of custody. In every type of correctional facility, some inmates cause trouble for the staff due to negative behavior—escape attempts, thefts, causing disturbances, assaults on staff and other inmates, etc. Other inmates adapt to being incarcerated and obey the rules. Some inmates need higher levels of staff supervision and secure custody based on their charges: murder, felonious assault, etc. For these reasons, custody is broken down into three types of security levels. In many institutions, particularly jails, all three types are incorporated into the same facility.

Maximum security: Facility or area designed to exercise maximum control over the inmate population. Through use of two officer escorts, prisoners in restraints when out of their cells, security cameras, high numbers of locked doors, solitary confinement, and frequent head counts and searches, escapes, violence and disturbances are minimized.

Medium security: At this level, the prevention of escapes, violence and disturbances are still goals. However, the security measures are less strict. Fewer cameras and the allowance of inmates to move unescorted and unrestrained typify some trust in the inmates. Inmates may live two to a cell or in a dorm.

Minimum security: Inmates are allowed greater degrees of movement and responsibility such as attending programs or in cases of CCC's, attending programs or working in the community.

A simple axiom is this—the higher the security—cameras, officers, razor wire on outside perimeters, checks, counts and searches, for example—the higher the level of custody.

Costs

When the public thinks of men and women locked up in jails and prisons, the costs associated with incarceration roughly come up. Tax revenues support local, state and federal institutions.

The United States is the world's "Number 1 jailer" due to the public's "lock em' up fever" (mandatory sentences, tighter parole laws, etc.). In the 1980's, harsh drug penalties made the United States incarceration rate increase to 455 per 100,000 citizens and an annual bill of $21 billion to construct prisons and house inmates. [Smolowe, 1994] In 1998, federal prisons, state prisons and local jails held 672 inmates per 100,000 citizens. [BJS, 1999]

Correctional Costs

- In FY97, 52 correctional agencies' budgets totaled $28.9 billion.
- On average, the operating budget was 93.8% of an agency's total budget.

> Source: *Corrections Yearbook 1997*, George Camille Camp, Criminal Justice Institute, Salem, NY, 1997

The public taxpayers or the average citizens, pour funds into prison operation and construction. These expenditures compete with other needed funding, such as money for roads and schools. In the United States, five states have a corrections budget of more than $1 billion! To meet the high demand of prisons, states divert money from welfare, education, etc., to prison costs.

- California annually spends $3.6 billion on prison operations. Another $500 million is spent per year on prison construction. [Donziger, National Criminal Justice Commission, 1996]
- Corrections, as a state spending category, increased 95% from 1976-89. [Gold, 1998]
- In Texas, the state government expended over $1 billion for an additional 76,000 beds in *two years*! [Donziger, National Criminal Justice Commission, 1996]
- States can build prisons, but can they operate them? In South Carolina, two prisons costing $80 million stood empty—there

SPRING CREEK CAMPUS

was no money to run them. [Donziger, National Criminal Justice Commission, 1996]

The costs of incarceration does not simply mean "build a prison and the convicts will come." Not only does costs mean feeding, clothing, and housing an inmate, costs also include:

Construction: The average cost of building a new prison cell is $54,000. When debt service (agency borrowing money or loans) and interest is added, the actual or real cost of a cell is significantly over $100,000.

Operating: It takes about $22,000 a year on average to operate a state prison bed per inmate per year. In the federal system, the cost of keeping an inmate in prison for one year equals all of the taxes paid by three average families.

Service costs: Corrections agencies pay businesses that provide services to the inmate, such as food services and medical care.

There are many more expenditures that add millions of dollars to the annual national correctional budget. The high costs of treating health problems in inmates such as AIDs, tuberculosis, and medical ailments of elderly inmates must be paid. Also, it is important to note the nearly *one million* children of inmates in foster care are supported by taxpayer dollars. [Donziger: National Criminal Justice Commission, 1996]

Jails, like prisons, are expensive to run, renovate and build.

- In 1993, the United States spent $6.8 billion to house inmates in jail, at an average annual cost of $14,667 per inmate. [Cornelius, 1996]
- Operating costs of local jails totaled a little more than $9.6 billion in FY93. [Cornelius, 1996]
- Operating costs (salaries, wages, food, supplies, contractual services) were 71% of expenditures in FY93. [Cornelius, 1996]
- The average cost of keeping an inmate incarcerated for one year rose 57% from 1983-1993. [Cornelius, 1996]
- For a planned bed in a jail system, the average *projected* cost is $44,514 per bed. [*Correctional Yearbook*, 1997]
- The jail system with the highest cost per planned bed was Travis County, Texas ($161,765 per bed). The lowest was Hillsborough County, New Hampshire, at only $103 per bed. [*Correctional Yearbook*, 1997]
- The overall average cost per inmate per day in United States jails currently is $55.41. [*Correctional Yearbook*, 1997]

While the two main types of correctional facilities, prisons and jails, have differences in function, when it comes to costs, they are expensive.

Summary

The main types of correctional facilities—prisons, jails, lockups, community corrections centers and juvenile facilities—all have a main goal of confinement. However, prisons house people for long periods, jails for shorter periods, and community corrections centers for periods designed to reintegrate the offender back to society.

The three custody levels are maximum, medium and minimum. In descending degree, they restrict surveillance and movement of the prisoner.

Correctional facilities are a big business from construction costs to operating costs. Besides just housing a prisoner, other factors influence the total costs—construction, operation and service costs.

Review Questions

1. Explain the differences between a jail, prison and lockup.

2. What are the eight main functions of a jail?

3. What are the functions of community corrections centers?

4. Explain maximum, medium and minimum security.

5. What are factors in the cost of incarceration?

Terms/Concepts

Lockup	Community Corrections Center
Jail	Maximum Security
Prison	Medium Security
Detainer	Minimum Security
Regional Jail	

References

Allen, Harry, and Clifford Simonsen, *Corrections in America, An Introduction*, 8th Ed., Prentice Hall. Englewood Cliffs, NJ, 1998.

Camp, George and Camille, *The Corrections Yearbook*, 1997, Criminal Justice Institute, South Salem, NY, 1997.

Champion, Dean J., *Corrections in the United States: A Contemporary Perspective*, Prentice Hall, Englewood Cliffs, NJ, 1990.

Cornelius, Gary, *Jails in America: An Overview of Issues*, American Correctional Association, Lanham, MD 1996.

Donziger, Steven R. (Ed.), *The Real War on Crime: The Report of the National Criminal Justice Commission*, Harper Perennial, NY, 1996.

"Drunk Driving Suspect Hangs Self in Waldorf State Police Barracks," *Washington Post*, 6/2/85.

Fox, Vernon & Jeanne Stinchcombe, *Introduction to Corrections*, 4th Ed., Englewood Cliffs, Prentice Hall, 1994.

Gilliard, Darrell K., and Allen J. Beck, Ph.D, BJS Statisticians, "Prison's & Jail Inmates at Midyear, 1996" *BJS Bulletin*, NJC 162843, January, 1997.

Mumola, Christopher, and Allen J. Beck, Ph.D, BJS Statisticians, "Prisoners in 1998," *BJS Bulletin*, NCJ 175687, August, 1999.

"Prison Construction in U.S. Grows," *Corrections Today*, 10/97, p. 14.

Smolwe, Jill, "...And Throw Away the Key," *Time*, 2/7/94, pp. 55-59, Vol. 143, No. 6.

Maguire, Kathleen, and Ann L. Pastore (Eds.), *Sourcebook of Criminal Justice Statistics, 1995*, Bureau of Justice Statistics, 1995.

Maguire, Kathleen, and Ann L. Pastore (Eds.), *Sourcebook of Criminal Justice Statistics, 1996*, Bureau of Justice Statistics, 1996.

Maguire, Kathleen, and Ann L. Pastore (Eds.), *Sourcebook of Criminal Justice Statistics, 1998*, Bureau of Justice Statistics, 1999.

Chapter 3

Correctional Officers: Personnel Issues and Training

The public image of a prison or jail usually focuses on the correctional officer. Sometimes they are called guards, jailors, turnkeys, etc. Thanks to movies and television, these men and women are sometimes portrayed as undereducated, out of shape (overweight), sadistic, and brutal. That is not the case. Our nation's jails, prisons and community corrections centers are staffed with trained, skilled and conscientious men and women who must perform a difficult mission—keeping people safely and securely locked up against their will.

This chapter will discuss five areas concerning correctional officers:

- number
- salaries
- duties of correctional officers
- training
- traits of a good correctional officer

Number: On January 1, 1995, there were 365,755 employees in adult correctional systems in state and federal systems and the District of Columbia. The Federal Bureau of Prisons had 26,708 employees *then*. [Bureau of Justice Statistics, 1995] North Dakota had the fewest (200) and Texas had the most (34,548). [Camp and Camp, 1997; Cornelius, 1996]

In terms of race and gender, most employees are white males.

Correctional Systems: State and Federal 1995

Total (reported 1/95)	Male	Female	White	Non-White
365,755 (total)	252,150	112,158	261,237	99,174
26,708 (federal)	19,615	7,093	18,447	8,261

These trends are also indicated in juvenile correctional systems. Out of 39,376 employees in juvenile correctional systems listed in 1994, 28,002 were white (or 71%). Blacks accounted for 10,598 (or 27%).

Correctional officers are the foundation of a correctional facility. Champion (1990) defined a correctional officer as a guard in a prison whose

Uniform Inspection.

function is to supervise or manage inmates. While the image of the correctional officer (or CO) is one of the traditional prison guard, the term is more complex. A more specific definition is:

> A trained law enforcement officer in a correctional facility whose function is to supervise and manage inmates, enforce the laws of the jurisdiction, enforce the rules of the facility, maintain the inmates in a safe and secure environment, and prevent escapes.

Correctional officers are employed by state and federal systems, and locally in county sheriff's offices and corrections departments. Juvenile facility workers have similar responsibilities—keeping juvenile offenders safely housed and preventing escapes.

The previous tables have reflected the total number of employees, including correctional officers. In reality, many employees having many different jobs comprise the staffs of correctional facilities.

Support staff: clerical, administrative workers

Maintenance workers: electrical workers, repair personnel

Food service workers: cooks, dieticians

Medical staff: physicians, dentists, nurses, correctional health care workers (usually called medics)

Treatment staff: substance abuse counselors, teachers, mental health workers, classification staff, teachers, vocational instructors

Religious staff: chaplains and assistants

In state and federal adult correctional systems, the number of correctional officers at the beginning of 1995 was 213,370 (state) and 10,932 (USBOP), for a total of 224,302. Also, most correctional officers are white males. The following table provides a snapshot of demographics concerning state and federal CO's:

Data: 6/30/94   Figures/%

System	Total CO's	White	Black	Hispanic	Other
State	205,453	142,031	46,650	12,913	3,859
	100%	69%	23%	6%	2%
Federal	10,248	6,582	2,324	1,157	185
	100%	64%	23%	11%	2%

[Source: *Sourcebook of Criminal Justice Statistics*, 1995, BJS]

It is interesting to note that the ratio of state correctional officers to inmates is one officer to four inmates while in the federal system it is one officer to eight inmates. The turnover rate, or rate of officers leaving the job, is lower in the federal Bureau of Prisons (5.30%) than the state average rate of 11%. The reasons for this possibly could be higher salaries and benefits in the federal system. Another aspect of this could be that corrections is a demanding, high stress profession which many officers find out is not for them. [Source: *Sourcebook of Criminal Justice Statistics*, 1995, BJS]

In juvenile systems, the breakdown is, as of mid 1994, and is similar to adult systems:

Data: 6/30/94   Figures/%

Total	White	Black	Hispanic	Other
39,376	25,351	10,598	2,651	776
100%	64%	27%	7%	2%

[*Sourcebook of Criminal Justice Statistics*, BJS, 1995]

The trend continues in jail staffing:

1993 Jails:

Total CO's	White	Black	Hispanic	Other
117,800	81,500	27,400	7,900	1,000
100%	69%	23%	7%	1%

[*Sourcebook of Criminal Justice Statistics*, BJS, 1995]

By gender, most CO's are male:

%	Federal Prisons (1995)	State Prisons (1995)	Juvenile Facilities (1994)	Jails (1993)
Male	89%	82%	65%	75.8
Female	11%	18%	35%	24.2

[*Sourcebook of Criminal Justice Statistics*, BJS, 1995]

Salaries: As indicated by 1995 statistics, annual salaries of federal and state correctional personnel averaged $19,907.00. Also, officers could reach an average maximum annual salary of $31,447.00. The entry level for the USBOP was $23,075.00 with a maximum of $35,067.00. Thirteen state correctional agencies do not increase the annual salaries after the probationary period (usually one year). Salaries for juvenile workers are not widely reported. [*Sourcebook of Criminal Justice Statistics*, BJS, 1995]

Concerning jails, entry level salaries for officers/sheriff's deputies have remained constant in the past several years. In 1996, Cornelius wrote that the average jail officer's starting salary was $21,542.00 and a maximum salary of $31,890.00. This was based on research by Camp and Camp, 1995. In 1997, the average starting salary was $23,699.00, the maximum salary was $35,122.00. [Camp and Camp, 1997]

Duties of Correctional Officers

Though correctional agencies, both adult and juvenile, have various general orders and procedures that govern officers and provide guidance, the basic goal of a CO and juvenile facility staffs is to *securely* and *safely* confine inmates/offenders in their care.

Secure and safe confinement simply means that the public is protected from escapes, staff and visitors are protected from aggressive acts by inmates, and the inmates/offenders are protected from each other (murders, assaults, thefts, etc.), and themselves (self-mutilation, suicide). If order is maintained, lives and property are not harmed.

According to the Honorable Helen Corrothers, former president of the American Correctional Association and former Commissioner of the United States Sentencing Commission, the goal of public safety can be achieved through the achievement by two objectives:

1. Preventing escapes and humanely incarcerating offenders until they are legally released; and

Correctional officer checking a segregation unit.

2. Provide an appropriate safe environment (for inmates *and* staff) which may influence inmates to learn and adopt positive values.

[Corrothers, 1992]

Hopefully, the second objective will create a will or desire in the inmate to stay crime free once released.

To achieve these two objectives, the duties of a CO take both a formal and an informal track. [Partial source: U.S. Department of Labor, 1994]

Formal Duties of a CO:

1. Perform regular checks and headcounts on inmates in living, programs, and work areas. These checks are performed at intervals (every thirty minutes, every fifteen minutes, etc.). Some checks, such as in inmate segregation or in jail booking/receiving are performed more frequently. These checks are logged or documented.
2. Perform searches on inmates' persons, living areas, and work areas; the purpose of these searches are to look for several things such as contraband or signs of illegal or self-destructive activity (needle tracks due to drug use, tattooing them-

Two correctional officers conducting a "shakedown," or cell search. One looks for contraband, and the other documents the search and records its findings.

selves, wrists, etc.). Contraband is defined simply as any item (illegal drugs, weapons, etc.) that is not authorized by the facility administration. Contraband can also be any authorized item in excess such as extra blankets, hoarded food, etc.

3. Process inmates into the facility: all correctional facilities have intake centers. Inmates must be properly committed—legal paperwork must be in order, the inmates must be searched, placed in confinement, have his/her property inventoried, and medically checked.

4. Observe inmate behavior and activities. CO's must observe inmates for rule violations, work performance, unusual behavior, hygiene, signs of depression, etc. The CO must observe inmates constantly in living units, segregation units, work assignments, in recreation, programs, etc.

5. Supervise inmates on work assignments. Inmates who perform work for the facility, called "trusties," must be supervised by officers. These officers must also provide direction and issue instructions.

6. Enforce rules and laws, investigate violations. Prisons, jails, community corrections facilities and juvenile centers have rules that must be followed. CO's must enforce these rules, show-

ing no favoritism. Violators must be reported. Also, inmates must obey the laws of the jurisdiction and may be criminally prosecuted. For example, if an inmate stabs another inmate, he/she can be charged with felonious assault and face criminal prosecution.

7. Inspect the facility security system and environment. COs inspect daily the cells, cellblocks, dormitories, program areas, recreation facilities, offices, lock window/door bars, gates, cameras, intercoms, radios, etc., for flaws. All areas are inspected for fire safety and/or sanitary violations. Incoming mail and packages are inspected for contraband.

8. Escort or transport inmates and admit authorized visitors. COs escort inmates to and from housing areas, court, programs, recreation, visiting, sick call, classification or other institutions. COs also escort authorized visitors inside the facility.

9. Participate in disciplinary hearings/administrative hearings.

All of the above functions require documentation. Checks, violations, escorts, and inspections usually require some kind of written report. Formal duties such as observation, looking into rule violations, crimes in the institution, and being part of hearings result in roles such as patrol officer, investigator, and judge.

Documentation of observations, events, and interactions with inmates is a critical part of the correctional officer's job.

Informal Duties of a CO:

Officers perform many functions informally in the facility; not all duties and jobs are formal. The informal roles that officers perform include:

Psychologist: recognizing symptoms of mental illness and referring inmates to appropriate mental health staff.

Legal advisor: when asked, providing answers to inmates' legal questions — sentence, court dates, bond, etc., or representing an inmate in a disciplinary hearing.

Parent: being a strong, positive role model for immature inmates, teaching inmates better hygiene. For example, correcting an inmate who exhibits a body odor problem, telling an inmate to clean his cell, etc.

Information agent: when asked, giving answers to inmates about facility policies, programs, rules, etc. Some officers conduct orientations for newly arriving inmates.

Counselor: giving advice to inmates on how to properly conduct themselves, how to handle a personal problem, etc.

Diplomat: intervening in and defusing inmate disputes, before verbal disagreements escalate into full scale physical altercations.

It has been said that working in a correctional institution can prepare one to deal with a variety of people. Corrections officers can learn first hand how to handle resistant people while maintaining a calm demeanor.

Training

All correctional officers must have training. Working with offenders and dealing with inmates require special skills. Research by Shannon in 1987 indicated that in a survey of correctional officers, the ten specific areas that most COs were trained in were (in descending order):

Firearms	97%	Self defense	84%
Housing and body searches	93%	Key/Tool control	78%
Searching for contraband	92%	General safety	68%
Report writing	88%	Riot control	67%
Facility rules & regulations	85%	CPR	66%

[Champion, 1990]

While these subjects are important and are critical to officers' safety, other important subjects were not so prevalent in officer training. Some subjects rated low, such as stress reduction (31%), ongoing physical fitness (21%), lawsuit liability (48%), and civil rights awareness (35%).

Corrections Officers at Roll Call.

Training for correctional officers comes in two basic types: [Camp and Camp, 1997]

1. *Introductory training*: the number of hours that an officer is required to attend before officially being allowed to perform the job. The officer is tested and must meet performance standards. This training is usually within the first year of employment.

2. *In-service training*: the number of training hours that an officer is required to complete during each subsequent year of employment. The officer may be required to complete a certain number of hours every year, or every two years, depending on mandates by the state. If the facility is accredited by the American Correctional Association (ACA), correctional officers must complete:

   - 40 hours of orientation and training *prior* to receiving an independent job assignment;
   - additional 120 hours of training during the first year on the job (or probationary year);
   - 40 hours of training each subsequent year.

[ACA, 1997]

The sources of training vary. Most agencies rely on a training academy to provide training. A training academy may be a branch of the agency or, as a cost saving move, be composed of staff from the several agencies it serves (regional academy). Other methods of providing training are roll call training where training is presented at shift change, or one- or two-day seminars held at the facility sponsored usually be the academy. Staff who meet certain criteria can become certified instructors in their jurisdictions. Training can also be in the form of seminars conducted by such correctional organizations as the American Correctional Association (ACA), the American Jail Association (AJA), and the National Sheriff's Association (NSA).

Specialized training in a particular subject can be obtained through seminars. For example, if a jail's booking system is becoming computerized, training in PCS is offered/required.

There is no limit to the subjects offered in training. The following is representative of areas of effective correctional training:

Security procedures: counts, searches, key and tool control

Supervising inmates

Use of lethal/non-lethal force

Defensive tactics

Inmate discipline

Inmates' civil rights

Report writing/documenting events

Fire procedures/safety

Escape prevention

Firearms training

Communicating with inmates

First aid/cardiopulmonary resuscitation (CPR)

Blood-borne/air-borne pathogens

Criminal code

Agency policies and procedures

Code of Conduct/ethics

Staff communications/use of computers

Emergency operation of motor vehicles

Suicide prevention

Crisis intervention

Handling special inmates (mentally ill, etc.)

Cultural diversity

Gangs

Prevention of riots and disturbances

Stress management and wellness

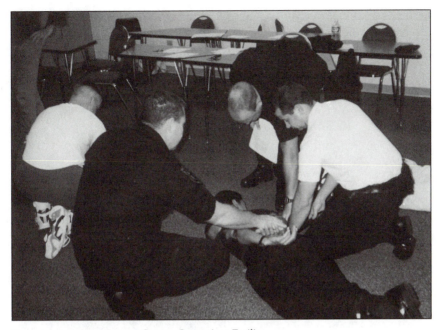

Restraints training, Manatee County Corrections Facility.

Physical fitness and agility

Juveniles in custody

Safe transport of inmates

Many states have standards of training which in detail describe subject areas to be taught, the required number of hours, and performance based objectives that the officer must pass. Academies may combine formal classroom-type training with on-the-job training, putting the trainee with veteran staff in the facility and grading them on job performance. These standards also govern the selection of training of instructors. Certified instructors must have formalized training in teaching techniques and lesson plan development.

Training Topics

Specialized topics, such as inmate con games, high risk prisoners, and defensive tactics, are offered at most training academies.

The actual number in pre-service training and in-service training varies throughout the nation. Training in the juvenile corrections system is very similar to adult corrections training—security issues and dealing with offenders are addressed. However, Camp and Camp in 1995 reported that in twenty-nine states, the average pre-service training was 102 hours. However, annual in-service training was forty-three hours, which is comparable to the forty hours for adult corrections officers required by ACA. [*Corrections Yearbook, 1995*]

Required Training Hours for CO's (Average)

	1995		1997	
	Pre-Service	In-Service	Pre-Service	In-Service
Jails	238	31	273	36
Prisons	224	43	229	39

[Source: Camp & Camp, *Correctional Yearbooks 1995 and 1997*, Criminal Justice Institute]

On the average, pre-service training has increased and in-service hours have remained nearly constant.

More attention is being given to the juvenile worker. According to a report in 1997 by Criminal and Juvenile Justice International, Inc., juvenile caseworkers are receiving less than half of the training as COs in adult systems. Training is critical to the juvenile worker because juveniles are more assaultive and impulsive than adult inmates. The report suggests that juvenile caseworkers training be improved drastically, especially skills training. [*Corrections Professional*, 6/6/97]

In the articles, "Preliminary Survey of Personnel Training in American State Prison Systems" by Dr. Elmer H. Johnson in the Summer, 1992 issue of *The Journal of Correctional Training*, thirty-two states responded to a survey concerning their training academies. Academies were categorized into independent (agency) academies, multi-agency academies, and states having a non-academy program. He found that:

- Independent academies with separate physical plants averaged the greater number of hours (189) to independent academies located in a prison (140) devoted to major topics;
- All academy systems surveyed devoted sixty hours plus to instructor certification;
- In all academies, security topics had the most training hours;
- All training academies emphasized emergency tasks.

The National Academy of Corrections established in Boulder, Colorado, in 1981 by the National Institute of Corrections, offers training seminars to local/state corrections as well as curriculum packages and technical assistance.

New Trends

North Carolina: For jail officers, the current training curriculum consists of twenty-four blocks of instruction with a total of 135 hours. Critical safety issues such as fire emergencies requires sixteen hours, unarmed self defense has eighteen hours, and trainees received twelve hours in legal rights and responsibilities. Training instructors are categorized into general, limited, and professional. General instructors teach all subjects with the exception of five limited blocks: first aid/CPR, medical care, unarmed self defense, fire emergencies, and physical assessment of jailors. Limited instructors teach these and professional instructors teach legal issues: civil liability, legal rights and responsibilities, and legal aspects of criminal investigations. Professional credentials are required and general instructors must undergo at least eighty hours (two weeks) of instructor training. To save staff time and money, training courses are available at fifty-eight community colleges, the North Carolina Justice Academy, and six sheriff's offices. [Yearwood, 1994]

Virginia: At the Clarke-Frederick-Winchester Regional ADC in Winchester, Virginia, training is emphasized in a Career Advancement and Development or *CAD* program. In order to improve eligibility for advancement and promotion, jail officers are strongly urged to utilize training offered by the regional criminal justice academy, local colleges, in-house agencies, and seminars offered by professional organizations. This program is representative of agencies who use outside sources to supplement training.

Alexandria, Virginia: the Field Training and Evaluation Program (FTEP) requires on-the-job training to be supervised by veteran personnel. New officers also must undergo eighty hours of new employee training.

Washington: At the Washington Department of Community Corrections, an in-house training program was developed to provide quality training within the agency. By the use of focus groups from different job sections, assessed training needs and developed implementation through a training advisory committee. This utilization of staff resources has saved money and provided staff with a way of having input concerning training needs. [*Corrections Professional*, 11/7/97]

Illinois: Juvenile services supervisors dress up staff members to look like a juveniles and run them through the yard to test staff reaction. [*Corrections Professional*, 6/6/97]

Correctional officer on rounds.

Traits of a Good Correctional Officer (CO)

While training methods have improved for workers who deal with adult and juvenile offenders, training alone does not make an effective correctional officer.

According to the U.S. Department of Labor, job opportunities for correctional officers are expected to be plentiful through 2005. [Baldwin, 1997] The reasons for this trend are clear—more facilities being built, and offenders being incarcerated for longer periods of time.

Not everyone or just anybody can become a correctional officer. It takes a special type of person to work with offenders. Staff development and training must bring out the best traits.

Much has been written and researched about what traits a correctional officer should have. The following is based on research from Karen Campbell, women's program manager at the Federal Correctional Institution in El Reno, California; Linda Zupan, researcher; and Susan McCampbell, former jail director, Broward Co., Florida:

- have a desire to help people
- have an ability to work without fear or anxiety

- have a knowledge of human behavior
- be able to maintain good health and an organized lifestyle
- have an ability to manage a safe and humane environment
- be able to handle inmate discipline and maintain order
- have a desire to respond promptly to inmates' requests
- have an ability and desire to build and maintain personal credibility with inmates, as well as developing an ongoing rapport with them
- be able to perform duties among inmates in a clear, well organized, attention-getting manner
- be able to resolve inmate conflicts and problems fairly and promptly
- have effective relations with the facility administration and staff

[Cornelius, 1994]

Correctional officers are required to manage the inmate population through face-to-face, interpersonal interaction with inmates. The ways that this is accomplished assists to maintain an orderly and safe environment. COs must have "job related competencies" in two areas: security and procedural skills, and human relation skills as listed below:

Security and Procedural Skills:

- knowledge of rules, regulations and procedures concerning custody
- ability to:
  — be a team player
  — locate and identify contraband
  — prevent escapes, riots and disturbances
  — prevent violent physical and sexual predatory behavior
  — when necessary, use appropriate degrees of physical force
  — accurately use weapons and to know under what circumstances deadly force can be applied
  — defend oneself if attacked
  — intervene in an assault, fight, confrontation, or argument between inmates
  — rescue inmates and staff from fire or smoke hazards
  — correctly use emergency equipment
  — protect the safety and lives of injured or sick inmates or staff through the correct application of emergency first aid and life-saving techniques

— to maintain control over inmates without creating hostility or compromising security
— to understand and describe inmates' rights and not violate them
— to communicate clearly verbally and write clear, concise and informative log entries, memoranda and reports
— by physically proficient in order to protect inmates and staff rights to health, safety and welfare

Human Relations Skills:

- ability to:
  — remain non-prejudiced, non-judgmental, humane, treat inmates as people, be consistently fair and honest
  — establish and maintain positive relationships with inmates, to be genuinely concerned as to the welfare of inmates and staff
  — listen, watch, and care about what happens to inmates
  — clearly, politely and understandably orally communicate to inmates
  — when confronted with an inmate problem, handle it calmly, being non-judgmental or abusive, offer counseling and practical advice
  — recognize physical and behavioral changes in inmates as signs of potential problems and offer assistance, if applicable
  — refer an inmate for help if he/she has a serious personal problem
  — be non-defensive and open to any honest dialogue
  — effectively manage people
  — defuse or de-escalate a crisis situation effectively and safely
  — through interviewing, determining what the inmate believes to be the causes of a crises
  — mediate and informally resolve conflicts and interpersonal disputes between inmates where practical
  — handle the rigors, pressures and stresses associated with correctional work

[Gilbert & Riddell, 1983]

To do these duties, correctional officers are hired through a careful screening process:

Corrections Officers Education and Training

In a study by the American Correctional Association, responding agencies reported the following (figures have been rounded):

Examination processes:

Written exam	79%
Psychological test	27%
Interview/oral exam	51%
Medical exam	64%
Background investigation	81%
Drug screens	42%
Other	12%

Education level required (entry):

High school diploma	60%
College (four years)	10%
Choice degree with experience	15%
Other	3%
None	10%

Total length of time in training:*

2 weeks	2%
3 weeks	2%
4 weeks	10%
5-9 weeks	48%
10-16 weeks	12%
17-24 weeks	4%
25+ weeks	23%

*Includes academy and on-the-job training.

Source: *Vital Statistics: 1994*, ACA, Laurel, MD, 1994.

It is correctional officers, through their interaction with inmates, who set the stage for whatever the correctional environment becomes.

Summary

Correctional officers are trained law enforcement officers. Recent trends have shown that COs are primarily male in gender. Pay rates for jail officers have remained constant recently, but overall pay averages are not that high. The main goals of correctional officers' work are to prevent escapes and maintain a safe environment. These goals are accomplished by formal and informal duties. COs receive training through pre-service and in-service schools and seminars offered by academies and in-house. Training is improving and becoming more specialized. Good COs must exhibit abilities in the security and human relations areas.

Review Questions

1. What is the definition of a correctional officer?

2. What groups comprise the staff of a correctional facility?

3. Describe the formal and informal duties of a correctional officer.

4. What are the two basic types of training for correctional officers.

5. What have researchers indicated are traits of a good correctional officer.

Terms/Concepts

Formal duties of a CO

Informal duties of a CO

Introductory training

In-service training

Career Assistance and
  Development (CAD) program

Traits of a good CO

Security and procedural skills

Human relations skills

References

American Correctional Association, Vital Statistics 1994, Laurel, MD, 1994.

Baldwin, Mary, "Correctional Officer Staff Development Research Paper," submitted at George Mason University, SOC 402, 4/14/97.

Bales, Don, Ed., *Correctional Officer Resource Guide*, Lanham, American Correctional Assocation, 1997.

Camp, George & Camille, *Corrections Yearbook*, 1997, Criminal Justice Institute, South Salem, NY 1997.

Camp, Geroge & Camille, *Corrections Yearbook*, Adult Systems, 1995, Criminal Justice Institute, South Salem, NY, 1995.

Camp & Camp, *Corrections Yearbook*, Juvenile Systems, 1995, Criminal Justice Institute, South Salem, NY, 1995.

Campbell, Kathleen, July 1985, "Sharing Career Perspectives, Four Stories from the LIne," *Corrections Today*, vol. 47, no. 4, pp. 12-18.

Champion, Dean J., *Corrections in the United States: A Contemporary Perspective*, Prentice Hall, Englewood Cliffs, NJ, 1990.

Clarke-Frederick-Winchester Career Advancement and Development Program (CAD), CFW Regional ADC.

Cornelius, Gary, *Stressed Out! Strategies for Living and Working in Corrections*, American Correctional Association, Lanham, MD 1994.

Cornelius, Gary, Twenty Minute Trainer: No. 22: "Direct Supervision: Who's Right For It?" *Journal of Correctional Training*, Fall, 1994.

Corrothers, Honorable Helen G., "Career vs. Job: Why Become a Correctional Officer?" in *The Effective Correctional Officer*, American Correctional Association, Lanham, MD, 1992.

Gilbert, Michael J. and Jack Riddell, "Skills for Achieving Security, Control, and Public Protection," in *Correctional Officers: Power, Pressure, and Responsibility*, American Correctional Association, College Park, MD, 1983.

"In-House Training Yields Cost Savings, Increase Staff Buy In," *Corrections Professional*, 11/7/97, Vol. 3, Issue 5.

Johnson, Elmer H., Ph.D., "Preliminary Survey of Personnel Training in American State Prison Systems," *Journal of Correctional Training*, Summer, 1992, pp. 7-11.

McCampbell, Susan, "Direct Supervision: Looking for the Right People," *American Jails*, Nov-Dec, 1990, Vol. IV, No. 4, pp. 68-69.

McGuire, Kathleen and Anna L. Patore (Eds.), *Sourcebook of Criminal Justice Statistics*, 1995, Bureau of Justice Statistics, 1995.

"National Survey Shows Juvenile Leaders Should Improve Training," *Corrections Professional*, 6/6/97, Vol. 2, Issue 18.

Stinchcomb, Jeanne and Vernon Fox, *Introduction to Corrections*, 4th Ed., Englewood Cliffs, Prentice Hall, 1994.

U.S. Dept. of Labor, *Occupational Outlook Handbook*, 1996-1997, Wash. D.C.

U.S. Department of Labor, Bureau of Labor Statistics, 1994-95, *Occupational Outlook Handbook*, http://ny.jobsearch.org/youth/occ8.htm.

Yearwood, Douglas, "Jail Officer Training in North Carolina," *American Jails*, Sep-Oct 1994, Vol, VIII, No. 4, pp. 53-59.

Chapter 4

Early Development: Punishment and Early Prisons

Today's corrections facilities and practices were not thought of overnight. The discipline of corrections as seen today is a product of hundreds of years of beliefs and opinions on what should be done with society's wrongdoers.

This chapter will explore how the concept of criminal punishment developed. This chapter, in conjunction with Chapter 5, will give the reader a clear insight into where corrections came from.

Early Behavior

Throughout the history of man on this planet, societies, whether they be in tribes, nomadic groups, city-states (such as in ancient Greece), countries, etc., have held that certain acts (or groups of acts) have been looked upon as wrong. Acts such as these are discouraged or proscribed. Examples of *proscribed behavior* are murder, rape, thievery, kidnaping, destruction of another's property, etc. Societies also encouraged certain acts which were deemed acceptable—marriage, bearing and rearing children, growing food, hunting, protecting the family, helping others, etc. These acts were called *prescribed behavior*. [Allen & Simonsen, 1998]

As societies developed, people learned that behavior, both prescribed and proscribed, could be controlled by social rules called folkways. [Allen & Simonsen, 1998] Folkways can also be described as customs or more simply, habitual, acceptable ways of doing things. Examples of this are well known throughout history—the Plains Indians of North America viewed as "taboo" (or against custom) to scare away buffalo, which was an important source of food and clothing. Eskimos viewed the harming of seals as taboo. [Fox & Stinchcombe, 1994]

We have folkways in everyday life such as working for a day's pay, paying for what one wants—purchasing, etc. Folkways are mildly encouraged (i.e., applause) or discouraged (i.e., a look of dismay or shock). If the behavior—prescribed and proscribed—was stronger, the encouragements (financial security, status) are discouragement (physical beatings, banishment) were more pointed and strong. These stricter rules were called mores. However, as society evolved and the protection of the group became more important, mores and their sanctions (or punishment) were written down and became laws.

Development of Society

Laws	(Written rules, codes)
↑	
Mores	(Rewards/sanctions)
↑	
Customs/Folkways	(Enforced good/bad)
↑	
Prescribed/Proscribed behavior	(Good/bad)
↑	
Early man: tribes, groups	

Retaliation

Early groups accepted and encouraged the *earliest* forms of punishment on a wrongdoer—personal retaliation. If a person committed a wrongful act against a person, he could simply seek personal revenge. This theme of vengeance on the wrongdoer continues as a theme in corrections today—long, harsh sentences, no parole, etc. The practice of seeking retaliation or revenge evolved into the *blood feud*—victims' families/tribes seeking revenge on the offenders' people and family. [Allen & Simonsen, 1998] These feuds or vendettas could continue for long periods of time—spilling much blood and causing suffering, much of it probably needless.

Men were "duty bound" by religious forces and expectations to avenge deaths of kinsmen by killing the offender's nearest male relative, who in all likelihood was not involved in the crime. [Kocoureh & Wigmore, 1915, Allen & Simonsen, 1998] Some people, sick of bloodshed and suffering, began to accept property—land, castle, goods, etc., or money in place of vengeance. Vengeance was still practiced, but as rulers needed to exert control, this practice of restitution became more widespread. If a wrongdoer stayed away by his choice, he became an *outlaw*.

A civilization developed, so did the practice of writing. Laws were written down. Tribal taboos and customs were written into codes, such as the Code of Hammerabi (1750 B.C.) In Babylon. In Rome, a great influence was wielded by the "Twelve Tables" of Wood. [Fox & Stinchcombe, 1994] Sumerian Codes appeared in 1860 B.C.

In the Code of Hammerabi and the Sumerian Code, the concept of *"lex talionis"* (an eye for an eye and a tooth for a tooth) was evident. Codes in these times were vengeful and very harsh. Both the Hammurabic and Sumerian Codes called for mutilation, whipping, or wrongdoers being made to perform forced labor. Slavery was also used as a punishment. The Romans used penal servitude as a way of getting manpower to row galleys, building public works or working in mines. Slaves had their heads shaved ("mark of the slave"). [Allen & Simonsen, 1998]

The "Scales of Justice" depicted in Roman art comes from the Emperor Justinian's efforts to enforce a code in sixth century A.D. where the punishment fit the crime. As is the case today, these laws, the *Code of Justinian*, had many administrative procedures which slowed it down. When the Roman Empire fell, this code did not survive, but it left building blocks on which today's Western Codes were built. In nearby Greece, the "Code of Draco" was harsh and included previous practices of blood feud, vengeance, and outlawry. The significance of the Greek Code is that any citizen could prosecute a wrongdoer in the name of the wronged citizen. [Allen & Simonsen, 1998]

Soon religion began to have an impact on the development of corrections. In the thirteenth century, the powerful Spanish Inquisition, described as a religious tribunal, punished those who disagreed with and did not conform to the church. [Champion, 1998]

During the Middle Ages, the church enjoyed great influence and reforming criminals was a religious process. An offender had to pay a debt to society and *another* debt to God. Accused people were subjected to "trials by ordeal" in which painful tests were administered. If an offender was innocent, it was believed that he would emerge unscathed and unharmed, the guilty would suffer excruciating pain and agony, and finally, die. The authorities did not care about rehabilitating an offender except through a painful punishment in the hope that God would be pacified. However, one lasting concept of the Middle Ages and its religious influence has been the term *"free will."*

Free Will

A concept whose basic premises are:
- A person chooses good or bad actions
- As a result of these choices, he/she must be held accountable for the consequences of them.

The church during the Middle Ages used this concept to reinforce harsh punishment. Its position was that harsh treatment would not be necessary if the wrongdoer had not chosen these actions.

Source: Allen & Simonsen, 1992.

The concept of free will echoes throughout our modern correctional facilities, but in a secular tone. Although many inmates have serious problems, such as substance abuse, etc., they have chosen illegal acts and must pay the consequences through doing time. Jail officers say frequently of prisoners—no one made them come here, they chose to do the crime.

Free Will v. Criminal Responsibility

Today's public thinks that many criminals will "get off" by using the criminally insane defense. While this defense is mentioned frequently in the media, it is only brought up in 1% of felony cases and is successfully in only one quarter of that amount. The courts have ruled that for an offender to qualify for the insanity defense, they must show suffering from a "serious mental disease or defect" which impairs their behavioral controls or somehow hinders the understanding of what they did.

The majority of criminals know what they did and understand the proceedings affecting them. "Criminal responsibility" takes the Middle Ages term "free will" to a modern plane—their mental state did not interfere with their understanding of what they did. It did not impair controls of their behavior. Simply, they acted on free will—the modern translation being: they *rationally* chose to commit an illegal act and should suffer punishment for their actions.

> Adapted from St. Lalley, "Drawing a Clear Line Between Criminals and the Criminally Insane, *Washington Post*, 11/23/97, p. C2.

Early Methods of Punishment

Early punishments of wrongdoers had two distinct characteristics: variety and brutality. Until the 1700's, the main rule of punishment was *corporal punishment* or as defined as "infliction of pain on the body by any device or method." [Champion, 1990] Methods of corporal punishment were numerous; brutality and pain were the rule of the day.

Methods of Corporal Punishment

- Flogging: whipping or "mortifying the flesh" on back or buttocks; accepted practice in schools, prisons and on naval vessels.
- Stocks: offenders were seated with their feet protruding through holes. Meant to be uncomfortable, the citizenry could jeer, taunt and humiliate them.

- Pillories: offenders were forced to stand with their heads and arms protruding through holes. Like in stocks, offenders were humiliated by townsfolk.
- Ducking stool: a device consisting of a chair at the end of a long lever; the offender seated in the chair is dunked in a pond or river to the point of almost drowning. [Champion, 1990]

Other methods included: adulterers having an "A" branded on their faces; tongues cut out of "liars;" mutilation (cutting off of hands, dismemberments), and branding. Authorities were inventive in devising ways of inflicting pain to force wrongdoers to "think." In America, corporal punishments were practiced well into the 20th century. Flogging was practiced in Delaware's prisons. As recently as 1937, only 60 years ago, Georgia inmates were placed in stocks that painfully secured both feet and hands. In Middle Eastern countries, mutilation is still a practice. [Leinwand, 1972]

Capital Punishment

When the authorities decided to take the life of an offender, the concept of *capital punishment* began. Like with corporal punishment, various methods were devised to ensure the wrongdoer suffered a very painful death. A simple rule was the more harsh and brutal, the better. Consider this account of an Indian tribal execution of a village sentinel which, because of his carelessness, the village had been burned:

> The chief sits alone, his principal men placed on a long semi-circular bench nearby. The executioner orders the sentinel to kneel down before the chief... He sets his left foot on the offender's back and with a sharp-edged club made of ebony or some other hard wood, he strikes him a blow on the head hard enough to split open the skull.

An explorer in Florida described this 1500's account and noted that other offenses warranted the same punishments. [Leinwand, 1972]

Early Methods of Capital Punishment

- burning at the stake: offender is tied to a wooden stake in a public area, kindling is piled around the offender and set afire.
- hanging: offender's neck is broken by dropping with a noose around the neck.

- starvation: offender is placed in a locked box to starve.
- beheading: taking off the offender's head by sword, ax, guillotine.
- iron maiden: victim is placed inside a box with a hinged door, when closed, spikes from back and front would pierce the body.

[Fox & Stinchcombe, 1994.]

In Colonial America, the death penalty had an interesting development. Colonial authorities used the death penalty for crimes against morality such as adultery and sodomy. In the Massachusetts Bay Colony in 1644, a married woman and her lover were executed. However, executions for adultery ceased in the mid 1600's due to the reluctance of juries to convict. [Friedman, 1993]

Overall the colonies sparingly used the death penalty. Before 1660 in the Massachusetts Bay Colony, only fifteen executions took place. In Pennsylvania, only 94 condemned prisoners out of 170 were pardoned or reprieved. On the whole, Pennsylvania executions averaged only one per year. Pardons were also a factor. Virginia and New York used it extensively. [Friedman, 1993]

Concerning capital offenses, murder was the most common capital offense. However, rape and statutory rape were also punishable by death. In Virginia, a 1748 law imposed the death penalty on repeat offenders or receividists. Livestock in those times was important property. For a first offense of hog theft, for example, the wrongdoer received a fine and twenty-five lashes; the second offense had a penalty of two hours in a pillory nailed by the ears; a third offense resulted in death. [Friedman, 1993]

Mitigating factors were considered in early times. The "two witness rule" in the Massachusetts Bay Colony said that no offender was to be executed without the testimony of two or three witnesses. But if the prisoner confessed, the rule did not apply. Another rule that was used by criminals to stay alive was "*benefit of clergy.*" Benefit of clergy was basically a "dodge." In the Middle Ages, priests accused of a crime could have their trials in Church courts. Ordinary citizens could not read, priests could, and by reading from the Bible, they proved that they were clergymen. Around 1600, benefit of clergy protected any wrongdoer from the hangman's noose if they could read at all; they then received a lesser penalty such as branding. This was practiced in the English colonies. [Friedman, 1993]

Of course, the practice of capital punishment has been refined; the "two witness rule" and "benefit of clergy" are no longer practiced. While a detailed discussion of capital punishment would be too much detailed for this work, the reader should note:

- in 1997, the Federal government and thirty-eight states had capital punishment statutes;
- forty-five inmates were executed in 1996;
- on January 1, 1997, 3,267 inmates were under a death sentence; and
- lethal injection was the most common method, followed by electrocution, gas, hanging and firing squad.

[Camp & Camp, 1997]

Corporal punishment was generally conducted in public view. The pillory, stocks, burning at the stake, etc., were public. It was hoped that not only the wrongdoer would suffer shame, but the punishment would serve as a warning and deter future wrongdoing. The debate as to whether capital punishment is a deterrent has continued for decades without a definitive conclusion. Some think that executions should be made public while others think that the spectacle of a public execution would commercialize and cheapen a process, though depressing — and it should maintain some dignity. The fact that in some jurisdictions victims' families are permitted to view an execution is a compromise.

Early Prisons and Methods of Confinement

In the early stages of civilized society, methods of punishment were numerous and brutal, as has been stated. Not much thought was given to humanely housing wrongdoers until trial and caring for their needs, as evidenced by today's modern facilities. Early places of confinement were horrible in methods of confinement and in the lack of decency. Early prisons were "self consciously punitive and controlling; their internal regimes were intentionally inhumane...[they] were haphazardly arranged, inflicting pain without purpose...meeting out pain for pain's sake." Prisoners were meant to be painful for the offender. [Johnson, 1996]

Probably the first prison was the *Mamertime Prison* built under the sewers of Rome in 64 B.C. This prison was nothing more than dungeons and its purpose apparently was to cause offenders great suffering due to "neglect, the darkness and the stench." [Peck, 1992; Johnson, 1996]

Underground Prisons

Early societies, such as Rome, used underground confinement as a convenient way to house criminals and keep them securely confined out of the public's view in squalid conditions. Prisoners were also housed in sulfur pits and quarries.

In Colonial America, this belief resulted in what some researchers say is the United States' first state prison, *Newgate Prison*, in an abandoned underground copper mine in Simsbury, Connecticut. Established in 1773, it became a permanent prison in 1790. Inmates were shackled at the ankles and worked long hours. Offenses such as burglary and counterfeiting drew sentences of up to ten years; a second offense resulted in life imprisonment. Administration buildings were built over the mineshaft; the "prison" was three excavated caverns with one pool of fresh water.

Sources: Champion, 1990; Fox & Stinchcombe, 1994, ACA, 1983.

As time went on, fortresses, castles, bridge abutments, and town gate-houses were all pressed into the service of housing prisoners. Feudalism of the Middle Ages ended and more people moved to urban areas. In London in 1557, *Bridewell*, a workhouse, was built to deal with wrongdoers by using them as cheap labor based on the Judeo-Christian belief that work benefits the soul and society (or the "work ethic").

Another institution that authorities used to house outcasts were debtors' prisons — "prisons" which housed the poor until their monetary debts were paid by family, friends, charity-minded groups or citizens. Some were housed until they died. [Fox & Stinchcome, 1994]

By 1576, the English Parliament had ordered every county in England to construct a workhouse or house of correction. Work was hard and discipline was harsh. [Allen & Simonsen, 1998]

Gaols

The term "jail" originated from the old English word *gaol* which is pronounced the same. In 1166 A.D., Henry II, King of England, established gaols as part of the Constitution of Clarendon. Gaols were locally operated by English "shire-reeves" (now sheriffs) and were meant to be holding facilities to confine or detain persons accused of breaking the law. They were held untill courts convened and guilt or innocence was established. [Champion, 1990]

Throughout the 16th and 18th centuries, an estimated 200 common jails were in operation in England, under the responsibility of the local sheriff and the justices of the peace. The justices of peace used county funds to repair and rebuild jails. The sheriffs were the keepers and legal owners of the jails. Like with early places of imprisonment, jails took many forms — parts of castles, rooms in old towers or gatehouses, or two or three dungeons under a public building. The sheriff appointed the keeper, who was not paid a salary. The fee system developed where fees were charged for every item (such as a bed, mattress) and process (being housed in squalid quarters or a private room). Also under the fee system, jail keepers could sell goods to the inmates and use them for forced labor. The jail business was corrupt and profitable. Prisoners had to support themselves through family, friends or begging. Extortion was practiced, resulting in pain and death for inmates who could not pay the required fees. [Kemble, 1996]

Conditions in jails were filthy, leading to outbreaks of *"jail fever,"* a form of typhus. An example of these conditions was London's Newgate Gaol, where the cells were poorly ventilated, gloomy and dark. Inmates suffered from an appalling stench and inadequate water supplies. The gaol was paved in stone, the prisoners had no beds and endured miseries by having to lay on the stones. Fees were even charged to inmates to warm themselves by a fire! [Moynahan and Burke, 1991]

Another type of early punishment that had a decidedly different aspect than just throwing inmates into squalid quarters was banishment into the wild or exile. The practice had English roots; errant children in Coventry, England, were sentenced to having all communications cut off with everyone — a practice knows as being placed "in Coventry." Criminal offenders heard sentences banishing them to unknown misfortunes such as storms, shipwrecks, famine or death by the hands of savages or wild beasts. With the onset of mechanization in the Industrial Revolution, slavery became less profitable. Countries began to export prisoners through transportation, sending them away. [Fox and Stinchcombe, 1994]

Transportation

A form of banishment, transporting inmates to remote areas or colonies, was widely used after the onset of the Industrial Revolution. Russia sent convicts to Siberia; Africa received prisoners from Spain and Portugal; France sent prisoners to South America.

England sent prisoners to the North American colonies beginning in 1630 and in 1717, Parliament officially ruled America was Britain's penal colony. By the start of the American Revolution in 1776, an estimated 100,000 prisoners had been transported to America. Transported prisoners were a free, thrifty, economical source of labor. Private contractors and businesses took advantage and allowed convicts to work as "indentured servants." Convicts satisfied their sentence by working for wealthy colonists for specific time periods. The American Revolution effectively closed the colonies to prisoners; England turned to Australia for use as a penal colony until 1879. Eventually the usage of prisons ended banishment and transportation.

Source: Fox & Stinchcombe, 1994.

In England from 1776 to 1858, the overload of convicts forced English authorities to house prisoners in old, abandoned transport ships anchored in harbors and rivers. These *hulks* housed young and old, hardened criminals and misdemeanants and men and women all together without regard to segregation, safety or hygiene. Because of practices such as flogging, use of inmate labor and squalid, filthy conditions, hulks were horrible places. Hulks were generally in use until 1858. However, they were used in the 19th century in California. The idea of housing inmates in ships was considered as recently as 1976 when Washington considered using decommissioned U.S. Navy warships. Old ferries and barges are used currently in New York. [Allen & Simonsen, 1992]

Improvement of Confinement

In the discussion of the history of corrections, two early cellular prisons bear mention—the *Maison de Force* at Ghent, Belgium, and the *Hospice of San Michel* in Rome, Italy.

The Maison de Force (House of Enforcement) fed prisoners well. Prisoners were also supplied with adequate clothing and lodged in a humane manner, separately at night. The institution was operated by administrator and disciplinarian, Jean Jacques Vilain, who had some revolutionary practices. He instituted a classification procedure—separating women and children from hardened prisoners and minor offenders from felons. Vilain's discipline was based on the Biblical rule that if a man [prisoner] will not work, he will not eat. [Champion, 1990; Allen & Simonsen, 1992]

The Hospice of San Michel was located in Rome and was built by Pope Clement XI. He placed the following inscription over the door which is still there to this day:

> It is insufficient to restrain the wicked by punishment unless you render them virtuous by corrective discipline.

Its target group was juveniles under age twenty. Inmates were exposed to hard work and lessons in Scripture. Strict silence was the rule; violators were flogged. Separate cells were used for sleeping and a large central hall was for work. This practice would influence discipline in later institutions. [Allen & Simonsen, 1992]

Three Key Philosophers

Not all observers and practitioners of corrections during the 1600's and 1700's were callous, brutal and harsh. Frenchmen like Montesquieu (1689-

1755) and Voltaire (1694-1778) called for penal reforms such as punishment fitting the crimes, more humane conditions for the imprisoned and judicial reform. In England, Jeremy Bentham (1748-1832) called for a unique form of punishment where criminals would see clearly the losses and pains of punishment due to punishment being swift, certain and painful. Bentham also developed the architectural concept of the *"panopticon."* The panopticon was a circular design for prisons that allowed correctional officers to observe and monitor many prisoner housing areas from a central location. This concept is in wide use today. [Champion, 1990]

Three philosophers of the field of corrections bear mentioning because their influence continues to this day. They are: Cesare Bonesana, Marchese de Beccaria or Cesare Beccaria (1738-94); John Howard, High Sheriff, Bedfordshire, England (1726-1790); and William Penn, Quaker, Governor of Pennsylvania (1644-1718).

Cesare Beccaria: An Italian jurist and economist, Beccaria opposed the death penalty, torture and harsh treatment of inmates. His philosophy was that the "true measure" of crime is the "harm [that is] done to society." He authored and published the book *Essay on Crime and Punishment* in 1764. His philosophies are summarized below and became known as the "classical school of criminology."

1. Laws alone determine the punishment of crimes, punishments stay within the law and cannot be increased by any one magistrate. Laws are to serve the needs of society, not moral virtues.

2. Punishments are to be determined by the injury done to society. The punishment of a nobleman (rich) should not differ from punishment to the "lowest member of society" (the poor).

3. Punishments should be swift and certain. Offender personalities and social characteristics are not considered.

4. Prevention of crime is more important than punishment and the mode of punishment should leave an impression on the citizens. Legal codes must define prohibited behaviors and their punishments.

5. All accused persons are to be considered innocent until proven guilty. They should be allowed to present evidence in their behalf and be treated humanely before trial.

6. Criminal procedures should not include secret accusations and torture. Trials should be speedy.

7. Concerning penalties, punishment against property should only be punished by fines. If the offender cannot pay, imprisonment is warranted. For the crimes against the state, banishment is acceptable.

8. Life imprisonment is a better deterrent than the death penalty. There should be no capital punishment because it is irreparable.
9. Imprisonment of offenders should be more widely used, but the mode should be improved. This can be done by providing better living quarters and by separating and classifying prisoners by sex, age and degree of criminality (the offense/their criminal histories). [Killinger & Cromwell, 1973; Champion, 1990; Allen & Simonsen, 1992]

Becarria's philosophies had a great influence on the jurisprudence and legal philosophies of many countries, including the U.S. Constitution. In jails and prisons today, his idea of separating offenders by sex, age and degree of criminality is practiced through classification procedures.

John Howard: Next to Beccaria, the contributions of John Howard (1726-1790) to the discipline of corrections are noteworthy and his influence is still felt in today's jails and prisons. Howard was Sheriff of Bedfordshire, England, and traveled outside of England to examine other prison systems. Impressed with the humane treatment of prisoners in the Maison de Force, he published *The State of Prisons* in 1777. This classical essay led to reforms in European and American correctional institutions. In 1779, the British government passed the Penitentiary Act. [Champion, 1990; Killinger & Cromwell, 1973]

This significant law dictated the creation of new correctional institutions, where prisoners would work *productively* at hard labor. Prisoners were to be adequately fed, clothed and housed singly in sanitary isolated cells. There were to be no fees for the prisoners' incarceration. Other reforms included regular inspections. Howard believed that hard and productive labor would result in prisoners realizing how serious their crimes were and the consequences of lawbreaking.

From these ideas of reform and penance came the term *penitentiary*, a Latin derivative suggesting a place that a man is sent to do penance for sins against society. [Champion, 1990; Leinwand, 1972]

The State of Prisons, 1777

The publication of this essay by John Howard helped to change the course of corrections. Howard's views on the management of inmates were unique.

Location and Construction of Prisons: areas that are "airy," near a clean river or brook in order to avoid "the stench of sewers." Men-felons wards should be raised on arcades; small rooms and cabins should allow prisoners to sleep alone and reflect in solitude and silence. Baths should be "comodius" with an adequate water supply. Ovens can be used for cleaning clothes. Day rooms should have a kitchen and fireplace.

Classification of Inmates: Women felons are housed separately from the men, the same separations apply for old, hardened offenders from young criminals.

Hygiene: Howard detailed how wards should be cleaned (scraped and then swept and washed), prisoners entering the gaol should be bathed and have his/her clothes washed. Prison uniforms should be worn for hygiene and to detect escapees. Bedding should be changed weekly.

Food: Food should include "good household bread," having good meals would encourage prisoners to behave.

Rules: No fighting, quarreling, abusive language, or gaming (gambling). Injured inmates could complain to the keeper who "must hear both parties face to face" and make a decision. The aggressor is then punished by "closer confinement." More serious offenses are examined by a magistrate or inspector. Rules should be "made known...and intelligibly drawn up."

Staff and Management: No fees are charged and no profit gained from the prisoners. Gaolors (jailors) are to be paid a suitable salary proportioned to "trust and trouble." They are to be "honest, active, and humane...sober"...having no contact with the sale of liquors. Inspectors must be appointed for every prison. They are to hear all complaints and correct serious wrongs. Inspectors should visit once per week without notice.

Security: Alarm bells, double doors, surrounding high wall, clothes of two colors, jailor's window looking into the yard.

The influence of this document is still felt today in penal housing, disciplinary procedures and hiring practices.

[Adapted from *Penology: Evolution of Corrections in America*, George Killinger and Paul Cromwell, editors; *State of Prisons - 1777*, West, 1973.]

The *State of the Prisons* influenced the establishment and operations of the goal at Wymondham, in Norfolk, England. The gaol, built in 1785, had cells for separating different types of prisoners and men and women. The founder of the gaol, Sir Thomas Beever (1786-1814), had prisoners sleeping and working in separate cells. Beever believed that this is more effective than corporal punishment, like whipping. This idea worked: prisoners earned double their maintenance by working at hard labor six days per week. Judges reported fewer offenders being committed to the gaol, so it was believed that it was a deterrent. Ironically, the founder of the gaol's principles, John Howard, died of jail fever (typhus) in 1790. Representative of the poor health conditions of English jails, this disease killed many prisoners. [ACA, 1983]

William Penn: Arriving in Colonial America in 1682, this Quaker governor of Pennsylvania instituted reforms. Penn established a penal code which did two things: (1) retained capital punishment only in cases of homicide; and (2) punished wrongdoers by hard labor instead of bloody corporal punishment. There were also other significant provisions.

All prisoners were eligible to be released on bail. Prisoners who were wrongfully incarcerated could recover double damages; and prisons could not charge fees for food and lodging. Injured parties could claim double restitution from the land and goods of felons and all counties were to erect "houses of detention" to replace such brutal methods as the pillory, stocks, etc. [ACA, 1983]

This code, or the *Great Law of 1682* took a humane approach to corrections. However, flogging was still used as punishments for the crimes of adultery, arson and rape. The Great Law and the policies that followed created a need that continues to today—the need to find housing for felons who are sentenced to a length of incarceration. Beginning in Pennsylvania in 1725, county jails began to emerge with sheriffs maintaining administrative and operational control. [Kemble, 1996] However, one day after Penn died in 1718, the Great Law was repealed and replaced by the English Anglican Code. Punishment began to be more harsh and to a large degree, capital and corporal punishments were re-established. [Allen & Simonsen, 1992]

Walnut Street Jail

The Walnut Street Jail in Pennsylvania was built in 1773 and closed in 1835. The reforms of William Penn had long since grown obsolete. By 1730, legislation had passed reinstating inmate fees. Extortion and corruption among inmates had grown. There was no classification of inmates with regard to age, gender, race, crimes or the physical and mental states of the inmates. [Kemble, 1996]

In 1790, reform-minded Quakers, trying to change the treatment of convicted criminals, requested that the Pennsylvania legislature declare a wing of the Walnut Street Jail a penitentiary house for *all* convicted felons. Exceptions were those prisoners condemned to death. [ACA, 1983]

This era spawned the birth of the prison reform movement and, in practicality, the first corrections volunteer organization. The efforts to change prisoner treatment were primarily due to the group formed in 1787—the Philadelphia Society for the Alleviation of the Miseries of Public Prisons. Members visited the prisons once per week bringing food, clothing, religious tutoring, and teaching basic reading and writing skills. They also made inquiries about inmates' conditions and reported abuses. The Society wanted to know if society's morals were influenced by punishment and confinement. The Society still exists today as the Pennsylvania Prison Society. [ACA, 1983; Champion, 1990]

The Walnut Street Jail was revolutionary. The reformers' efforts had resulted in humane treatment for prisoners and genuine concerns for their welfare.

In practice, the Walnut Street Jail treated inmates well by doing the following:

- More serious offenders were separated from others in sixteen large solitary cells, other inmates were separated by degree of offense and by sex.
- Inmates were assigned productive work according to gender and the offense conviction. Women made clothing, mended clothes and did laundry. Inmates who were skilled could work as carpenters, shoemakers or craftsmen. Unskilled prisoners also worked by beating hemp or jute for caulking in ships. Prisoners who worked, except women, received a daily wage, which was applied to defray the cost of their incarceration.
- Religious groups provided religious instruction for offenders. [Champion, 1990]

Medium, maximum and minimum security institutions can trace their roots to the Walnut Street Jail. The jail also was the forerunner of the usage of solitary confinement.

During the next several decades, many institutions and management practices were modeled on the Walnut Street Jail. [Champion, 1990] Other innovative practices included weekly inspections of the jail by city inspectors and inmate behavior was controlled by a disciplinary system of rewards and punishments. By the beginning of the 1800's, prisons were being built in the eastern states of the United States. Prisons in New York, Massachusetts, Maryland, Vermont, Kentucky, Ohio and Virginia followed the premises of the Walnut Street Jail.

Summary

Early methods of punishing wrongdoers developed from early views of vengeance and inflicting pain. From early civilizations through the establishment of the Walnut Street Jail, criminal offenders suffered the pais of capital punishment, corporal punishment, and housing in unsafe and unsanitary structures. Enlightened philosophers such as Bentham, Beccaria, Howard, and Penn set the course for change. While many institutions were not conducive to positive treatment of prisoners, institutions such as the Maisons de Force, Hospice of San Michel, and the Walnut Street Jail started penal reform.

Review Questions

1. What were the views of Beccaria's Classical School of Criminology?
2. How did churches influence the punishment of wrongdoers?
3. Describe methods of capital and corporal punishment.
4. What were the views of John Howard concerning jails, prisons and the treatment of inmates?
5. Why was the Walnut Street Jail revolutionary?

Terms/Concepts

Prescribed behavior	Corporal punishment
Proscribed behavior	Capital punishment
Retaliation	Benefit of clergy
Lex talionis	Mamertime Prison
Code of Justinian	Newgate Prison
Free will	Bridewell
Gaol	Maisons de Force
Transportation	Hospice of San Michel
Hulks	Panopticon
Great Law of 1682	Walnut Street Jail
Penitentiary	Jail Fever
Blood Feud	Outlaw

References

Allen, Harry and Clifford Simonsen, *Corrections in America: An Introduction*, 6th Ed., Prentice Hall, Englewood Cliffs, NJ, 1992.

Allen, Harry and Clifford Simonsen, *Corrections in America: An Introduction*, 8th Ed., Prentice Hall, Englewood Cliffs, NJ, 1998.

American Correctional Association, *The American Prison from the Beginning: A Pictorial History*, Laurel, Maryland, 1983.

Camp, George and Camille Camp, *Corrections Yearbook, 1997*, Criminal Justice Institute: South Salem, NY, 1997.

Champion, Dean J., *Corrections in the United States: A Contemporary Perspective*, Prentice Hall, Englewood Cliffs, NJ, 1990.

Fox, Vernon and Jeanne Stinchcombe, *Introduction to Corrections*, 4th Ed., Prentice Hall, Englewood Cliffs, NJ, 1994.

Friedman, Lawrence, *Crime and Punishment in American History*, N.W. Basic Books, 1993.

Johnson, Robert, *Hard Time: Understanding and Reforming the Prisons*, 2nd Ed., Wadsworth, Belmont, California, 1996.

Kemble, Tod, *Jails in America*, Texas Journal of Corrections, May-June, 1996, pp. 14-19.

Killinger, George G. And Paul Cromwell, Editors, *Penology: The Evolution of Corrections in America*, St. Paul, Minn, West, 1973.

Kocourek, Albert, and John Wigmore, *Evolution of Law, vol. 2, Punishment and Ancient Institutions*, Little; Brown, Boston, 1915.

Lally, Stephen, "Drawing a Clear Line Between Criminals and the Criminally Insane," *The Washington Post*, November 23, 1997, p. C2.

Leinwand, Gerald, Editor, *Prisons*, 1972, N.Y. Pocket Books.

Moynahan, J.M., and Burke, Troy, "London's Famous Newgate Gaol (1188-1902), part of "Some Old English Institutions," in *American Jails*, May-June, 1991, pp. 76-77.

Peck, H.T. (ed.), *Harper's Dictionary of Classical Literature and Antiquity*, NY, American Book, 1922.

Chapter 5

The Development of the Modern Correctional Facility

The development of the modern correctional facility in the United States has its roots in three penal systems—the Pennsylvania system, the Auburn system, and the Reformatory system. By understanding the philosophies and daily operations of the institutions in these systems, one can see the reasoning behind today's penal facilities.

The Pennsylvania System

The Pennsylvania system was a result of the disciplinary system of the Walnut Street jail. This school of thought was primarily developed by the penal reformer, Dr. Benjamin Rush (1745-1813), a famous physician, politician, and signer of the Declaration of Independence. Dr. Rush believed that dangerous, assaultive prisoners should be housed singly from the rest of the inmate population. He advocated gardens for food and exercise. Prisons should sell goods that were manufactured in the prisons in order to help financially support the prisons. Dr. Rush believed that prisoners must reform and be prevented from committing crimes. Dangerous criminals must be removed from society. Dr. Rush's ideas were incorporated into the *Pennsylvania system* of discipline at the Walnut Street Jail—an inmate was to be in solitary confinement with no work. The objective was to get offenders to repent and reflect on their crimes all day. However, such isolation and inactivity was detrimental to the inmate's well being so minimal labor such as handicrafts and piecework was allowed. Inmates also received moral and religious education. [ACA, 1983]

Two institutions were constructed. The Western State Penitentiary in Pittsburgh was built in 1826. It had an octagonal shape, based on the cellular isolation wing of the Walnut Street Jail. Inmates were kept in isolation without work. The cells were replaced with larger, outside cells in 1833. Inmates were allowed to work in their cells in 1829. The Eastern State Penitentiary was influenced by the Western State Penitentiary and was built in 1829. It became the model for the Pennsylvania or "separate" sys-

59

tem. It had seven cellblocks radiating from a hublike center. This central structure had a rotunda equipped with an alarm bell and observation tower. The entire prison was surrounded by a wall. [ACA, 1983]

For an inmate, life inside a Pennsylvania system prison was not easy. The routine has been described as "one of solitary confinement and manual labor, a simple monastic existence in which the prisoners were kept separate from one another as well as from the outside world." [Johnson, 1996]

Inmates lived in solitude—eating, sleeping, and working alone. Exercise was alone in private yards and they saw and spoke to only visitors who the staff carefully selected. The only reading material allowed was the Bible. Officials would not let inmates see or speak to each other for fear of contamination. The goal of total solitude was to arrest or deter the progress of corruption, thus receiving no additional contamination. Inmates could receive labor as a welcome diversion after a time and learn regularity and self discipline. If an inmate showed good behavior, he could receive books and visitors more frequently. Security was maintained due to close confinement and no communication with the other inmates was allowed. [Rothman, 1971]

This system was expensive. Solitary confinement mandated the construction of large cells. Crafts and piecework could not generate much income to the prison, although prison staff was minimal due to the isolation of the inmates. [Johnson, 1996]

The Auburn System

While some prison authorities embraced the Pennsylvania system as the answer to the question of how to reform the criminal, others believed in another system first developed at a prison in Auburn, New York.

Built in 1816, the Auburn prison was modeled after other prisons using solitary confinement. An experiment to test the separate system was tried from 1821 to 1823. A test group of inmates was confined to their cells without participating in labor. The majority became ill and insane; also, the majority of the test inmates were pardoned. Authorities then began a policy of inmates sleeping in their cells at night, but worked and ate meals together during the day. This system became known as the "congregate system"[ACA, 1983] or the *Auburn system*.

The Auburn system developed a system of cell construction that continues to this day: the *interior cellblock*. This economical building of prison cells simply was constructing cells back to back in tiers. The tiers were constructed in a large, hollow building. The cell doors opened out on a gallery or "catwalk" which was eight to ten feet from the exterior wall of the building. Thus, many prisoners could be "stacked up." [ACA, 1983]

Inmates in the Auburn type prison system slept singly and congregated for eating and working. Like the Pennsylvania system, there was no communication with other prisoners. Silence was the rule in order to have a monastic type environment by night and a military type of routine by day. [See box] Inmates labored all day and the only sounds they heard were guards' orders, machines and tools. They were in a "prison within a prison." [Johnson, 1996]

Discipline: Silence and Regimentation

Both the Pennsylvania and Auburn prison systems believed in order to prevent contamination and cross-infection from prisoners and to encourage improved behavior, silence and penitence must be enforced. Authorities in the Pennsylvania system believed that silence and penitence resulted in more control of prisoners, a prisoner's individual needs could be addressed, and he would not be "contaminated" from other prisoners. An inmate could be released with his background known only by a few penal administrators.

In the Auburn system, inmates ate with backs straight at attention in silence. Corporal punishment for rule breaking was common. Maine prisons used the ball and chains; Connecticut used the cold shower. Whipping was used. Regimentation in daily routines became the mainstay. Bells signaled when the prisoners could leave their cells. Tasks such as emptying chamber pots were done in line formation. Marching to and from meals and work was done in *lockstep* (close order, single file, each prisoner looking over the shoulder of the man in front, facing towards the right, feet stepping in unison).

It was believed that existing in silence, thinking about their crimes, and severe discipline and regimentation would teach proper behavior and good habits.

Sources: *The American Prison from the Beginning*, ACA, 1983; Rothman, David, *The Discovery of the Asylum: Social Order and Disorder in the New Republic*, 1971; Johnson, Robert, *Hard Time: Understanding and Reforming the Prison*, 1996.

Eventually a debate took place as to which system was better. While Pennsylvania system advocates argued control and anti-contamination, Auburn supporters showed that it was cheaper to construct interior cell-

Manatee County Corrections Facility.

blocks, vocational training was offered in congregate shops, and as a result, more money was earned for the states. The Auburn system won. From 1825-1870, twenty-three Auburn type prisons were built in the United States. [ACA, 1983]

The Reformatory Influence

As Auburn type prisons flourished in the 1860's, a prison reform movement began to develop. From 1870 to 1900, the reformatory movement arose and left a definite mark on corrections. The *Reformatory system* advocated education, vocational or trade training, grades and marks, the indeterminate sentence, and parole. [ACA, 1983]

Two things influenced the reformatory type of inmate management: the *Mark system* under Captain Alexander Mconochie and the *Irish system* under Sir Walter Crofton, an Irishman. [ACA, 1983] Both systems believed that inmates through proper behavior and participation in rehabilitative activities could earn their release from prison *early*.

McConochie was an Englishman who took charge of the penal colony of Norfolk Island in the South Pacific Ocean in 1840. Conditions were brutal. He believed that an offender can be reformed if given an incentive for good behavior. While determinate sentencing fixes a flat maximum term (i.e., ten years) that the inmate must serve, indeterminate sentencing fixes a range of time (i.e., five to ten years). Prisoners in McConochie's charge could be released sooner by earning marks for proper behavior and hard work. Discipline decreased as inmates earned marks and received privileges. McConochie believed that the Mark system better prepared inmates for early release. His policies were not well received as many businesses relying on convict labor opposed him. As a result, he was removed from his post. [Fox & Stinchcombe, 1994]

Crofton developed the "Irish system" in which the indeterminate sentence was used as an incentive for inmates to move through stages toward release. The first stage consisted of solitary confinement combined with dull, routine work. In the second stage, inmates were assigned to public works and several grades, each of which shortens the stay. In the final stage, inmates were assigned to an "intermediate prison." In this stage, the inmate worked and *without supervision* could go into the community and return, similar to today's work release. If a prisoner found work and continued to behave, the prisoner could be conditionally released on a pardon or *ticket of leave*. If the prisoner violated the conditions of this ticket, it could be revoked and the inmate would return to prison to finish the original sentence. [ACA, 1983] These ideas and the "ticket of leave" concept evolved into what we now know as parole. [Fox & Stinchcombe, 1994]

One key event that occurred during this period of American penology is the 1870 National Prison Congress held in Cincinnati by corrections professionals. In this unprecedented conference, twenty-two resolutions were adopted in a "Declaration of Principles." Included in these principles were promotions of reformation of inmates, classification based on the Mark and Irish Systems, rewards for good conduct, endorsements of religion, education, vocational training, and improvements in penal management and architecture. These principles are still advocated today by the organization born at that Congress—the American Correctional Association. [ACA, 1983]

The Reformatory Movement and the use of indeterminate sentencing started with the 1870 National Prison Congress and in 1876 with the opening of the *Elmira (New York) Reformatory* under the leadership of Zebulon Brockway. Targeting young offenders aged 16 to 30 years of age, this prison placed inmates into one of three classes or grades. If they behaved, they could move to the first grade and parole eligibility. Moving to the third grade was a demotion. As a result, sentences to this prison were indeterminate. Movement from grade two to grade one was based on earned "marks" and education and trade training was available. However, by 1910, the Reformatory movement was on the decline due to not luring adequate staff to maintain high quality rehabilitation programs and staff feeling that old style discipline was easier than the grade system. [ACA, 1983]

The Industrial Type Prisons

A common myth or mistaken image of the 20th century prison is that only large state and Federal prisons used inmates as a type of "factory worker." In reality, prisons have been used by government and private industries for the production of goods.

After the Civil War (1861-1865), the South was in economic ruin. Slavery was gone so a new source of labor had to be found—the convict.

In the South, states leased out their convicts to contractors. Another method was for prison administrators to take in contracts. Convict labor was cheap and cost effective. Many Southern convicts were black plantation workers and were exploited. Leasing continued into the 1920's. [Allen & Simonsen, 1992] Conditions were brutal. If a business leased convicts, they were transported in *prison wagons* to the work site. These "mobile cages" could hold up to thirty convicts and provided sleeping quarters. If a prison "contracted" out work, the convicts worked inside the prison. The chain gang and guard dogs became widely used. [ACA, 1983]

The goal of turning profits and producing goods for the state gave rise to the prison farm and the prison camp. Both provided work for convicts in agriculture, road building, and prison construction. Prison farms began to decline by 1973; privately produced food was cheaper than convict grown. Some states still use the camp system. [ACA, 1983]

From 1900 through the 1920's, prisons were used as factories. The expansion of railroads and the development of the automobile resulted in convicts building and maintaining roads—working for long hours under conditions less favorable than in private industry. The zenith of prison industries came in 1924 where $74 million of convict-made material was produced. From 1929 to 1940, the Congress and the states passed laws that severely restricted the manufacture of prison goods which were competing on the market with private goods. Today, there is inmate labor, but it is restricted to goods that are sold in restrictive markets within the state, goods for usage in state agencies and institutions, and public works projects such as construction and maintenance of roads, parks, public facilities, etc. [Fox & Stinchcombe, 1994]

The Big House

Beginning in the early 20th century and lasting primarily through the 1950's, a type of prison known as the *Big House* developed. These prisons were walled institutions with large cellblock buildings. These build-

Inmate Housing Unit, Manatee County Corrections Facility.

ings contained stacks of three or more tiers of one or two inmate cells. The average institutional population was about 2,500 inmates. [Irvin, 1980]

The "Big House" prison was maximum security where custody was strictly enforced. Very little was offered in terms of rehabilitative programming. Punishments were brutal; routines were monotonous. According to Johnson, three things made life in the "Big House" bearable—tobacco, abolition of corporal punishment, and some internal freedoms. Convicts could smoke, they were not beaten or tortured, and they could move around the prison. But cells were drab, food was part of a monotonous menu, and the work and leisure routines were devoid of any goals or initiative. Prisoners were told to keep silent and guards could use force to maintain control. [Johnson, 1996]

The era of the "Big House" resulted in the construction of well known prisons such as San Quentin (California), Sing Sing (Ossining, New York), and Stateville (Illinois). [Irvin, 1980] It also ushered in the "isolation" type prison such as Alcatraz in San Francisco and more recent models of Pelican Bay (California) and Marion (Illinois).

Isolation Type Prisons

Alcatraz, Pelican Bay and Marion are representative of super maximum security, isolation type prisons.

Officially known as the United States Federal Penitentiary, Alcatraz Island, *the Rock* was known to famous criminals such as Al "Scarface" Capone and George "Machine Gun" Kelly. Formerly a fort and a military prison, Alcatraz was a Federal prison from 1934 to 1963. The majority of the inmates imprisoned at Alcatraz were problems in other Federal prisons—troublemakers, escape risks, etc. Security was tight not only by guards, but by its location, an island surrounded by cold water and a swift current in San Francisco Bay. There were fourteen attempted escapes, the last being in 1962. Due to increasing maintenance costs, Alcatraz was closed in 1963 and is now a tourist attraction. Contrary to the image portrayed in movies, Alcatraz was clean, the food was good, and the inmates were not mistreated. Also, the operational capacity was 336; the average population was 260; the maximum population was 302.

Pelican Bay State Prison is located in a remote area of Northern California. Its Security Housing Unit (SHU) holds approximately 1,200 of the worst inmates in the California system. The prison is set in a 270 acre clearing and built of reinforced concrete in an "X" shape. SHU prisoners are monitored, escorted and cared for under very tight security. All recreation, exercise and leisure activities and programs are strictly controlled. [Hentoff, 1993]

The United States Penitentiary at Marion, Illinois, replaced Alcatraz. Marion inmates are considered the most dangerous security risks in the Federal system. The average sentence is 39.5 years. In 1990, 98% of the inmates had violent histories and 51% were convicted murderers. Inmates are restricted to their cells for twenty-two hours per day and restraints are applied when the inmate is moved inside the prison. Searches are very frequent and extremely thorough. Marion is located 100 miles southeast of St. Louis near a wildlife refuge.

Sources: *Discover Alcatraz: A Tour of the Rock* by the Golden Gate National Parks Association, 1996; Hentoff, Nat, "Buried Alive in Pelican Bay," *Prison Life*, Sept. 93, Vol. 1, No. 9, pp. 21-27; Dickey, Christopher, "A New Home for Noreiga?" *Newsweek*, 1/15/90, pp. 66-69.

Development of the Modern Jail

Jails in the United States from the 1800's to today have had a colorful and diverse history. Since jails were under the authority of local sheriffs,

Inmate Dining Area, Manatee County Corrections Facility.

jails in the United States have been in different sizes and modes of operation.

Early American jails practiced what is called *rabble management* or housing people such as drunkards, vagrants, public nuisances, and the mentally ill. These people were not a criminal threat, but it was convenient to just lock them up. [Stojkovic & Lowell, 1997]

During the 19th and early 20th centuries, there was no recognizable system or area of corrections that could be labeled as jails. Jails took the form of sheriffs' homes in some jurisdictions. In others, workhouses, barns, and other buildings confined wrongdoers and were sometimes called jails. Little interest was paid to jails because they were operated locally and little communication existed between sheriffs' agencies. [Champion, 1990]

The keeping of jail statistics started in 1880 under the United States Census Bureau. The Bureau obtained statistics every ten years concerning race, ethnicity, gender and age. In 1923, this information was incorporated into jail statistics. Joseph Fishman, a Federal prison inspector, reported "horrible" conditions in the 1,500 jails he visited. [Cornelius, 1996]

By the mid 1960's, studies reported that jails built prior to George Washington's inauguration in 1789 still were in use. Also, 25% of jails were built more than 50 years ago. Most jails reportedly were not administered properly, were overcrowded and poorly staffed. Services such as medical care and recreation were substandard and funds were lacking. [Kemble, 1996]

Starting in the mid 1960's, the Federal courts began to take an interest in jail and prison conditions based on lawsuits filed by inmates. Conditions began to improve in many U.S. jails. As a result of the Federal Bureau of Prisons policy of maintaining a "normalized living environment" for inmates, the concept of direct supervision was born and the first direct supervision jail—the Contra Costa County Detention Center—opened in 1981. [Kemble, 1996]

In the 1980's, primarily due to inmate lawsuits and court rulings [See Chapter 14], jail management and design underwent a significant overhaul with conditions beginning to improve. Jails now fall into one of the following types of inmate management—linear/intermittent, podular/remote surveillance, and podular/direct supervision.

Even though overcrowding remains a problem, jails' operations and quality of life for the inmate will continue to improve into the next century.

Development of Community Corrections Facilities

While the roots of community corrections can be traced back to MacConochie's Mark system and Crofton's Irish system, today's corrections' systems—Federal, state and local—operate a variety of *community based corrections programs* and facilities. These facilities can be part of the main correctional facility (such as a dormitory or wing) or can be a separate facility.

While community based corrections is defined as "non-institutional," programs for offenders [McCarthy & McCarthy, Jr., 1991], it includes a diversity of programs. Several programs such as diversion, pretrial release, probation, restitution, community service and fine options programs allow the offender to remain in the community or a treatment program, while others have a direct impact on the CO.

Partial incarceration programs such as work release, weekend confinement, home incarceration and service programs require the inmate to be inside the facility if not engaged in work. For example, inmates selected or court ordered into a work release program may go unsupervised into the community to work, subject to random checks by staff. Weekend confinement programs require that inmates sentenced to weekends in jail perform work which produces cost saving labor to the jurisdiction.

The goal of community-based programs is *reintegration*. In 1967, the President's Commission on Law Enforcement and Administration of Justice defined reintegration as "...building or rebuilding ties between offender and community...restoring family ties, obtaining employment and education." [McCarthy & McCarthy, Jr., 1991] Community-based corrections makes use of community programs and resources.

Probably the most well known of the community-based programs or community corrections is work release. In the 20th century, modern work release dates back to 1913 in Wisconsin, where by statute, misdemeanants could work their jobs while serving short sentences in jail. By 1957, North Carolina enacted a similar law, followed shortly by Michigan and Maryland. In 1965, the Federal Prisoner Rehabilitation Act took effect allowing Federal prisoners to take part in work release, furloughs, and community treatment centers. [Allen & Simonsen, 1998] By the 1950's and 1960's, programs in community-based corrections began to be accepted as alternatives to traditional modes of incarceration. [McCarthy & McCarthy, Jr., 1991]

From the 1960's through the 1990's, community corrections programs and facilities have been put into operation for two purposes — to attempt to treat inmates' problems using people and resources in the community and to give Federal, state and local correctional systems a cost saving alternative to traditional incarceration. Community corrections inmates working at gainful employment and paying room and board are generating revenue more than the inmate existing in a cell draining tax dollars.

Community corrections programs such as diversion programs and day reporting centers are usually handled by probation officers or a court treatment program. There are, however, several types of facilities/programs that are usually staffed by correctional officers. They are: [Camp & Camp, 1997]

- *work/study release*: Inmates reside in a community corrections center or pre- release center and work or attend school in the community. Inmates can wear civilian clothes, have their urine and breath tested for substance abuse, and are subject to on-site checks. Inmates can be court ordered or be placed in the program through a screening process in the agency in accordance with statutory guidelines. These facilities have rules and regulations and a disciplinary system.
- *electronic monitoring*: Inmates may reside in their homes and leave in order to work, attend treatment programs, or attend school. While confined at home, inmate is tracked electronically through a transmitter that is worn on wrist or ankle. Schedules and time in the community are subject to staff approval. Inmates may apply, be screened, or court ordered. Inmate is subject to checks and tests similar to work release.
- *halfway house*: Facility in the community used to reintegrate offenders nearing the completion of their sentences from incarceration to living in society. Halfway houses may be similar to work release centers.

Several types of local programs require correctional officer security. Public works projects using inmates with short sentences performing work in public areas (parks, schools, etc.) use correctional officers to escort and guard inmates. Correctional officers may supervise offenders completing community service hours or working off fines.

Trend wise, fewer inmates per correctional agency are being placed on work release. In 1993, 1,589 inmates were placed; in 1996, the placements were 1,140. [Camp & Camp, 1997]

As correctional facilities become more and more overcrowded, community corrections programs may provide "breathing room" by keeping less hard core offenders in alternative programs and putting the more serious offenders behind bars.

Boot Camps

Another type of correctional facility that has received much press in the past decade is the *boot camp*. This facility is based to a degree on the strict basic training regimen used in our armed forces. Sometimes called *shock incarceration* programs, boot camps stress discipline, routine and obedience to others. This concept of harsh, strict incarcerations has caught the public's interest. [Bassett, 1996]

Boot camps can be most simply defined as follows:

> An incarceration program operated by adult correctional, jail and probation/ parole systems as an alternative to traditional incarceration. Boot camps may be used as a "pre release" program. Emphasis is placed on discipline and physical training; many include educational and substance abuse programs.
[Camp & Camp, 1997].

The concept of boot camps is not unique to the last few years. The roots of boot camp regimens can be traced to 1888 at the Elmira Reformatory where military type training was instituted; in 1915, Elmira inmates were trained in preparation for duty in World War I. Elmira's program ended in 1920. [Robertson, 1995]

Ohio passed the first shock incarceration program in 1965; its goal was to give the offender a brief taste of prison life and then release him under parole supervision or probation. The first boot camps opened in Georgia in 1983 and Oklahoma in 1984. [Osborne, 1994, Hoybach, 1995]

As of January 1, 1997, thirty-two adult correctional agencies had 7,250 offenders in boot camp programs. Most offenders were male rather than female (91.9% to 8.1%). New York had the most offenders in boot camp (1,480); New Hampshire had the least (16). The average cost per boot camp inmate per day was a low $56.77. Also, in January 1997, thirty-five agencies were operating fifty-four boot camps. While the length of boot camp programs varied from three to six months, the average length of stay reported was five months. [Camp & Camp, 1997]

Many jails operate boot camps as part of a jail system. Boot camps cannot be considered "super-maximum" facilities; the average accommodation ability for each program is 100–250 inmates, thereby making each a medium-sized facility. [Joelsson, 1996]

While different states have different procedures for putting offenders in boot camps (direct sentencing or Department of Corrections screening), the whole idea of shock incarceration has six main goals: [Robertson, 1995]

1. *Deterrence*: giving the offender a clear, blunt and unpleasant taste of prison life, threatening imprisonment for future crime.
2. *Treatment and rehabilitation*: providing programs and educational opportunities to improve the inmate, many programs require aftercare when the inmate leaves the boot camp.
3. *Reducing recidivism*: since 1988, numerous studies have been supported *and* discredited boot camps concerning repeat offenders. Some researchers suggest that boot camps can curb recividism only with care, programs and aftercare. [Brandenburg, 1995]
4. *Reducing overcrowding and costs*: boot camp supporters feel that some inmates are better served in camps rather than prison. Costs have been previously mentioned, but a recent study in Louisiana said that $8,000.00 was saved for each inmate in a boot camp rather than prison. [Allen & Simonsen, 1995]
5. *Punishment*: media portrayals of a harsh military atmosphere, drill instructors and inmates being treated like raw recruits appeal to politicians and citizens who advocate inmates not having it "easy."
6. *Safe environment*: shock incarceration programs have low rates of inmate-on-inmate violence and/or assaults on staff.

Boot Camp: Manatee County, Florida

One example of a modern "boot camp" for multiple offenders ages 14 to 18 is the Manatee County (Florida) Sheriff's Office Boot Camp. In providing long-term residential treatment, inmates are exposed to role modeling, physical training, practical problem solving and training in educational and social skills.

Six hours per day is spent in school and recruits (offenders) are ordered into the program for a minimum of six months. An average day starts at 5:00 a.m. and ends at 9:00 p.m. The nineteen basic rules are strict, as are the two levels of rules. Recruits are also appraised of their rights — visitation, health care, phone use, etc. To successfully complete the program, recruits must meet goals set by the program and develop the skills necessary to return to the community and family.

Source: Manatee Co.: Sheriff's Office *Boot Camp Recruit Handbook*, Juvenile Justice Division pamphlet.

The Rise of Private Correctional Facilities

Privatization of correctional facilities began during the 1980's and has become a controversial issue. Private prisons did exist prior to the 20th century, using inmates for cheap labor. Also, the government has contracted with private firms (such as food service and medical) to operate within facilities. [Weiss, 1996]

Early contracts between small firms and Federal agencies such as the Immigration and Naturalization Service (INS) and the U.S. Marshals were negotiated in the early 1980's. In 1984, the first county level contract was reached between the Corrections Corporation of America (CCA) and Hamilton County, Tennessee (representing the city of Chattanooga), and Bay County, Florida. Another company, the United States Corrections Corporation, was awarded the first state level (Kentucky) contract in 1985. [Weiss, 1996] The rated capacity of private facilities continued to grow from 2,620 in 1986 to 63,595 in 1995. [Weiss, 1996]

In recent years, the business of privately managed correctional facilities at the federal, state and local levels is apparently very profitable. In the first six months of 1996, two leading companies in the field, CCA and Wackenhut Corrections Corporation, reported recent increases of 37% and 36%, respectively. [Lubby, 1997]

In the United States, only approximately 4% of the more than 1.6 million incarcerated inmates are held in private prisons. [Lubby, 1997]

Statistics about private facilities are now gathered by the U.S. Justice Department. The following data was reported in the Sourcebook of Criminal Justice Statistics, 1995:

- Fifteen private correctional facility management firms reported a total of 99 facilities under contract with nineteen facilities being planned to open in the near future.
- All of the facilities under contract had a rated capacity of 61,400 inmates; facilities in actual operation had a rated capacity of 42,721, with an occupancy rate of 85.6%.

- Ninety-two federal, state and local facilities were listed with the following security levels:

— All levels	14
— Maximum	2
— Medium/maximum	2
— Minimum/medium	20
— Medium	23
— Minimum	30
— Arraignment	1
	92

Also, the Census of State and Federal Correctional Facilities, 1995 reported that almost three of every four private correctional facilities were community-based—over half the offenders allowed to enter the community for work or study. The number of private facilities under state and federal contract increased from 67 in 1990 to 110 in 1995—an increase of 65%!

There is a heated debate over the effectiveness of private prisons in terms of cost savings and the caliber of personnel. In a 1997 report of comparisons of private and public prisons, no evidence was reported that private prisons save money. The report is being opposed by several companies saying operating and construction costs can be reduced. Prisons' biggest expense are staff salaries. Private companies say that they pay competitive benefits and salaries to attract the state of the art technology (sensors, monitors, etc.) to lower the number of staff positions necessary for operations. [Lubby, 1997]

Opponents of privatization feel that "prisons for profit" will result in companies being concerned with revenue instead of inmates' well being. [Weiss, 1996] The training and professionalism of officers is debated, as well as the possibilities of private workers going on strike. Supporters point to training programs, inmate programs and the lack of worker strikes. Perhaps the most realistic view is of the American Correctional Association which feels that private facilities have a place in the correctional field, but they must meet professional standards. Also, they must provide equal or *better* services than government facilities as well as proving cost effective. It is projected that over the next few years, the private prison industry will grow from 20% to 30%! [Lubby, 1997] A typical event concerning private facilities is in Wisconsin where a tentative agreement with CCA was reached in early 1998 to transfer 200 inmates to a private prison in Tennessee and possibly 1,200 during 1998! [*USA Today*, 1/7/98]

The usage of private correctional facilities is not without controversy. In August of 1997, a privately run jail in Texas was under scrutiny due to allegations of brutality by guards. The alleged brutality was captured on videotape and was obtained by the media. In a 1996 National Institute of

Corrections study, states had identified "potentially troubling aspects" of the use of private prisons, including the improper use of force. [Johnson & de la Cruz, 1997]

Prisons Today: State and Federal

Correctional facilities today come in a myriad of large, small and intermediately-sized physical plants. Types of facilities vary from minimum security to "super max" such as Pelican Bay or Marion. The following data, taken from the *Census of State and Federal Correctional Facilities, 1995*, shows significantly the state of federal and state prisons in the late 1990's:

- From midyear 1990 to midyear 1995, the number of state and federal correctional facilities increased 17% (1,287 to 1,500).
- Additional facilities were built during the early 1990's — one in eight state facilities; one in three federal.
- The capacity for state prisons expanded on an average annual of 6.9% from 650,000 (1990) to 910,000 (1995).
- Federal capacity grew annually at an average of 9.3%.
- Most facilities were of the confinement type, more than the community corrections types: 80% to 20%.
- From 1990 to 1995, the number of inmates in both systems increased from 715,649 to 1,023,572 or 43% (average 7.4% annually).
- Overcrowding is a serious factor: 103% of state capacity and 124% of federal capacity were occupied in 1995.

Summary

Today's prisons, jails and community corrections facilities were born out of well meaning conflicts among learned men as to how inmates should be housed and treated. Out of the Pennsylvania and Auburn systems' debate came new ways to house inmates (the interior cellblock). The reformist ideas of MacConochie, Crofton and Brockway resulted in rehabilitative programs for inmates. Though the original programs were short lived, their philosophies resulted in community corrections programs such as today's work release. Not all was positive as the brutal conditions in southern prisons attest.

Isolation-type prisons developed as did the "Big House," large prisons that warehoused inmates. However, in the last twenty years, alternatives such as community corrections facilities, boot camps, and privately run prisons started to save funds and reduce overcrowding.

Even with the advancement of corrections since 1900, today's state and federal facilities are filled to capacity and are mostly confinement oriented.

Review Questions

1. Explain the philosophies of the Pennsylvania, Auburn and Reformatory Systems.

2. How was prison discipline maintained by silence and discipline?

3. Describe the Mark and Irish Systems and their influence on the Reformatory Movement.

4. Describe the development of the Industrial type prison.

5. What is the goal of community corrections?

6. What are the six main goals of boot camp or shock incarceration?

Terms/Concepts

Pennsylvania system	MacConochie's Mark system
Auburn system	Crofton's Irish system
Interior cellblock	Ticket of leave
Reformatory system	Prison wagons
Elmira Reformatory	Big House
Isolation-type prisons	Work study release
The Rock	Electronic monitoring
Rabble management	Halfway house
Community-based programs	Shock incarceration/boot camps
Lockstep	Reintegration

References

Allen, Harry, and Clifford Simonsen, *Corrections in America, An Introduction*, 6th Ed., Prentice Hall. Englewood Cliffs, NJ, 1992.

Allen, Harry, and Clifford Simonsen, *Corrections in America, An Introduction*, 7th Ed., Prentice Hall. Englewood Cliffs, NJ, 1995.

Allen, Harry, and Clifford Simonsen, *Corrections in America, An Introduction*, 8th Ed., Prentice Hall. Englewood Cliffs, NJ, 1998.

American Correctional Association, *The American Prison from the Beginning*, ACA, Laurel, MD, 1983.

Bassett, Melinda, *Correctional Boot Camps*, Research paper: George Mason University, SOC 402, (Spring, 1996).

Brandenburg, Leslie, *Boot Camps*, George Mason University, SOC 402, 11/95.

Camp, George & Camille, *Corrections Yearbook: 1997*, Criminal Justice Institute: South Salem, NY, 1997.

Census of State and Federal Facilities 1995, Bureau of Justice Statistics, NCJ 164266, 8/97.

Cornelius, Gary, *Jails in America: An Overview of Issues*, 2nd Ed., American Correctional Association, Lanham, MD 1996.

Dickey, Christopher, "A New Home for Noriega?", *Newsweek*, 1/15/90, pp. 66-69.

Fox, Vernon & Jeanne Stinchcombe, *Introduction to Corrections*, 4th Ed., Englewood Cliffs, Prentice Hall, 1994.

Golden State National Parks Assoc., *Discover Alcatraz: A Tour of the Rock*, 1996.

Hentoff, Nat, "Buried Alive in Pelican Bay," *Prison Life*, 9/93, Vol. 1, No. 9, pp. 21-27.

Hoybach, Brandon. "Boot Camps," Research paper: George Mason University, SOC 402, 4/25/95.

Irwin, John. *Prisons in Turmoil*, Little, Brown, Boston, 1980.

Joelsson, Charlotte, "Correctional Boot Camps," Research paper: George Mason University, SOC 402, 4/12/96.

Johnson, Kevin and Bonna M. de la Cruz, "On Video: Inmates bitten and beaten," *USA Today*, 8/20/97, p. 3A.

Johnson, Robert, *Hard Time: Understanding and Reforming the Prison*, Wadsworth, 1996.

Kemble, Tod, "Jails in America," *Texas Journal of Corrections*, May-June, 1996, pp. 14-19.

Lubby, Tami, "Private Prison Industry," *Keeper's Voice*, Spring, 1997, Vol. 18, No. 1, pp. 25-26. IACO.

Manatee County (Florida) Sheriff's Office Boot Camp Recruit Manual/Juvenile Justice Division, 1998.

McCarthy, Belinda and Bernard J. McCarthy, Jr., *Community Based Corrections*, 2nd Ed., Pacific Grove, CA, Brooks-Cole, 1991.

See Osborne, William N. Jr., "Shock Incarceration and the Boot Camp Model: Theory and Practice," *American Jails*, July-Aug, 1994, pp. 27-30.

Robertson, L., Jr., *Shock Incarceration: Boot Camps: Good Alternative on Good Public Relations? An Overview*, Research paper: George Mason University, SOC 402, Sp. 95.

Rothman, David, *The Discovery of the Asylum: Social Order and Disorder in the New Republic*, Scott Foresman, Glenview, Ill., 1971.

Stojkovic, Stan and Rick Lovell, *Corrections: An Introduction*, 2nd Ed., Cinncinnati, Anderson, 1997.

Sourcebook of Criminal Justice Statistics, 1995, Bureau of Justice Statistics, NCJ 158900, 1996.

USA Today, 1/9/98.

Weiss, Lea, "Private Correctional Facilities," George Mason University, SOC 402, 11/96.

World Almanac and Book of Facts: 1999, World Almanac Books, Primedia, Mahwah, NJ, 1998.

Chapter 6

An Examination of Today's Inmate

The conventional term for persons housed in correctional facilities is inmate. More specifically, persons incarcerated but not yet convicted of a crime are called "pre-trial detainees;" those adjudicated and sentenced are "convicts." For the everyday correctional worker, all prisoners in the facility are collectively called "inmates." In some minimum security facilities such as community corrections centers, inmates may be called offenders, residents or clients.

Inmates come in various ages, races, physical sizes and social backgrounds. No two inmates are alike. While the average correctional officer may find it easy to "lump" all the inmates in one basket and try to treat them all the same, the reality is that inmates have different personalities and tolerances for frustration. Correctional officers must realize this and adjust their styles of dealing with inmates accordingly. This will be discussed more in Section IV.

Correctional officers are not paid to be psychologists and try to get into the minds of inmates in their care, but to deal with today's inmates, a correctional officer should understand their backgrounds. The nature of work in today's correctional facilities is the same as it has always been — adversarial, or "us v. them." Correctional officers *must* know their adversary.

In this chapter, we will look at the relationship of officers to inmates from a knowledge point of view: knowing inmates' problems, backgrounds and limitations socially; and the "survivalist" part of inmates: how they adapt to and survive incarceration.

Sociological Characteristics of Today's Inmate

While the numbers of prisoners incarcerated in the United States has been previously discussed, this section will deal with age, sex, race, educational level, prior history of criminal behavior, and type of offense. It is meant to give the reader a concise "snapshot" of who is locked up currently in the United States.

Age: Several studies in recent years have shown that adult inmates in the United States are young. According to the United States Bureau of Justice Statistics in 1991, the breakdown of ages among U.S. inmates are:

Age of Inmate	Percentage of Inmate Population
21-24	19%
25-29	26%
30-39	37%
40-49	13%
50-59	3%
60+	1%

Source: *Profile of Inmates in the United States and in England and Wales, 1991*, released October 1994.

There is a large percentage of inmates ranging in age from 21-39. Other studies are similar: in South Carolina, 55.3% of inmates admitted to the Department of Corrections were between 17 and 29 years old in Fiscal Year 1996. [So. Carolina DOC, 1997] A BJS Survey of state inmates in 1991 found that 46% of inmates were ages 25-34; 22% were age 24 and younger. [Hall & Watson, *USA Today*, 5/20/93] Both male and female inmates' average age at admission were in the early 30's: 31 years old for males and 32.5 years old for females. The average age was 31.3 years of age. [Camp & Camp, 1997]

It is hard to gauge what the age indicators mean to the average correctional officer. As one veteran jail officer with twenty years experience said:

> I have noticed in my career that many of the inmates I see in jail are older, late 30's through 40's. While there are still younger inmates, sometimes the older ones act more immature and manipulative. While chronological age is important, behavior depends on the individual.

Sex: The gender breakdown in state, federal and local agencies is as follows:

- In 1998, 1,217,592 men and 84,427 women were incarcerated in state and federal correctional institutions. [BJS, 1999]
- In mid 1995, U.S. jails held 455,400 males and 51,600 females or 89.8% to 10.2% of the entire jail population, respectively. [BJS, 1997]
- In 1996, the number of female inmates grew almost twice as fast as the males. [BJS, 1997]

Race: In a "snapshot" of inmate populations on January 1, 1997, it was reported that 47.2% were black, 42.2% were white, Asian/Pacific Islanders were 0.7% and Native Americans numbered 8.9%. Hispanic prisoners accounted for 17.5% of the inmate population. [Camp & Camp, 1997]

Concerning black prisoners, in recent years reports of the high rates of young black males have caused concern. In 1997, the National Center on Institutions and Alternatives published a report stating that nearly half the black men in the District of Columbia ages 18-35 were incarcerated, on parole or probation, in a pre-trial status or were being sought by police with an arrest warrant. This report caused a stir among civic leaders and the Department of Corrections director. The lack of drug treatment and rehabilitative programs were mentioned as causative factors. [Thompson, 1997]

The 1995 figures on jail inmates concerning race and ethnicity are similar: white inmates (non-Hispanic) 40.1%, black non-Hispanic 43.5%, Hispanic 14.7%, other 1.7%. [BJS, 1997]

One concern among the corrections field is the high rate of Hispanic inmates, especially almost one-fifth of prison inmates (17.5%). Language barriers between these inmates and non-Spanish speaking staff are only one problem. Officers learning how to deal with the behaviors of incarcerated Latinos is being discussed and dealt with more by conducting cultural diversity training. [See Chapter 7.]

Educational level: According to a survey of state inmates in 1991, 22% graduated from high school, 46% had some high school education and 12% had some college and higher. Almost one-fifth or 19% had eighth grade education or less. [Hall & Watson, BJS, 1993] Allen and Simonsen reported in 1995 that more than 50% of jail inmates had less than a high school education. [Cornelius, 1996] In 1994, Gonzales, writing in *American Jails*, reported results of a study of inmates at the Northampton County Prison (Pa.). The inmates' average grade level was tenth grade; their average reading level was 5.9 grade. [Cornelius, 1996] Federal inmates surveyed in 1991 were found to have a higher level of education, i.e., some college, than state inmates: 28% to 12%. [BJS, 1997]

A general rule in society is that education is a must in achieving success in life, but according to Dr. Stanton Samenow, a clinical psychologist and author of *Inside the Criminal Mind*, the delinquent youths and future criminals do not appreciate school and the value of education. They use school to exploit others, engage in criminal activities and stake out territory. [Samenow, 1984]

Minnesota is taking a progressive view. About 35% of the inmates are functionally illiterate and must take a reading course before joining other classes. In 1994, a reported 90% of those illiterate inmates had enrolled. [Smolowes, 1994]

Prior history of criminal behavior: Recidivism or inmates being released and reincarcerated for committing new crimes is the "scourge" of the field.

While the most idealistic of corrections professionals believe that inmates can be rehabilitated, the fact that some always will be rearrested cannot be ignored. The 1991 Survey of State Prison inmates [BJS, 1993] found that among the inmate population, 45% of recividists had *three* or more prior sentences, 19% had six or more, and 6.6% had *eleven* or more. It could be argued that the answer to the inmates' problem of recurring criminal behavior is elusive. For inmates, incarceration is an "occupational hazard" of the criminal profession. For others, the lack of coping skills when faced again with a criminal environment (low income neighborhood, drugs, criminal peers, etc.) is a factor. Statistically, the rates of recidivism are still high. The Correctional Yearbook 1997 reported that among forty jurisdictions and tracking released inmates for an average of four years, the recidivism rate was 32.6% following release from prison. [Camp & Camp, 1997]

A study in 1996 of prisoners in Washington, D.C., found that nearly 99% *were* repeat offenders! [Anderson, 1986]

Type of offense: According to the Bureau of Justice Statistics, the four major offense categories are violent, property, drug and public order offenses.

- Violent offenses include murder, manslaughter, rape, other sexual assault, robbery, assault and other offenses such as extortion and criminal endangerment.
- Burglary, larceny, motor vehicle theft, fraud and miscellaneous offenses such as possession/selling of stolen property, etc., comprise property offenses.
- Drug offenses encompasses offenses with illegal substances.
- Public order offenses are crimes involving weapons, drunk driving, escape, court offenses, liquor law violations and morals charges. [BJS, 1997]

1995

Type of Offense	State Inmates	Federal Inmates
Violent offenses	47.0%	13.1%
Property offenses	23.3%	8.7%
Drug offenses	22.7%	59.9%
Public order offenses	6.6%	18.3%
Other/unspecified	.4%	0.0%
	100.0%	100.0%

Source: *Correctional Populations in the U.S., 1995*; BJS, May 97; tables: 1.12 and 1.14.

Concerning state inmates in the ten years from 1985 to 1995, violent offenses fell from 54.5% to 47% and property offenses fell 31% to 23.3%. However, drug offenses rose from 8.6% of state inmates in 1985 to 22.7% in 1995, clearly indicating the problems of drug abuse among the nation's criminal offenders. [BJS, 1997]

Concerning jail inmates, the Bureau of Justice Statistics reported in 1991 that almost 23% of jail inmates were charged with a violent crime. Property crimes numbered 30%, drug offenses were 23%, as were public order offenses (23%). About one out of four jail inmates were locked up because of a drug offense. [Cornelius, 1996]

As in prisons, drug offenses are responsible for a significant number of jail arrests. As veteran jail and prison officers realize, as well as treatment personnel, many offenses "spin off" from substance abuse, but are not labeled drug offense by the ordinary public. For example, grand larceny, selling stolen goods or robbery may all have a goal of obtaining drug money. Reactions to drugs or the influence of alcohol may result in assaults.

Inmates as Survivors: The Pain of Incarceration

There are two ways to look at inmates: in a detached, statistical way as we have done, and as human beings who live an atypical lifestyle and learn to adapt to the harsh rigors of prison life. They learn to survive.

To work everyday with inmates, correctional officers must learn about how they think, how they adapt and how they do their time. By doing so, they can *emphasize* with the inmate and can understand what they go through. The benefits are better communication and a lessening of tensions between staff and inmates.

Prisonization

When working with inmates, no matter what type of facility, correctional officers must realize that offenders are not "born" inmates, they *become* inmates through a process called prisonization.

First coined by Donald Clemmer in 1940, the term *prisonization* means "...the process by which the inmate learns, through socialization, the rules and regulations of the penal institution, as well as the informal values, rules and customs of the penitentiary culture." In other words, the inmate learns how to be an inmate: how to sleep, eat, dress and talk differently in order to survive. [Allen & Simonsen, 1995, Clemmer 1940]

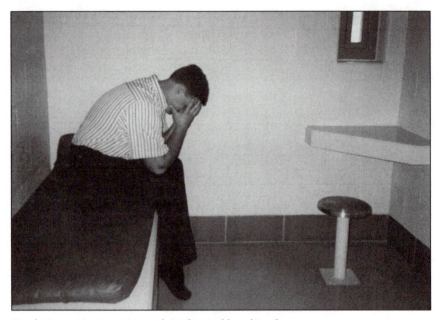

For the inmate, incarceration can bring his world crashing down.

Observers of the process note that not only does the inmate learn behaviors, they learn things about the staff from other inmates around them —what officers are "easy" to lie to, manipulate or influence; and what officers are "hard," sticking to policy, procedures and are not easily manipulated. Also, inmates will learn quickly which inmates are predators, thieves, liars and untrustworthy. They learn from inmates they befriend and who are similar to themselves; inmates trying to survive.

Prisonization besides the learning of everyday habits, is influenced by three things: the needs of inmates, the development of niches and the "inmate code."

A Lesson in Prisonization

Not all lessons an inmate learns through prisonization are negative and destructive. Ralf Dean Omar, an ex-convict, advises inmates to avoid these eight pitfalls:

1. *Gangs*: An inmate may be considered a gang member if he associates with a gang; gangs engage in illegal activities. Inmates should not accept favors from a gang and should decline tactfully any offers to join a gang.

2. *Drugs*: Using drugs impedes an inmate's judgment and ability to defend oneself.

3. *Sex*: Inmates entering the homosexual prison culture may be victims of rape, violence and sexually transmitted diseases.

4. *Debts and gambling*: Inmates should not lend things or gamble. If they cannot collect, it may be considered a sign of weakness.

5. *Stealing*: Inmates should guard their own property and not steal from fellow inmates.

6. *Snitching*: Inmates should stay away from illegal activity and not believe staff promises. Inmates observing such activities may be labeled a snitch by the guilty inmates.

7. *Trickbags*: When opportunistic inmates let an inmate borrow something and say it's broken or not the same upon its return, they have the naive inmates in a "trickbag" — indebted to them. Omar says that "if a [prison] deal looks too good to be true, it probably is."

8. *Riots*: Inmates should avoid becoming a spokesperson or being in areas where hostages are held. Avoid speaking to the media. Do not cross prisoner picket lines.

Adapted from: "Eight Pitfalls to Avoid in Prison," by Ralf Dean Omar, *Prison Life*, May-June, 1995.

The Needs of Inmates

Inmates have needs, needs beyond the simple everyday necessities of a bed, food and clothing. To safely manage inmates, officers must realize these needs and try to have them met in a positive way without jeopardizing security.

These needs can be viewed as "seven ecological dimensions" that serve to express the preferences and needs of inmates. Research by Hans Toch in 1977 described these dimensions or needs as:

1. *Activity*: to be occupied, do something to pass the time, be entertained and distracted. In jails and prisons, programs, recreation, television and radio serve this purpose as well as trustee (inmates performing work for the prison) jobs.

2. *Privacy*: to be alone, to try to survive in peace and quiet, away from noise, crowded living conditions, and immature, both-

ersome inmates. Inmates generally crave privacy and will ask at times to be transferred to single housing, away from the pressures of crowding. In certain cases, such as an inmate "on the edge" mentally, this may be possible so as to avoid future problems. Generally, in an overcrowded facility, inmates living alone is not a luxury that can be granted. Classification staff generally have the burden of finding such housing; inmates must be told if that is not possible.

3. *Safety*: inmates are concerned about their physical well being and that their belongings are left alone.

4. *Emotional feedback*: all of us want to be loved, liked and looked upon as a worthy person deserving of others' appreciation. Inmates do not want to be considered just inmates, they want to be loved, appreciated and cared for. There is loneliness in prison and inmates will find emotional support in friendship and relationships with other inmates.

5. *Support*: some inmates *do* take advantage of programs, counseling, volunteer assistance and other tools that can aid rehabilitation. Those inmates wish to have such support available to them.

6. *Structure*: inmates prefer predictability when it comes to rules, regulations and routines. Rules must be clear-cut, according to Toch. Enforcement of them must be consistent and fair. A common complaint from inmates is that one team or shift (squad, etc.) works differently from another.

7. *Freedom*: all inmates want freedom in the usual sense of the word. Toch states that inmates want minimal restrictions, minimal supervision and to be able to govern their own conduct. For example, many inmates covet trusty jobs to escape the restrictiveness and staff surveillance of the housing units. Being a trusty gives them more freedom of movement. Inmates who have been transferred to jails from prison for court hearings, for example, find the county jail housing more confining and do not like the increase in staff presence.

[Johnson, 1987, Toch, 1977]

Niches

Everyone has his or her own niche and inmates are no exception. The average citizen has a job, home and family — important things that can bring happiness and assist in survival. Inmates in prison look for the same supports. In 1977, J. Seymour (in Toch, 1977) defined niches as they fit in the prison setting. A *niche* is:

> A functional subsetting containing objects, space, resources, people and relationships between people.

[Johnson, 1987]

Inmates, by forming their niches, will try to have the seven needs Toch described met. They will form friendships, make arrangements with each other to look out for danger, engage in recreational activities or procure a work assignment in order to be active and in essence will try to cope with incarceration as best they can using the people and resources around them.

The corrections officer must realize that niches not only give an inmate relief from stress, they can also serve to keep the institutional climate calm. Niches must then be viewed as a realistic aspect of prison life.

However, niches can be both good and bad. While positive objects that Seymour mentions in his definition could be commissary items, family pictures, etc., they could also mean smuggled drugs or weapons. Space could be a private cell gained through lying to staff or manipulation. Resources could be a contraband smuggling operation trafficking in drugs. People and their relationships could mean power through membership in a gang or extremist group. While activity means positive distraction and entertainment, it could also mean using staff, lying and manipulating staff — entertainment for the inmates.

The Inmate Code

Much has been written about the *inmate code* or the social rules in prisons and jails that inmates live by. This code permits inmates to live by *their* own rules, not so much the institution's. Violations of this code could result in physical assault, murder or ostracism, at the minimum. Violators can be labeled weaklings or snitches. One of the best descriptions of this code is from the Kansas Department of Corrections training manual:

1. *Be loyal*: Keep silent about what other inmates do, including criminal acts. Lie if you must. Never take a problem to the institution staff. Be loyal to your fellow inmates no matter what the cost.

2. *Be cool*: Be calm and in control, no matter what the pressure you receive from staff. Do your time — don't make waves.

3. *Be straight* (with fellow inmates): Don't take advantage of another inmate — don't steal, don't lie, don't break your word. Inmates should share goods and do favors. It is permissible to tell staff "half truths" to get your way or avoid a problem.

4. *Be tough*: Don't be weak, don't whine, don't say that you are guilty. Inmates must "take it." The code says that inmates should not start fights, inmates should not run from a fight that another inmate starts.

5. *Be sharp*: Correctional officers must not be trusted, suspect them. Concerning a conflict between an officer and an inmate, the officer is always wrong.

Recently, some penal reformers and convicts have been speaking out against the code saying that through silence, it protects inmates who are brutal and should face the consequences of their actions. One convict said that he will accept responsibility for his actions and never would burden another. Bo Lozoff, director of the Prison-Ashram project, relates the true story of a convict who witnessed a vicious gang rape of a young inmate. The convict, a year later, said that the incident still bothered him, but has said nothing because of the "code." Lozoff says that his "biggest problem with the old convict code is that even at its best, it has been basically selfish. Its rule of silence allows all manner of brutality to take place."

Clearly, any revision of the code is in the hands of the inmates. Could a revision of the code be a twinge of conscience?

> Adapted from: *Helping Hands: A Handbook for Volunteers in Prisons*, and *Jails* by Daniel Bays, ACA, 1993; "Revising the Convict Code: One Step Further," by Bo Lozoff, *Prison Life*, July-August, 1985.

The Pains of Imprisonment

Being locked up away from families, loved ones and children is painful. No matter what prior record an inmate has or how many years of experience in prisons, prison life is uncomfortable and many inmates think about life on the outside and what they are missing. Many try to compensate by developing their niches.

Correctional officers must realize that for all the inmate "bravado" and cockiness, being incarcerated, especially at a younger age, can be devastating to the inmate. Robert Johnson wrote:

Imprisonment is a disheartening and threatening experience for most men. The man in prison finds his career disrupted, his relationships suspended, his aspirations and dreams gone sour."
[Johnson, 1976, 1987]

Some inmates will deal with this pain by acting tough, exhibiting a tough veneer or mask. When wearing this mask, inmates will act like nothing bothers them — not other inmates, not the staff and their rules or, in general, being locked up. According to Johnson, based on 1954 research by McCorkle and Korn, inmates feel a need to "reject their rejectors" and live as though the pains of incarceration are of little or no consequence. To illustrate how weak society is having to "cage" its "manly" outlaws, inmates may flaunt big muscles and tough behavior. [McCorkle and Korn, 1954, Johnson, 1987] To the average law abiding citizen, contact with authorities (from being given a warning to receiving a traffic citation or being arrested) is a traumatic, fearful experience. To many inmates, being written up in prison on a disciplinary charge is nothing; for some it is a way to verbally defy authority by appearing before a hearing acting like "it's no big deal."

However, when looking inward, many inmates realize their situation. Two quotes from two 18-year-old inmates both convicted of murder illustrate: [Buckley, 1997]

It dawns on me every day, I'm going to be in here for life.
Jail ain't a place to be. It's the emotional pain of being without your family.

In order to cope in this negative world, many prisoners will follow a "prison career." These careers had their origins in the Big House type prisons, but are evident today in our nation's correctional facilities. They are:

Doing time: The inmate's concern is doing his/her own time, getting out with minimum pain in the shortest time.

Jailing: Learning the inmate culture, similar to carving out a niche, getting very familiar with inmate life, looking on other inmates like family.

Gleaning: Taking advantage of any available resource, programs, counseling, etc., to better themselves and prepare for life after prison.

Improvisation: Gathering whatever items or materials that are available and substituting them for "luxuries" on the outside, i.e., making homemade alcohol, making weapons, etc.

Fantasy: Fantasies, daydreaming, etc., is conducted in private to shut out the drabness and despair.

Stupefaction: Due to the deprivation of outside contact, especially with long-term inmates, inmates learn to "blunt their feelings," fantasize and turn inward. Incarceration numbs them.

[Irwin, 1980]

Being incarcerated affects different types of inmates in different ways. The inmate prone to suicidal behavior may try to take his own life, the female prisoner with small children may cry a lot, the substance abuser may try to smuggle drugs. This will be discussed more in Chapter 7.

Summary

When discussing the question of who inmates are, the answer must be approached from two directions: social characteristics and a humanistic view.

Socially, inmates generally are young, lacking in education, are mostly male, and are almost evenly divided in the rates of white versus black. Violent offenses comprise the most number of state inmates, drug offenses the most in the federal system. High numbers of inmates have had previous problems with the law.

From a humanistic view, inmates are people who learn the culture of the prison through prisonization. Inmates have needs, as we all do, and these needs are met through niches. Incarceration is painful, resulting in the prisoner finding coping mechanisms, including exhibiting a tough shell.

The much discussed inmate code apparently gives inmates guidelines to live by. However, recent research has indicated that the blind loyalty to this code may be waning.

Review Questions

1. What is a niche?

2. Describe the seven inmate needs as researched by Toch.

3. What pitfalls of prison life should inmates avoid?

4. Define prisonization.

5. Describe the inmate "code" and explain how it may not be beneficial to inmates.

Terms/Concepts

Prisonization	Structure
Activity	Support
Privacy	Freedom
Safety	Niche
Emotional feedback	Doing time
Improvisation	Jailing
Fantasy	Gleaning
Stupefaction	Inmate code

References

Allen & Simonsen, *Corrections in America: An Introduction*, 7th Ed., Englewood Cliffs, NJ, Prentice Hall, 1995.

Anderson, John Ward, "Most District Convicts are Repeat Offenders," *Washington Post*, 9/5/86.

Bayse, Daniel, *Helping Hands: A Handbook for Volunteers in Prisons and Jails*, ACA, 1993.

Buckley, J. Taylor, "Growing Up and Growing Old in Prison," *USA Today*, 4/19/97, pp. 6D-7D.

Camp & Camp, *Corrections Yearbook 1997*, Criminal Justice Institute, South Salem, NY, 1997.

Clemmer, Donald, *The Prison Community*, Rinehart, NY, 1940.

Cornelius, Gary, *Jails in America*, 2nd Ed., ACA, Lanham, MD, 1996.

"Correctional Population in the United States," BJS, 1995, NCJ 163916, 5/97.

"Criminal Offenders Statistics, 1997," BJS, Internet: http://www.ojp. usdoj.gov/bjscrimoff.htm#inmates (rim off. H&m # inmates)

Hall & Watson, "Typical Inmate: Abused, Abuser, Repeater," *USA Today*, 5/20/93, p. 8A.

Irwin, John, *Prisoners in Turmoil*, Little Brown, Boston, 1980.

Johnson, Robert, *Hard Times: Understanding and Reforming the Prison*, Monterey: Brooks-Cole, 1987.

Lozoff, Bo, "Revising the Inmate Code—One Step Further," *Prison Life*, July-August, 1995, p. 32.

McCorkle, J.W., Jr., and R. Korn, "Resocialization Within Walls," *The Annals of Political and Social Science*, 293, May 1995, 88-98.

Omar, Ralf J., "Eight Pitfalls to Avoid in Prison," *Prison Life*, May-June, 1995.

Lynch, James P., Ph.D, Steven K. Smith, Ph.D, Helen A. Graziadei, and Tanutda Pittayathikhun, "Profiles of Inmates in the U.S. and England and Wales, 1991." BJS, NCJ 145863, Octobert, 1994.

Mumola, Christopher, and Allen J. Beck, BJS Statisticians, *Prisoners in 1998*, Bureau of Justice Statistics, NCJ 175687, August, 1999.

Mumola, Christopher, and Allen J. Beck, BJS Statisticians, *Prisoners in 1996*, Bureau of Justice Statistics, NCJ 164619, June, 1997.

"Profiles of Inmates Admitted," So. Carolina DOC, FY 1996, http://www.state.sc.us/scdc/admit.htm.

Renaud, Jorge, "Challenging the Convict Code," *Prison Life*, July-August 1995, pp. 30-33.

Samenow, Stanton, "Inside Criminal Mind," *Times Book*, NY, 1984.

Smolowe, Jill, "And Throw Away the Key," *Time*, 2/7/94, Vol. 143, No. 6, pp. 54-59.

Thompson, Cheryl W., "Young Blacks Entangled in Legal System," *Washington Post*, 8/26/97, B1, B5.

Toch, Hans, *Living in Prison: The Ecology of Survival*, Free Press, NY, 1977.

Chapter 7

Special Populations and Methods of Handling

In keeping with the theme of this text in presenting a useful information guide to the correctional officer, this chapter will focus on eight special types of inmates.

Each group will be discussed, including guidelines for correctional officer management.

Substance Abusers

Realistically, drug abuse by male and female offenders continues to be a decisive factor when discussing inmates. The "war on drugs" accounted for many commitments since 1980—46% of the increase in court commitments. Tests of inmates at adult male prisons and correctional facilities indicate an ongoing usage of drugs behind the walls. At least 1% tested positive for cocaine and heroin, 2% for methamphetamines, and approximately 6% for marijuana. [Allen & Simonsen, 1998, Beck, 1992] Correctional officers in both jails *and* prisons have to be aware of the "pull" that illegal substances have on inmates. While jail staff see the effects of substance abuse when inmates are booked in under the influence, prison correctional officers must be aware that inmates can use drugs and alcohol that are smuggled in.

In January 1998, a landmark three year study on incarcerated inmates and substance abuse was released by the National Center on Addiction and Substance Abuse. The study gives a clear picture of substance abuse patterns among the nation's inmates:

- 80% of inmates were involved with alcohol or other drugs at the time of their offenses (1.4 million inmates out of 1.7 million);
- among inmates serving time for violent crimes (including murder, rape, spouse and child abuse, assault), 21% were under the influence of alcohol at the time of the offense compared to only 3% of violent offenders under the influence of crack cocaine;

Booking area at a local jail. Correctional staff never really know if a newly admitted inmate will or won't be a problem; observation is critical.

- criminal activity due to drugs and alcohol caused a 239% increase in the U.S. prison population since 1980;
- recidivism rates are directly linked to drug abuse—41% of first time offenders in state prisons were regular drug users compared to 81% of inmates with five or more convictions who were habitual users.

[Fields, 1998]

Correctional officers must be able to recognize the signs and symptoms of alcohol and drug abuse, but do so cautiously. Diabetic emergencies, serious illness/injuries, and mental and emotional conditions can also exhibit similar symptoms. These symptoms are:

confusion/disorientation	abscesses/scars on arms and legs
delirium/hallucinations	needle marks (tracks) on arms and legs
cannot walk/stand	odor of alcohol
slurred speech	restlessness/agitation/aggressiveness
lethargic behavior	rapid and/or shallow breathing

pupils dilated/pinpoint   nausea — cramps, vomiting, diarrhea

inmate feels very hot or
  very cold

[Va. Dept. of Mental Health & Mental Retardation, 1986.]

The withdrawal from alcohol and drugs can pose serious health and management problems for the inmate. Inmates undergoing drug withdrawal (especially from heroin) may complain that they are "sick" and want medical help. Most jails observe inmates under withdrawal going *cold turkey* — withdrawal without maintenance doses of the drug. Correctional officers must take note of these alcohol and drug *withdrawal* symptoms.

fear/anxiety	sweats
tremors (shakes)	hallucinations
agitation	nausea/vomiting
insomnia	pupils pinpointed
talkativeness	difficulty breathing
delirium — violent excitement	

[Va. Dept. of Mental Health & Mental Retardation, 1986.]

Any inmate undergoing withdrawals or showing signs of alcohol and drug abuse must be *closely observed*; all interactions with staff, meals, medical checks and behaviors must be documented. The inmate must be reported *immediately* to the medical staff and mental health staff, if applicable.

For substance abusers in our nation's correctional facilities, programs are available if the inmate wants help. Alcoholics Anonymous (AA), Narcotics Anonymous (NA) and *therapeutic communities* where inmates live as a group and undergo treatment and therapy (in cellblock programs) are available.

SLU: Sobering Prisoner's Lives

In 1988, the Alexandria, Virginia, Adult Detention Center initiated the Sober Living Unit (SLU) — a housing unit ninety-day program using AA's twelve-step approach. Daily routines are rigidly structured; inmates must go by the rules. It is a non-stop, intensive program that helps inmates that want to live a "drug free life."

Adapted from "Program Sober
Prisoner's Lives," Buzz Mclain,
Fairfax Journal, 8/31/90.

Prisoners offer treatment for longer periods of time due to inmates' sentences. Some jail systems are offering revolutionary treatment programs in order to change the offender into a recovering chemical-free person from the outset of incarceration in the local jail.

Suicidal Inmates

One special group of inmates that all correctional officers and staff should be aware of is the inmate prone to suicide. Inmates may become suicidal due to the trauma of being arrested, loss of stable resources in their lives (such as job, family, etc.), shame, fear, depression, or withdrawal from drugs or alcohol. Whatever the reason, the suicidal inmate, if successful at self-destruction, can cause the institution embarrassment, scrutiny and liability. Correctional staff have the responsibility to protect inmates not only from other inmates, but from themselves.

Training in suicide prevention must be ongoing. Correctional officers, with heavy workloads and demands from inmates, may become indifferent. This indifference is not conducive to helping a suicidal inmate, who is looking for help.

Researchers have identified four types of suicidal inmates:

1. Morality shock: becomes suicidal shortly after admission; has to come to terms with criminal behavior and the losses and consequences that it has caused;
2. Chronic despair: in post-sentencing incarceration, has become depressed and hopeless about the future, feeling disconnected and distant from family, friends and attorneys;
3. Manipulative anti-social inmate who, by non-lethal acts, attempts to gain a softer assignment (hospital/infirmary), sympathy, or *escape* (during transport to the hospital).
4. Self-punishment: inmate wishes to humiliate him/herself and make life painful and miserable.

[Lester and Danto, 1993]

Methods include hanging, ingesting hoarded medications or slashing. Correctional officers must be aware that critical times for inmates include before/after court, after visiting, first few hours after admission and before release. Staff, when confronted with a suicidal inmate, should move the inmate to a high observation area, observe *very* frequently, such as every 5-10 or 15 minutes, and get the inmate to talk while staff are supportive listeners. Correctional officers should document their observations and call in qualified mental health staff to intervene.

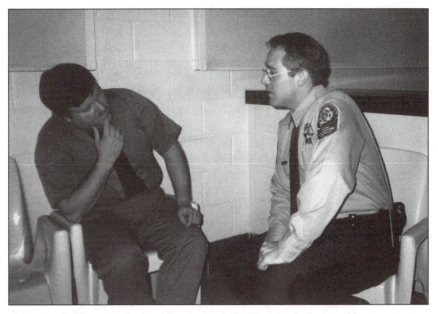

Correctional officers must be good listeners; assisting inmates who have problems promotes a positive climate in the facility.

The following is a general list of suicidal behavior symptoms:

depression	suicide threats
crying	suicide attempt
varying moods	tenseness
withdrawal	feelings of self-blame/ worthlessness/guilt

[Va. Office of Mental Health and Mental Retardation, 1986, Cornelius, 1996]

In the past twenty years, much information has been made available about suicidal inmates. Every facility should have entry level and in-service training.

Gangs and Extremist Groups

Recently, the prevalence of gangs in jails and prisons have posed a serious security problem for correctional staff. In a parallel development, the existence of extremist groups also poses a security nightmare for correctional officers.

Most gangs originate from street gangs and are based on racial attitudes and ethnic origins. Gangs group together for power and protection. [Allen & Simonsen, 1998]

For correctional officers to deal with gangs, their origins must be examined. Up until the early 1980's, "gangbanging" meant gang members "hung out" with neighborhood toughs or homeboys. Gang violence and fights occurred with fists or baseball bats. With the crackdown on crime, street gangs had their power bases relocated from the street to prison. Conversely, some gangs that have started in prison have relocated to the street. Prisons have become the new recruiting and training group for our nation's gangbangers. [Cozone, 1995]

In 1989, the U.S. Department of Justice Office of Legal Policy provided funding for a Criminal Justice Institute Study of prison gangs. The study included all state prison systems and the Federal Bureau of Prisons. Thirty-three agencies reported the presence of prison gangs. At the time of the study, gang members comprised 3% of all inmates. Undoubtedly, the number now is higher. [Littman, 1995]

While many may think that prison gangs disrupt the institution, the truth is that prison gangs apparently are not interested in disrupting facility operations. Gang activity, according to correctional administrators, is directed at conducting gang business using the institutional activities and routine. Authorized activities, clubs, programs and visiting all allow gang members to meet, convey messages, and to plan activities. The actual problems created by prison gangs consist of drug smuggling, drug dealing, intimidation and preying on weak inmates, extortion, fights (usually racial) and contracted inmate murders. Results of these activities are inmates requesting authorities for transfers and/or protective custody, [Littman, 1995], staff/gang confrontations and injuries/death to staff.

Not all groups of inmates who congregate together can be called a gang. Researchers Harland, Buentello and Knox in 1993 advocated applying four criteria to determine if an inmate group is a gang. [Porter, 1995]

- Does the group have an organized leadership and a clear chain of command structure?
- Through good times and bad (including conflict) does the group stay cohesive and unified?
- Does the group demonstrate or exhibit loyalty in obvious, recognizable ways?
- Are the group activities criminal and/or threatening to the operations of the facility?

Gangs are mostly in male institutions and female gangs are rare. Women serve as runners who supply husbands and boyfriends with information, intelligence, contraband (drugs, weapons, etc.) from the outside. [Porter, 1995]

As reported by Silberman in 1995, gangs grow by recruiting street gangs into prison gangs, recruiting/absorbing gang members transferring into the institution and recruiting inmates by force and intimidation. If an inmate wishes out of the gang, he risks his life. [Porter, 1995, Silberman, 1995]

Correctional officers must be cognizant of the signs of gang activity as researched by Greene in 1996:

- frequent gathering and associating of inmates having a common bond — street gang ties or ethnic origins;
- displays of gang colors, tattoos, hand signals and graffiti;
- increase in inmate on inmate violence;
- activities of inmates transferring from the western United States where prison and street gangs are strongly entrenched.

To combat gang activity, intelligence gathering is a must. Informants can supply good information. [Silberman, 1995, Porter, 1995] Recently, policy departments and other law enforcement agencies have started sharing gang information with correctional staff. Other measures include tracking known gang members in the prison population, on-going staff training concerning gangs, and using criminal and in-house disciplinary charges to the fullest extent possible. Gang leaders can be placed on administrative segregation away from population whenever possible.

For all the information and media attention given to gangs in movies, books, etc., the exact definition of a gang is commonly thought to be a group of "toughs" disrupting society through violence. The state of California defines in clear terms both the criminal street gang and the gang member.

These definitions can be helpful to the correctional officer who has to be on the lookout for gang activity.

Criminal street gang: Any organization, association or group of three or more persons, whether formal or informal which

- has a continuity of purpose;
- seeks a group activity.

Members of criminal street gangs engage in criminal activities either individually or collectively engage in patterns of criminal activities.

A *gang member* participates in the gang and has knowledge of members engaging in criminal activities. A gang member also is one who assists members' criminal behavior and promotes and furthers such activity.

Adapted from: *Controlling the Influence of Gangs in our Jails,* by Sgt. Roger Ross, LA Co. Sheriff's Dept. of Safe Jails Unit, Large Jail Network, Longmont Col., 1/23/95

Gangs and extremist groups can be designated a security threat group or *STG.* An STG is two or more inmates who, by acting together, pose a threat to staff and inmate safety as well as disruptive to the operation of the facility. These groups have an organizational structure and a propensity towards violence and criminal acts. [Ross, 1995]

Correctional officers must be trained to identify inmates as possible STG members. The research by Levinson and Ross is a good foundation for an effective checklist on STG identification:

1. *Self-admission by inmate*: Inmates may boast about gang affiliation, either among inmates in living areas or during an intake or classification interview.
2. *STG markings or tattoos*: Inmates who possess marks or tattoos such as gang emblems, colors, etc., are easily identifiable.
3. *Possession of STG paraphernalia*: Paraphernalia could be certain clothing and jewelry. For example, Laron Douglas (aka "Scoobie G") describes his "Gangster Disciple Nation" uniform: black sweatshirt over a long blue T-shirt, black tweed belt turned to the right, saggy black Levis, black ProModel cap turned right. The jewelry worn is a Turkish gold rope and a ring in the shape of a six-pointed star on the right index finger. [Douglas, 1995]
4. *Information from Law Enforcement*: Law enforcement sources does not mean only the police, there are many agencies that participate in gang intelligence. Information could be gathered from local police, neighboring agencies, probation and parole and the U.S. Bureau of Prisons.
5. *Information from Internal Investigations*: Any investigation conducted regarding gang activities should be released to all sections who deal with inmates on a daily basis.
6. *Information from Confidential Informants*: Not all inmates want to be caught up in gang activities. Informant information must be initially taken seriously and confirmed.

7. *Inmate Mail/Outside Contacts*: While correctional officers cannot usually read private mail or listen to personal visits except by court order, they can observe the visitors, especially if they are sporting gang colors or emblems. The outside of envelopes may have gang symbols drawn on them.

8. *Individual or Group Pictures*: Some inmate gang members are proud of their affiliation and may be the affiliation of friends. Their cells may contain photos of them or those close to them in gang pictures. These photos can be in plain view and can be easily seen by the officer.

[Levinson, 1995]

Another type of STG group is the racial supremacist groups or, more commonly thought, the racist, bigot groups that have members in our corrections facilities.

Research by George Wilcox in 1992 resulted in a six-point classification system to identify if a group is extreme. These points are:

1. They are absolutely certain that they have the truth, their way is the *only* way.
2. Some evil, conspiratorial group controls to a greater or lesser degree the United States.
3. The group hates their opponents openly. They make no secret of their animosity.
4. Group members have little or no faith in the democratic process. Compromise is scorned.
5. The group believes that its enemies are to be denied basic civil liberties; they do not deserve them.
6. Groups will irresponsibly accuse opponents and engage in "character assignation." Opponents will be charged with having wicked motives and agendas.

[Mason & Becker, 1994, George and Wilcox, 1992]

In addition to this list, these groups assume that they have the absolute right to revolt or reform the "corruption" of the social system and members who are inspired or hailed are elevated to martyrdom or sainthood. [Mason & Becker, 1994]

Gangs and extremist groups are often linked. In 1984, the Federal Bureau of Investigation (FBI) stated that two white supremacist prison gangs, the Aryan Brotherhood and the Aryan Special Forces, participate in loan-sharking, extortion, gambling and suspected murders of guards and fellow inmates. They are linked to the Church of Jesus Christ Christian, whose action arm is the Aryan Nations. The Aryan Nations denounces blacks, Jews, communists, civil rights activities, and the U.S. government, nicknamed the Zionist Occupational Government or ZOG. [Thorton and Reid, 1984]

Tattoos and markings are excellent clues that an inmate is a member of an STG. Crude tattoos in black or dark blue ink often are done in prison, due to the lack of commercial dyes which are used on the outside. Tattoos are symbolic of gang affiliation and beliefs. Swastikas are symbolic of the Aryan Brotherhood; shamrocks or clovers represent the white race; skulls, demons and serpents state that the wearer is alienated from society's social values. The number of murders committed for the "cause" is indicated by the number of dots between the thumb and forefinger. [Mason & Becker, 1994] Only a well-informed security network can get such information on STGs to the line staff.

To the correctional staff, STGs cannot be thought as basic white and black groups. There are Asian gangs consisting of Chinese, Korean and Vietnamese subgroups who form separate gangs. Asian gangs tend to keep to themselves and appear quiet and respectful. The number of Asian gangs in the U.S. jails is predicted to increase. Hispanic gangs are considered the most structured with leaders who tightly control operations and discipline. [Ross, 1994]

A General Guide to Security Threat Groups (STG'S)

Mexican Mafia: Formed in 1958, it is thought to be the most powerful gang in the California penal system. Membership is for life, restricted to Mexican Americans. Criminal activities include gambling, drugs, homosexual relations and crimes in the community such as murders ordered from prison.

Black Guerilla Family: Follows a revolutionary philosophy, its goal being to control the destiny of the black inmate through education about racism and advocating pride and dignity. It is highly organized and correctional authorities are its number one enemy. This group is responsible for serious murders and assaults on California correctional staff.

Christian Identity: Racist theology based on religion. Provides justification for all white supremacist groups. Identity churches in jails and prisons serve to recruit members. Identity members believe that non-whites are "mud people" and are on the same spiritual level as animals; Jews are Satan's descendants and are imposters; British people are true Israelites; and a race war which will destroy all non-whites is predicted in the Bible.

Black Gangs: Crips and Bloods: Very little formal structure and strong leadership. Members may act for themselves instead of the gangs. Correctional staff enforcing rules are taken as a personal affront. File many complaints, members will not hesitate to use violence against inmates or staff.

Adapted from: *Controlling the Influence of Gangs in Our Jails* by Sgt. Roger Ross, LA Co. Sheriff's Dept., at Large Network Jail Mtg., Long Mount Col., Jan, 1995; *Know Your Bigots* by Mason & Becker, 9-10/94; Fox & Stinchcombe, 1994.

Trends involving STG's are not good. In a 1992 study, an estimated 47,445 inmates in the U.S. are affiliated with a known 755 STGs in the U.S. In 1989, an estimated 80-90% of inmates in the Illinois correctional system had gang affiliations. Some gangs on the rise have been identified as Bloods, Crips, Vice Lords, Hell's Angels, Skinheads and Latin Kings. In 1984 and 1985, in the Texas correctional system, there were fifty-two inmate homicides and 7,000 assaults on inmates and staff. Gang-related activities were linked to 92% of the murders and 80% of the assaults! [Fox & Stinchcombe, 1998, Buentello, 1992]

In the mid 1980's, a new type of STG emerged—roving gangs of Vietnamese criminals who specialize in home invasion, car theft and robbery. What is different about this type of group is that they are loosely organized with 3-10 members, ages 16-25, have no group name and have no permanent leaders. Apprehension is difficult due to members using multiple identification and adults claiming to be juveniles. [Carton, 1986]

What can correctional staff do about STG activities? One positive trend in corrections has been the increase of informative studies and articles on STG activities (see References). This material contains some useful steps to curb STG activity:

- All correctional facilities should develop policies and procedures concerning STG's. [Littman, 1995] All staff should be trained in STG identification and activities.
- Violent acts should be aggressively prosecuted [Fox & Stinchcombe, 1994] both by the use of in-house disciplinary sanctions and criminal code prosecution.
- Confirmed prison gang/STG members should be placed in administrative segregation whenever possible, [Fox & Stinchcombe, 1998] especially when the inmates are very active in STG activities.
- Aggressively and frequently pursue such existing security measures such as strip searches, cell shakedowns, [Ross, 1995] incoming property searches, visitation monitoring, etc.

- Prohibit contact visits to known STG members, restrict visitors if necessary. [Ross, 1995]
- Monitor incoming and outgoing mail and telephone calls. Court orders likely will be needed. Inmate financial accounts should be monitored. [Ross, 1995]
- Credits for good time and work time credits could be cancelled as a result of STG activity. [Ross, 1995]
- All indicators of STG activity, such as tattoos and hate literature, should be photographed and documented. *All* behavior and activity should be documented by memorandum, incident report or log entry in the inmate's file. [Mason & Becker, 1994]
- All material found in inmates' property, such as tattoo patterns, ink, material marked with tattoos, boots/heavy footwear (can be used for weapons), should be placed in the inmate's property, sent out at the inmate's expense, or if the inmate signs a waiver, destroyed. [Mason & Becker, 1994]
- Develop an STG intelligence network consisting of several components:

    — A very detailed classification procedure that asks the inmate detailed questions about tattoos, markings, gang activities, etc. Also, the staff should ask the inmate such questions as:
    * Are you a racist?
    * Will/can you freely associate with members of other races and religious groups on an equal basis, including being housed with them?
    * Do you think that you have been a victim of political, racial or religious persecution? [Mason & Becker, 1994]

    — A mechanism for trained STG intelligence personnel to analyze all STG information, recommend proactive strategies, and to regularly brief the institutional staff. Also, continuous training should be provided.

Progress is being made. For example, the New York City Department of Corrections initiated a gang tracking program that shares computerized data with other law enforcement agencies. Correctional officers collect intelligence on gangs and maintain a digitized photo data base. Gang members who commit crimes are aggressively prosecuted and the crimes are examined for intelligence gathering. The message to the inmate population is that gang violence *will not* be tolerated. [Nadel, 1997]

Mentally Disordered Inmates

It is no secret that our jails and prisons house inmates that are mentally ill. In nearly the past forty years, the care of the mentally ill has changed. According to Vesey, Steadman and Salasin in 1995, the development of new medications, changes in treatment philosophies, the civil rights movement and federal funding for a nationwide network of community mental health centers has resulted in a decline of patients in state mental hospitals. The philosophy has been for people with mental illness to get treated at the local level, thus, the deinstitutionalization of the mentally ill. Another result is that treatment varies from jurisdiction to jurisdiction — a fragmented approach. [Vesey, Steadman & Salasin, 1995]

Mentally ill people do get arrested and come into the criminal justice system. They come in all genders, ethnic groups, ages and socio-economic levels. Many people think that most mentally disordered people are violent. Some are, depending on their illness and symptoms. However, research indicates that most are not violent. [Vesey, Steadman, Salasin, 1995]

According to estimates, approximately 10% of inmates have severe or significant psychiatric disabilities. [Steadman, 1991; Allen & Simonsen, 1995] Not all correctional facilities have the capability to treat the mentally ill inmate. In jails and lockups, the general concern is the safety of the staff, the inmate and his/her stabilization. In the short term, inmates in jails are screened for medical problems and in well operated jails, mental problems. However, the mentally ill inmate in jails may often be released after being stabilized back into the community without adequate supports such as discharge planning, social services, and treatment. [Steadman, Vesey and Salasin, 1995]

However, the prison is a different environment than jails in terms of treating mentally ill inmates. Inmates are there for much longer periods of time and the approach should include these areas, according to a 1989 report of the American Psychiatric Association: mental health screening, evaluation, crisis intervention, treatment and discharge/transfer planning. [Steadman, Vesey & Salasin, 1995]

These positions and philosophies are on a much higher level than the level on which the line correctional officer operates. The correctional officer should be aware of this information.

According to the Virginia Department of Mental Health and Mental Retardation in 1986, mental disorders may be categorized as disturbances in behavior, thinking (cognitive) or emotion (affect). Schizophrenia and paranoia are cognitive disorders while mania and depression are affective.

Symptoms: Symptoms may range in severity, depending on the seriousness of the disorder. The best rule to follow is that the inmate is not acting normally. The following are general symptoms that may indicate mental illness:

fear	depression/suicidal thoughts
withdrawal	manic behavior: non-stop energy
confusion	delusions (think they are God)
anxiety	hallucinations: hears voices, sees visions
anger	thinks others are plotting against him/her

[Va. Dept. of Mental Health & Mental Retardation, 1986]

Abuse of alcohol and drugs can contribute to odd behavior. The correctional officer, if possible, should try to ascertain if there is any history or sign of substance abuse and notify qualified staff.

Some inmates may suffer from *"prison psychosis"* or a form of mental disorder where the inmate cannot cope with prison life any more. This could be due to prison routine, assault, fear of rape/assault, depression, falling apart of social life (family, marriage, etc.). Not all inmates who suffer from mental illness are new arrivals—the overwhelming problem of being incarcerated can contribute to a breakdown of mental health. [Allen & Simonsen, 1995]

A Thumbnail Guide to Mental Disorders

The science of psychology covers a wide range of material. Often, the correctional officer must be able to ascertain that something "isn't quite right" with an inmate. Ongoing training by qualified mental health staff is crucial.

The following will serve as a general guide which can be expanded upon by in-depth training:

Substance Abuse Disorders: Caused by alcohol and drug abuse which affects behavior and functioning. Depression can be induced by alcohol, heroin and its derivatives (narcotics), inhalants, barbiturates, etc. Stimulants (cocaine, amphetamines) can result in mania, while hallucinogens (LSD, PCP, marijuana) can alter one's sense of reality. As the person sobers up, the symptoms disappear.

Mood Disorders: Non-substance abuse and appear abnormal-depression (sadness, despondent), bipolar disorder (manic depression) and mania (rapid speech, agitation, no need for sleep). These disorders are treatable with drugs.

Anxiety Disorders Involve being overly anxious and exhibiting repetitive behavior — general anxiety disorder (fear or worrying about non-specific problems), obsessive compulsive disorder (doing things a certain way such as washing hands repeatedly, etc.), post-traumatic stress disorder (PTSD anxiety resulting from a past event like an assault, etc.) and phobias such as fear of certain things (i.e., insects) or situations. These disorders are treatable with medication and counseling.

Thought Disorders: Schizophrenia, delusional disorders and para-noia are frequently aggravated by stress such as coming into a jail. Hallucinations can tell an inmate to commit suicides. Treatment in-cludes anti-psychotic medications.

Sexual Disorders: Include exhibitionism, voyeurism, froteurism and sadism. Information such as this needs to be kept confidential to ensure the safety of the inmate.

Personality Disorders: Five that are of concern to the correctional officer are: anti-social (deceitful, lack of remorse, lack of respect for others), borderline personality disorder (lacks self-identity, may act suicidal, empty feelings), histrionic personality (draws attention to self through physical appearance, seductiveness, etc.), narcissistic personality disorders (overblown sense of self, being special) and paranoid personality disorders (believe they are being used, distrust people, hold grudges, feel like they are being attacked).

Adapted from: "Identifying and Referring Inmates with Mental Disorders. A Guide for Correctional Staff," by Gary L. Lupton, *American Jails*, May-June, 1996, pp. 49-52.

Handling of the Mentally Disordered Inmates

Documentation is of primary importance. Staff should document through reports, logs, memos, etc., all behavior and symptoms of mentally ill in-mates. Inmates should be referred to the mental health staff in the facility. However, some jails do not have full-time mental health personnel. In such cases, arrangements must be made with local community mental health centers or hospitals to have a qualified mental health therapist come in to assess inmates. Under no circumstances should correctional officers diag-nose inmates; they should only report what they observe.

Inmates who are ascertained to be behaving irrationally due to a mental disorder should be housed near an officer's post and checked at least every fifteen minutes, or sooner in some cases.

Inmates who are suspected to be mentally ill should be treated with caution. Though the inmate may be on medication and/or in treatment, his/her behavior may be unpredictable. Caution is a must. Also, to keep the inmate on a calm level, correctional officers should speak to inmates calmly, listen to what they have to say and not be sarcastic and condescending.

The Developmentally Disabled Offender

A recent development in the subject of mentally disordered inmates is the study of the developmentally disabled offender or "mentally retarded." These inmates are characterized by low intellectual ability (IQ) and show an inability in social or life skills. Estimates of the rate of developmentally disabled inmates in the general inmate population run from 3-10%.

Developmentally disabled offenders may distrust the system or become angry when asked to read or sign something. They do not understand what is happening to them. For example, in South Carolina, out of forty-five such inmates who were evaluated, seven did not know what the word "guilty" meant.

Guidelines for correctional officers include observing appearances such as clothing and hygiene for unusual characteristics. Also, the inmate may have problems with motor skills such as using a pen. Communications should be calm and clear and precautions should be taken against the inmate from becoming a victim for predators. Referrals concerning such inmates should be made to the mental health staff, courts and attorneys.

> Adapted from "Working with the
> Developmentally Disabled in Jail,
> by Wendy R. Jones, *American Jails*,
> Nov-Dec, 1995, pp. 16-20.

Female Offenders: More attention has been devoted in recent years to the problems of the female inmate. More females are going to prison. According to Meia Chesney-Lind, Director of Women's Studies at the University of Hawaii at Manoa, mandatory minimum sentences combined with new sentencing guidelines have decreased how much discretion judges have in sentencing. Ten to twenty years ago, female offenders may have received probation due to pregnancy or dependent children. Now, more are receiving incarceration. Between 1980 and 1992, the number of female inmates incarcerated increased 276% compared to 163% of male inmates. [Ragghianti, 1994]

Recent studies have resulted in this profile of the typical female offender:

- Approximately 13% of female jail inmates are incarcerated for a violent offense and one in three are first time offenders. [Allen & Simonsen, 1998]
- Drug use is high. More than 50% used drugs in the month prior to being jailed; about 39% used cocaine or crack during this; nearly 40% use drugs daily, according to a 1989 survey of jail inmates. [Allen & Simonsen, 1998, Snell, 1992]
- Drug and alcohol abuse began at about age thirteen. [Ragghanti, 1994]
- Unemployment is a factor. The typical female inmate is unemployed at the time of arrest. Her annual income was less than $10,000. [Ragghianti, 1994]
- Her life has not been easy. Depression is common; she may have attempted suicide. The average female inmate is three times more likely than a male inmate to be physically or sexually abused. [Ragghianti, 1994]
- Many incarcerated females are mothers. In 1991, according to a study by the National Council on Crime Delinquency, there were about 167,000 children who had mothers in U.S. jails and prisons. [Ragghanti, 1994]
- Researcher Barbara Bloom found that 54% of the children never visit their mothers. Children of incarcerated females have trouble in school, trouble with peers, and possible long-term psychological effects. [Ragghanti, 1994]

While females have been traditionally viewed as the "fairer sex," veteran correctional officers know that there are female inmates who are as hard core and streetwise as males. However, female inmates should be encouraged to enroll in vocational and educational programs while incarcerated. Since many are mothers, such rehabilitation programs can assist in maintaining a crime-free life for them and their children. Correctional officers must remember that family ties are important and not being able to see their children or participate in their upbringing can lead to despair and depression.

Conditions of confinement and programs for female inmates are improving. Class action lawsuits on the behalf of female inmates can have an effect. At the Huron Valley Correctional Institution in Ypsilanti, Michigan, female inmates could receive minimal job training as housekeepers, cooks and craft workers—the traditional "female" jobs. Male inmates in the Michigan system could choose from *twenty* job training courses such as auto repair, air conditioning service and repair, commercial baking and drafting. A 1979 class action suit improved jobs training for females. In 1981, another class action suit improved conditions for females at the Women's Prison in Rehee Valley, Kentucky. Until the suit, new inmates could not set their hair or display photos of their children in their cells. By 1987, the availability of programs for women was not at the same level for male inmates, but conditions have improved. [Rubin, 1987]

In the past 10-15 years, more attention has been given to the female inmate who is a mother. Programs have been developed to allow visits with dependent children and parenting. Another aspect of "inmate motherhood" is that some babies are born while the mother is incarcerated—an estimated 9% of women inmates. [Harris, 1993] The common practice in most states after birth is to give the baby to relatives or social services. New York is the only state where the infant can stay with the female inmate until their first birthday or for an eighteen-month period if the mother will be paroled during that time. The criteria for this decision is if the mother is determined to be emotionally and physically fit to care for the child, has resided with her other children and most likely will be the principal care giver upon release. [Harris, 1993] Hopefully, this trend of keeping mothers and babies together combined with rehabilitative programs will keep the female from returning to prison.

Juvenile offenders: To the correctional officers in our nation's jails and prisons, some juvenile offenders are as hard core and streetwise as some adult offenders. Felonies by juveniles increased alarmingly from 1985 to 1995, due to trafficking in crack cocaine and activities of armed gangs. Violent offense arrests of juveniles increased 67% in that ten-year period and about a fifth of violent crimes in the U.S. can be attributed to teens. [Lacayo, 1997]

The plan of attack on juvenile crime has been in the past several years to certify more juvenile offenders as adults so they can be tried and punished in adult courts. The debate continues as to whether this approach is the right answer. About 12,300 juvenile offenders, or about 9% of all juveniles arrested for violent crimes, are prosecuted as adults annually. Apparently the affects are not as marked as anticipated. Connecticut has the highest rate of transfer from juvenile to adult status; Colorado has the lowest. Youth crime rates in both states remain the same. New York automatically prosecutes youths age 16 and older for serious crimes, but New York juvenile crime rates have doubled. [Lascayo, 1997]

In 1986, juvenile justice experts recommended strategies to deal with the juvenile offender. Upon release, juvenile offenders should be given effective caseworker attention in community-based programs with positive peer group activities and responsible citizens acting as role models. Chronic offenders should receive long-term incarceration if other strategies fail. Courts, schools and juveniles' families must work with the offender together. If the juvenile's family situation is negative and contributes to a lack of supervision and crime, the youth should be placed in foster care. Finally, courts must sentence consistently and fairly. The juvenile should not be able to "skate by" on an offense and manipulate the system by false promises of rehabilitation. [Santoi, 1986]

Novel Approaches to Juvenile Crime

Several studies have taken some unique approaches to battle juvenile crime. In 1994, Minnesota passed a law that gives a "last bite of the apple" to violent juvenile offenders. The juvenile receives a "dual sentence," one as a juvenile, including restitution and community-based strategies (intensive probation, for example) and an adult sentence—prison. If the juvenile violates the conditions of sentence one or repeats criminal behavior, sentence two is implemented.

Arizona and Colorado laws resulted in secure juvenile facilities being built for violent youths. Judges can sentence offenders to fixed terms which is unprecedented. Parents are pressured to participate in court proceedings and treatment plans.

Adapted from: "The Assault on
Juvenile Justice" by Penelope
Lemov, *Governing*, Dec. 1994

Handling juveniles in adult facilities is not easy. "Juvies" may be impulsive and immature. Some are drug abusers and gang members. Problems associated with these offender characteristics must be dealt with the same as with adult offenders. Hard core juveniles also engage in disciplinary violations and get into confrontations with staff. Young offenders need daily recreation and leisure activities; energy levels are higher. Correctional officers must take time and exhibit patience in dealing with juveniles due to immaturity and emotionally not being able to handle the situation. While a juvenile may be cocky, a realization may set in that once incarcerated, he has hit the "big time" and the situation is serious.

Juveniles confined to adult jails are generally handled separately from adult inmates by sight and sound. Inmates need social contact and juveniles are no exception. Staff should check juveniles at least every fifteen minutes and should watch for signs of suicidal behavior. Suicides of juveniles in jails occur four-and-one-half times more (450%) than juveniles in secure juvenile detention facilities. [Va. Dept. of Mental Health & Mental Retardation, 1986]

If a juvenile is transferred by the court to an adult jail from a juvenile facility for security or behavioral reasons, the jail staff should find out the offender's criminal history and institutional record.

Elderly inmates: Due to the current trends of abolishing parole and handing down tougher sentences, the fact that inmates will be growing old in prison is becoming a concern among corrections professionals. These trends will result in young inmates getting convicted and doing time into middle age and beyond for serious crimes. In 1988, there were less than 15,000 state prison inmates age 55 and under; in 1994, there were 22,495 inmates fitting that category. [Walsh, 1996]

There are definitive concerns about the management of geriatric inmates. Older inmates may be vulnerable to attack by younger, predatory inmates. Older inmates cannot be housed with inmates who are younger, less mature and more noisy.

Other concerns are about mental and physical health. Elderly inmates may suffer from depression as spouses pass away and/or family members reject them. Nutritional needs change: less protein, fewer caloric intake, soft foods and increased fiber may be required. Health problems do not stop at the prison wall: gastrointestinal problems, cardiac problems, hypertension, diabetes, strokes, cancer, lung diseases, etc., all can lay claim to the elderly inmate. By the year 2005, elderly inmate health care costs may increase to *fourteen times* today's levels! [Allen & Simonsen, 1998]

In 1994, the Center on Juvenile and Criminal Justice released a study, stating that the annual cost of an inmate to the California Department of Corrections was $21,000.00; average age was 30. Other research estimated that Department of Corrections cost of keeping an inmate over age 50 was three times that amount! Some steps are being taken. Michigan's Lakeland Correctional Facility is specifically designed for the care of geriatric prisoners; the POP's (Project for Older Prisoners) project in Washington, D.C., has worked to win the release of over 100 older prisoners with none committing another crime. [Walsh, 1996]

Medical Issues: The state of an inmate's health is important to all who work and live in the institution. Inmates have a right to basic medical care. More importantly, some illnesses and ailments can spread throughout an overcrowded facility.

Some inmates receive good medical care only when they come into a jail or prison. Alcoholics and drug addicts may be malnourished or suffer from various maladies resulting from their lifestyle. Some inmates have bad teeth, skin problems, colds, abscesses, etc., because they do not take care of themselves. As one veteran correctional officer states:

> I have seen inmates come into jail with rashes, sores, bleeding gums, rotten teeth, infected ears, severe colds and flu, venereal diseases,

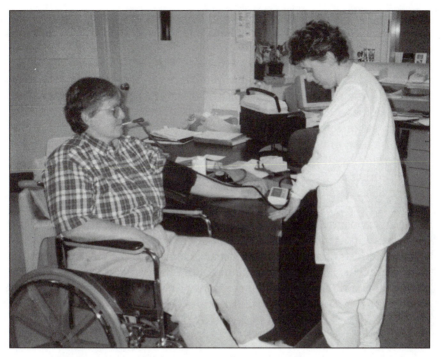

Most jails and prisons have qualified medical staff in order to treat a variety of medical problems and physical conditions.

etc. It appears that the only time some see a medical practitioner is when they are locked up.

While a very detailed examination of inmates' medical afflictions would take up a book in itself, this section will consist of an overview of the more serious disease: AIDS, tuberculosis and hepatitis.

AIDS (Acquired Immune Deficiency Syndrome): AIDS is a disease resulting from the Human Immunodeficiency Virus (HIV). AIDS is a bloodborne disease and it defeats the human body's ability to fight off infections and diseases. Some people become infected with the HIV virus and show no signs of illness for years while others become sick and die in a shorter period of time. Individuals infected with HIV have a 50% greater chance of developing "full blown AIDS" over a period of 10-20 years. AIDS infections vary from pneumonia, cancers and central nervous system disorders. [Hyzer, 1989]

Recent estimates state that at least 2% of jail and prison inmates are HIV infected. In Florida and Michigan, AIDS is the leading cause of death of prison inmates ahead of heart disease and cancer. [Faiver, 1998]

Tuberculosis (TB): This disease which can be contracted simply by breathing infected air is very contagious. The closer the quarters with an infected person and the longer the exposure the greater the risk. TB was in decline for 30 years, but resurfaced in 1985 with an 18% increase in cases from 1985-1991. High rates of HIV and AIDS was a causative factor. One concern is the multi-drug resistant strain of TB. Rates of TB in correctional facilities are 6-11 times the rates in the general population. A person can become infected with the TB bacteria and may not develop an active case for a long time. Treatment includes antibiotic and isolation in negative pressure isolation rooms, where the air inside the room does not ventilate to other areas. [Faiver, 1998]

Hepatitis: Viral hepatitis is caused by five viruses: hepatitis A, B, C, D and E. The hepatitis B (HBV) and C (HCV) strains are transmitted by needle stick exposures to blood and/or sexual contact. Hepatitis D (HDV) is also transmitted in this manner, but only to persons infected with HBV. The A and E strains are spread by fecal/oral route and a chronic infection does not occur. HBV infection damages the liver which becomes the site of infection and reproduction of the virus. Correctional workers have recognized the dangers of HBV infection for years and more information about HCV has become available. [ACA, 1997]

Transmission

The three diseases discussed here—HIV/AIDS, TB and Hepatitis B and C represent dangerous diseases in correctional facilities and correctional workers must always keep in mind how they are transmitted and take preventative measures.

HIV can be spread by blood to blood contact by infected needles or by infected blood coming into contact with an open cut or wound. It can also be spread by sexual fluids to blood contact, primarily through anal sexual intercourse or, as is now being documented, vaginal intercourse. [ACA, 1997]. The HIV organism does not live long outside the body. The primary transmission method is intimate transfer of certain bodily fluids, particularly from inside an infected person to the bloodstream of another. [Hyzer, 1989] Homosexual/bi-sexual men, persons who engage in casual, unsafe sex and intravenous drug users all run the risk of getting HIV.

TB is spread through breathing the air that contains the bacteria put there by an infected person. Hepatitis B and C are primarily spread by needle stick exposures to infected blood and sexual contact. However, HBV has been found in lower concentrations in semen, saliva, vaginal fluid and sweat. [ACA, 1997] A good rule to remember is TB by air, HIV, HBV and HCV by exposure primarily to blood or sharps (needles) containing infected blood.

Symptoms of AIDS

There is a lot of information to remember about deadly diseases. Medical staff should conduct periodic training; most agencies and facilities require training in blood-borne pathogens and TB. The following is a compilation of symptoms of AIDS.

- Persistent fatigue;
- Persistent fever, chills, night sweats lasting for a few weeks, not linked to a known ailment;
- Weight loss: unexplained, ten pounds in less than two months;
- Swollen glands/lymph nodes, especially on side and back of neck, not linked to a known ailment, lasts over two months;
- Thrush: fungal or yeast infection, creamy white patches on tongue or mouth;
- Frequent dry cough, breathing difficulty, shortness of breath;
- Unexplained diarrhea;
- Loss of vision;
- Blotches: pink or purple, raised or flat, that do not go away and do not pale when pressed;
- Persistent memory loss, changes to gait or loss of equilibrium, mood changes, blurring of vision, loss of hearing, unexplained psychiatric symptoms.

Adapted from: AJA Jail Operations Bulletin: "Infectious Diseases in the Jail," Vol. 1, No. 9, by Capt. Walter Hyzer, 1989, American Jail Assoc.

Correctional officers today can be vaccinated against Hepatitis B and also can get a TB skin test to ascertain if they have been exposed to the disease. All inmates entering a correctional facility should be asked about their medical history at a minimum. If an inmate is sick or is showing the symptoms of a serious disease, he or she should be examined by a qualified medical staff person as soon as possible. Inmates should be tested for TB and if there are symptoms present or they request it, HIV/AIDS.

Inmate access to quality health care in a correctional facility really begins with intake screening upon arrival, either at a jail or prison. Beginning with the correctional officer who meets the incoming inmate, all staff should be trained to recognize a medical emergency or to ask basic questions to ascertain if there are medical problems. [Faiver, 1998] Procedures must be in place for medical staff to do a comprehensive medical history and refer problems to the facility physician.

Medical Screening Forms

Correctional facilities' medical staff operate "sick call" where inmates that complain of medical problems can see the nurse or facility physician. Some jails charge the inmate for this service with the fee coming from the inmates' financial account. Placing the inmate in a dispensary or an outside hospital under guard may be necessary if the medical condition warrants it. Security and transport must be tight as some inmates have escaped or attempted escape from hospitals. Correctional officers *must* be at a heightened level of security.

Medication can be dispensed by calling the inmate to the medical station or by the medical staff making rounds or "medication [med] runs" to the inmate housing areas. Medication can be placed into envelopes with the inmate's name and dispensed or can come ready to dispense in a "blister pack;" each inmate has his/her own pack. The medication is popped out and given to the inmate.

Over the counter (OTC) medications such as headache remedies, antacids, etc., are sold through the inmate commissary in some facilities.

Giving an inmate a pill and proceeding on is not adequate security. Inmates have been known to fake taking their medications, thus hoarding them for sale to other inmates or taking them in a large quantity in order to commit suicide. Medical staff must exercise patience and caution, observing the inmate taking the pill/liquid, and then observing an open mouth to make sure the substance was ingested properly.

Prompt Intake Health Processing

The American Correctional Association (ACA) has strict accreditation standards on time intervals for inmate medical and dental screenings and appraisals in correctional facilities.

Dividing types of correctional facilities into prisons, jails and juvenile facilities, ACA recommends the following:

Arrival Mental Health Screening: immediately at all facilities.

Arrival Dental Screening: Fourteen days at prisons and jails, seven days at juvenile facilities.

Intake Health Appraisal: Fourteen days for prisons and jails, seven days for juvenile facilities.

Intake Mental Health Assessment: Fourteen days for prisons and jails, seven days for juvenile facilities, if problems evident at booking.

Intake Dental Exam: Prisons — three months; fourteen days for jails; one month for juvenile facilities.

Adapted from: *Health Care
Management Issues in Corrections,*
by Kenneth Faiver, MPH, Ch. 6
Ensuring Access to Care, ACA, 1998.

Foreign/Ethnic Groups: Correctional facilities have no control concerning what foreign born or ethnic inmates become incarcerated. At the local jail level, for example, a Latino inmate who speaks little or no English could be booked in for drunk driving, followed an hour later by a Vietnamese person charged with assault.

Generally speaking, almost 10% of the United States population is foreign born or about 25.8 million residents, according to a 1998 Census Bureau report. Trends in immigration show that most immigrants come from Central America, South America, and the Caribbean. The second largest group comes from the Phillippines, then from China and Hong Kong. In California, almost one in four residents are foreign born; in New York, it is one in five. A high volume of immigrants come from Mexico. [Vobejda, 1998]

For correctional officers to effectively deal with inmates of different cultures and ethnic groups, they must understand them. This can only be accomplished through cultural diversity training which is an emerging trend of corrections in the 1990's. Law enforcement officers, including corrections personnel, need to understand the cultural aspects of inmates' communication and behavior. If they do not, frustrations will mount as staff ignore the fact that inmates come in all cultures. [Weaver, 1992]

Staff must develop a mind set of putting themselves in other people's "cultural shoes." This concept is called *cultural empathy*. A key point to remember is that America is not "all the same;" we are a diverse society. [Weaver, 1992]

Here is an example of misreading an inmate's behavior due to a lack of cultural empathy from a jail officer:

I remember a time where we booked in a Vietnamese inmate, about 30-35 years old. He spoke no English. We noticed that he kept turning away food. He was charged with a felony and we all thought he was on a hunger strike. After a few days, the classification staff managed to get a Vietnamese interpreter as we had no Vietnamese speaking officers on the department. Through the interpreter, we discovered that the inmate had only been in the United States a very short time and could not digest American food. He requested rice; the jail cook made up a batch. The inmate ate and started to interact more with the staff.

Correctional officers tend to "lump" foreign inmates together by using common terms—Hispanics, Asians, etc. However, most Asians prefer *not* to be called Orientals, but by their nationality, such as Korean-American, Japanese-American, etc. Instead of "Hispanic," Spanish speaking inmates prefer "Chicano" (Mexican-American), Latino (Central American), or El Salvadoran, Costa Rican, etc. American Indians do not like the term "Native American" because it is an invention of the United States government. They prefer "American Indian" or being called by their trial ancestry such as Sioux, Cherokee, etc. African-American and black American are used often; most younger people prefer African-American. [Weaver, 1992]

It is impossible to cover all aspects of all the different cultures and ethnic backgrounds of inmates. Training must be afforded to all correctional staff who deal with inmates from different ethnic backgrounds. Staff must not develop an attitude of *ethnocentrism* or a belief that one's own culture is "inherently superior." Inmates should not be viewed as an inferior class. [Fernandez, 1992] In general, training should focus on these points:

1. People from different cultures can react in different ways to interactions with staff. For example, an Arab inmate may be reluctant to talk to an American correctional officer sitting cross-legged with a shoe near the inmate's face or having his feet up on the desk. Americans usually do not casually touch each other, but in Italian or Spanish cultures, it is all right. [Weaver, 1993]
2. In some cultures, families may cut ties with the inmate. In Asian families where parents cling to traditional customs, the family's reaction to a member being arrested may be total ostracism or disowning. Sometimes a family member keeps a "secretive" contact with the offender. [Cooke, 1990]
3. Ethnicity or common culture traditions or a sense of identity becomes important to the inmate. They become loyal to other inmates in a similar culture. For example, Hispanic inmates are loyal to their ethnic subgroup (Mexican, etc.) for brotherhood and protection. [Fernandez, 1992]
4. Training should stress that there is no place in corrections for ethnocentracism or prejudice. Being bigoted is not a good practice for correctional officers in overcrowded institutions where staff and inmates must engage in positive interactions and communications.

5. Cultural diversity training cannot be "glossed over" in roll calls. Seminars of at least two to four hours are recommended. Trainers should request that community leaders from ethnic groups in the community provide training to correctional staff.

Summary

Correctional staff must deal daily with many different types of inmates, each with their own unique characteristics and problems. Substance abusers, mentally disordered, females, elderly, juveniles, foreign, medically ill inmates, and suicidal inmates must all be understood and handled. AIDS poses a challenge as does the increasing number of aging inmates. In-depth training must be provided to the correctional officer.

Concerning substance abusers, recent studies show high rates of alcohol and drug abuse among inmates. Mentally disordered inmates are not to be merely labeled as "mentals," but may be suffering from a variety of disorders that the correctional officer should be aware of.

Female inmates pose problems due to drug abuse and being mothers. Elderly inmates are increasing in number as our society becomes more conservative in sentencing offenders to longer sentences.

Juveniles require special handling, especially concerning suicide. Foreign inmates should not be lumped together in a group—each ethnic group poses its own concerns.

Medically, AIDs, HIV, hepatitis and TB all pose a threat to the correctional officer, but training has improved greatly.

Review Questions

1. What are several general signs of alcohol and drug abuse?

2. What are several drug and alcohol withdrawal signs?

3. What four criteria determines if an inmate group is possibly a gang?

4. What signs of gang activity should correctional officers be aware?

5. Name five identification indicators that may tell a correctional officer that an inmate is in a gang.

6. What are several general symptoms of mental illness?

7. What are some concerns about elderly inmates?

8. Identify several symptoms of AIDs.

9. Identify several symptoms of suicidal behavior.

Terms/Concepts

Cold turkey

Therapeutic community

Criminal street gang

Gang member

STG

Personality disorders

Prison psychosis

Developmentally disabled
  offender

Substance abuse disorders

Mood disorders

Anxiety disorders

Sexual disorders

Thought disorders

Cultural empathy

Ethnocentrism

References

Allen, Harry, and Clifford Simonsen, *Corrections in America, An Introduction*, 8th Ed., Prentice Hall. Englewood Cliffs, NJ, 1998.

Bales, Don, ed., *Corrections Officer Resource Guide*, 3rd Ed., American Correctional Association, Lanham, MD, 1997.

Beck, Caroline W., *Drug Enforcement and Treatment in Prison, 1990*, U.S. Department of Justice, Wash. D.C., 1992.

Beuntello, Salvador, "Combatting Gangs in Texas," *Corrections Today* vol. 54 no. 5, July, 1992, p. 58.

Carton, Barbara, "Roving Vietnamese Bands Seen as New Crime Pattern," *Washington Post*, 9/25/86, pp. C1, C5.

Cooke, Kim, Cultural Sensitivity Seminar, Northern Virginia Criminal Justice Academy, 4/12/90.

Cornelius, Gary F., *Jails in America: An Overview of Issues*, 2nd Ed., ACA, Lanham, MD, 1996.

Cozone, "Gangbangers Speak Out, Part I" *Prison Life*, March, 1995, pp. 44-55.

Douglas, Laron, "In the Mind of a True Disciple," *Prison Life*, March, 1995, p. 46.

Faiver, Kenneth L., MPH, MLR, *Health Care Management Issues in Corrections*, ACA, Lanham, MD, 1998.

Fernandez, Victor, "Cultural Diversity Training in the Correctional System," *Journal of Correctional Training*, Winter, 1992.

Fields, Gary, "Study links drugs to 80% of incarcerations," *USA Today*, 1/9/98.

Fox, Vernon & Jeanne Stinchcombe, *Introduction to Corrections*, 4th Ed., Englewood Cliffs, Prentice Hall, 1994.

George, John and Laird Wilcox, *Nazis, Communists, Klansmen and Others on the Fringe Political Extremism in America*, Prometheus Books, Buffalo, NY, 1992.

Greene, M.S., "Prisoners of Violence: Street Gangs in Cellblocks," *Washington Post*, 9/9/96, A1.

Harland, A.T., S. Buentello, & G. Knox, "Prison Gangs," *Prison Journal*, 71(2), pp. 1-66, 1993.

Harris, Jean, "The Babies of Bedford," *Prison Life*, 7/93, pp. 30-32.

Hyzzer, Walter, Capt., "Infectious Diseases in the Jail," *Jail Operations Bulletin*, American Jail Association, Vol. 1, No. 9, 1989.

Jones, Wendy, "Working with the Developmentally Disabled in Jail," *American Jails*, Nov-Dec 1995, pp. 16-20.

LaCayo, "Teen Crime," *Time*, 7/21/97, Vol. 150, No. 3, pp. 26-29.

Lemor, Penelope, "The Assault on Juvenile Justice," *Governing*, 12/94, Vol. 8, No. 3.Lester, David, Ph.D., and Bruce L. Danto, M.D., *Suicide Behind Bars: Prediction and Prevention*, Philadelphia, Charles Press, 1993.

Levinson, Robert B., Ph.D., "Security Threat Groups," presented in "Controlling the Influence of Gangs in our Jails," Large Jail Network Meeting, National Institute of Corrections, Longmont, Colorado, 1/23/95.

Littman, Leah, *Gangs, Women and AIDS in Jail and Prison*, George Mason University, SOC 402, 11/29/95.

Lupton, Gary, "Identifying and Referring Inmates with Mental Disorders," *American Jails*, May-June, 1996, pp. 49-52.

Mason, John J. And Paul Becker, "Know Your Bigots: Identifying and Supervising White Supremacists in a Correctional Setting," *American Jails*, Sep-Oct 1994, pp. 61-65.

Mclain, Buzz, "Program Sobers Prisoner's Lives," *Fairfax Journal*, 8/31/90.

Nadel, Barbara A., AIA, "Slashing Gang Violence, Not Victims," *The Keeper's Voice*, Winter, 1997, Vol. 18, No. 4, pp. 16-19.

Porter, Desiree, *Prison Gangs*, George Mason University, SOC 402, 1995/see Harland, A.T., Buentello S., and Kno, G.W., 1993 *Prison Gangs*, Prison Journal, 71(2) 1-66.

Ragghianti, Marie, "Save the Innocent Victims of Prison," *Parade*, 2/16/94, pp. 14-15.

Ross, Roger D., Sgt., L.A. Sheriff's Office, "Controlling the Influence of Gangs in Our Jails," Large Jail Network Meeting, National Institute of Corrections, Longmont, Colorado, 1/23/95.

Rubin, Nancy, "Women Behind Bars," *McCalls*, 8/87, pp. 36-42.

Santoi, Al, "How Should We Handle Young Offenders?" *Parade*, 4/20/86, pp. 16-17.

Silberman, M., *A World of Violence: Corrections in America*, Belmont, Wadsworth, 1995.

Snell, Tracy, *Women in Jail 1989*, Bureau of Justice Statistics, Wash. D.C., 3/92.

Steadman, Henry, et al., "Estimating Mental Health Needs and Service Utilization Among Prison Inmates," *Bulletin of American Academy of Psychiatry and the Law*, 19(3)(1991), pp. 297-307.

Thornton, Mary and T.R. Reid, "Aryan Group, Jail Gangs Linked," *Washington Post*, 12/18/94, p. A3.

Trainer's Manual: The Mentally Ill, Mentally Retarded and Substance Dependent, Va. Dept. Of Mental Health and Mental Retardation, Project Consultant: Joseph Rowan; Project Director: Frank Patterson, 6/86.

Vesey, Bonita, Ph.D., Steadman, Henry, Ph.D., and Susan Salasin, "Double Jeopardy: Persons with Mental Illnesses in the Criminal Justice System," Center for Mental Health Services, U.S. Dept. Of Health & Human Services, Exec. Sum. 2/95.

Vobejda, Barbara, "Survey: U.S. Population About 10% Foreign-Born," *Washington Post*, 4/10/98, p. A11.

Walsh, Edward, "Growing, Graying Inmates Tax Prison System," *Washington Post*, 7/5/96, p. A1.

Weaver, Gary Ph.D., "Cultural Diversity," seminar, Fairfax Co. Office of the Sheriff, 4/2/93.

Weaver, Gary Ph.D., "Law Enforcement in a Culturally Diverse Society," *FBI Law Enforcement Bulletin*, Sept. 1992.

Chapter 8

Physical Plant

The word "security" is heavily used in the field of corrections. Correctional staff familiarize themselves with security procedures and officers take actions to preserve institutional security. This chapter will examine what is meant by the "physical plant" of a correctional institution. Also, since such an institution is mostly comprised of inmate housing areas, the process of housing inmates in different population areas will be examined. Finally, emergencies such as fire and power outages will be discussed. Another way to think of security is to think of safety — safety of the institutional staff, the inmate population and the public (by guarding against escapes).

Layout of Facilities

While prisons, jails and community corrections facilities are different in functions and goals, many are unique in design to themselves. For example, a maximum security prison can differ in design from another prison one hundred miles away or two jails can be designed differently in neighboring counties.

However, all correctional facilities have these areas in their physical plant:

Entry/exit points: These points are throughout the facility: the entry points are for staff entry, receiving inmates, receiving personal visitors (families, etc., of inmates), receiving professional visitors (attorneys, probation officers, etc.) and receiving services (deliveries, trash removal, etc.).

Procedures must be in place for receiving visitors. Personal and professional visitors must check in with the staff and show identification. Some institutions search visitors' bags, briefcases, etc., for contraband (illegal items, drugs, etc.).

Entry points for inmates are the receiving areas, commonly called "booking." Incoming prisoners must be searched, photographed, and certain data such as the charge or sentence must be recorded. The commitment paperwork *must* be in order. The receiving area is separate from personal visiting and the public entrance. Newly arrived inmates can receive professional visits. Concerning services, facilities receive shipments of supplies, food, etc., as well as maintenance visits. Trash is removed. It is cru-

127

Entrance door to the Maryland House of Correction.

cial to security that *all* such visitors be identified and escorted by staff. Records should be maintained of visits by professionals, personal family and friends of inmates.

Perimeter: While jails and community corrections facilities generally are near to public streets, prisons are usually located in open, relatively remote areas for security purposes. Some facilities are, however, located in urban areas. The goal of perimeter security is that the facility is sealed—no one gets out, nothing or no one gets in. Devices such as alarms, motion sensors, chainlink and mesh fences, walls and rolled razor wire maintain a physical security barrier. Visual observation from strategically placed towers and mobile patrols (walking and vehicle) maintain a presence from the correctional officer. Blind spots can be overcome by closed circuit television cameras and mirrors. Areas around the perimeter must be clear; overgrown vegetation provides hiding places for weapons, drugs, messages and other forms of contraband that someone could leave for an inmate. While not all inmates may have access to the fence, an inmate in a work crew may have an opportunity to smuggle contraband in. [Henderson, Rauch and Phillips, 1997] Perhaps the most memorable security perimeter of this century has been San Francisco Bay, which surrounded Alcatraz Federal Penitentiary.

Administration areas: Administration areas consist of a main records section, staff offices, mail rooms, property rooms, etc. Good security practices do not allow inmate workers in these areas unless they are escorted by staff. Also, administrative offices are located throughout the facility. Counseling offices, medical exam rooms and other rooms in which staff can see inmates may be located in different buildings. Locker rooms and weapons/emergency equipment storage areas are administrative areas and are located away from inmate housing areas.

Control centers: Control centers are the hub of any good institutional security system. Modern correctional facilities have closed circuit television systems, intercoms, fire/smoke alarms, door alarms, etc., for maintaining security. Phone lines to police and fire departments are located in these centers and provide instant access to outside help in case of emergencies. Staff in these centers must be constantly alert for security violations and in constant contact with staff members, especially those posted in inmate housing areas.

Visiting areas: Visiting in correctional facilities are located near entry points and are divided into two types: personal and professional. Personal visiting involve friends and family members of inmates coming to visit; professional visits consist of visits from attorneys, social workers, police officers, psychologists, etc. Generally, each type of visiting has its own area. In jails, personal visiting areas are no contact, but professional visiting areas have no physical barriers between visitor and the inmate. Visitors and their possessions, such as a purse or briefcase, are subject to search.

Entrance, Clarke-Frederick-Winchester Regional Adult Detention Center.

Metal detectors are being used more frequently. Good security policies dictate that packages, purses, etc., of personal visits must be left in another area. While visitors are usually not required to go through a body search, a visit may be denied if the correctional staff suspect that the visitor possesses contraband. The staff may call the local law enforcement agency to investigate at the direction of a supervisor. Visitors can volunteer for a body search, but this is rare. Each institution has its own rules and regulations concerning visiting. These rules should be posted where the public and visitors can see them. [ACA, 1997]

Service areas: These areas are operated by staff who provide services to the inmate population such as medical, laundry, janitorial, food service and maintenance. These areas are located away from inmate housing, but medical staff may have exam rooms located throughout the facility. Inmate workers or trusties may work in these areas under staff supervision.

Programs and recreation areas: Programs areas (classrooms, law/leisure libraries, gyms, exercise rooms) are located away from inmate housing areas. Only inmates authorized by staff can participate. Programs staff offices may be located here. In the new direct supervision style jails, each housing unit may have an adjacent exercise area.

Inmate Housing

In a correctional facility, inmate housing is divided into these areas: intake, general population, administrative segregation and disciplinary segregation. All of these housing areas are linked to one key section of the facility: the classification section.

Classification is more than just separating inmates into different housing areas. The classification process has three important objectives:

- to assess the inmate's background (social, economic, criminal, etc.) and behavior. The inmate is assigned to the appropriate custody level/housing in the facility or to the appropriate institution in a large correctional system. The proper assignment aids the staff in supervising the inmate;
- to develop a program or treatment plan for the inmate based on a prior assessment and staff input; and
- to periodically review and calculate the inmate's progress. The program and housing/custody level could be modified.

[ACA, 1997]

Classification sections perform additional duties, such as holding disciplinary hearings, holding administrative segregation hearings, assign-

Interior of a cell, Clarke-Frederick-Winchester Regional Adult Detention Center.

ing/removing inmates from inmate worker (trusty) status, conducting inmate orientations and communicating inmates' jail adjustments to concerned personnel such as a probation/parole officer.

Classification decisions can be handled by either the institutional classification committee (or ICC) or a unit team. [ACA, 1997] The ICC is a committee consisting of various sections of facility staff who have a vested interest in the inmate—namely background, behavior and housing status. The committee make up is from the custody, mental health, medical and classification staffs. As a result of this varied input, the decisions made about the inmate are well discussed and thought out. Other staff such as sociologists, chaplains, programs personnel or supervisors that deal with inmate treatment and housing may also be contributing members of the ICC. [ACA 1997]

If the facility uses the unit management approach where each housing unit has a team that decides housing and programs issues, classification decisions are handled by a unit team. This team is comprised of the unit manager, case manager, unit education staff, unit psychologist and unit officer(s). [ACA 1997]

As stated before, inmate housing assignments are based on classification decisions.

In *receiving/intake*, the inmate is interviewed by the classification staff. This in-depth interview is crucial. The inmate is asked about his/her:

- criminal history and prior incarcerations

- mental history/medical background
- education
- social history: addresses, etc.
- job history
- sexual preference
- offense

The inmate is housed in an intake area if they are cooperative and exhibit no problems. If an inmate refuses to be interviewed; is mentally disordered; is on special custody, such as a witness, escape risk, etc., he/she may remain in receiving until they cooperate or the matter is discussed by the classification staff. Generally, in intake, no visiting is allowed, except for attorneys, bondsmen, police, etc., and the inmate is observed for a period of time and receives an orientation.

If the ICC/unit team reviews the inmate's file and decides that *general population housing* is appropriate, the inmate is assigned to a cellblock or unit with other inmates. The committee decides on the custody level: maximum, medium, minimum. Some facilities do a subjective "gut feeling" approach while more sophisticated use an objective, numerical scale approach.

Classification, an ICC or unit team, can also assign an inmate to *administration segregation*. It is defined as where the inmate is housed separately from inmates in general population for other than disciplinary reasons. These reasons may include mental state, incompatibility, at their own request or for any reason for increased attention, surveillance or supervision. As much as is possible, the inmate receives the same privileges as inmates in general population. [Cornelius, 1996]

As a rule, disciplinary procedures against an inmate usually handled by the classification section, but some institutions may assign staff solely for that purpose. Classification handles the assignment of inmates to *disciplinary segregation* which is defined as when an inmate is isolated as a result of rule breaking. After a finding of guilt in a hearing, the inmate is placed in isolation and loses privileges such as commissary, personal visiting, programs, television, and possibly accrued good time. [Cornelius, 1996]

Inmates on segregation status must be reviewed periodically by the classification staff to ascertain if they are experiencing any problems. Also, inmates on administrative segregation may be re-classified to the general population if circumstances change.

Classification, in addition to assigning inmates to custody levels and suitable housing, also has much input in the correctional process. Court staff, probation/parole officers and other agency staff can inquire as to an inmate's background, conduct, etc. All facility staff should be made aware of the fact that the classification interview and assignment creates a file that has valuable information about the inmate. All staff should be encour-

Inmate in prison uniform, Maryland House of Correction.

aged to submit documented incidents about inmates to the classification staff, such as behavior observations, minor infractions and information only reports or memos. Disciplinary actions are filed usually in the classification file.

Fire Safety

In any building where people work and live, there is a genuine concern for fire safety. Correctional institutions are no exception to this rule. The role of the correctional staff is to provide for the *safe* custody of inmates. A fire could result in serious injury or death to both staff and inmates. In the confusion of a fire, an inmate may escape. While more institutions in recent years have become smoke free, fires can start due to inmate mischief, electrical failure, etc.

The American Jail Association reported that in a ten-year period prior to 1988, the National Fire Protection Association reported 132 fire fatalities in jails and prisons. Facility staff should be aware that many items in

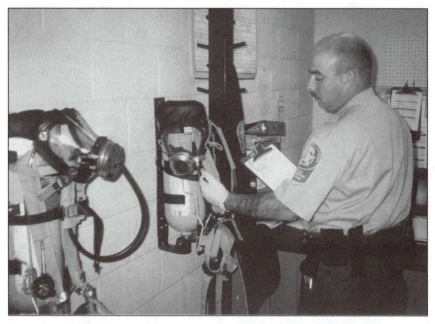

Inspection of fire safety equipment.

the building, such as mattresses, cell furnishings and wall padding may contain materials that, when ignited, produce deadly gases. Also, a key factor in fire prevention is constant detailed monthly inspections in *all* areas. These inspections should be in *addition* to inspections by the local fire department. Each facility should have several fire safety officers to help in inspections and conduct staff training. [Catanese, 1988]

Fire safety inspections should include, but not be limited to, the following items:

- styrofoam and plastic eating utensils: can produce a smoke if ignited which contains toxic gases;
- newspapers, books, magazines: should not be stock piled in dayrooms and cells;
- clothing and bedding: overcrowding means more of these items, which should be stored neatly and folded;
- commissary and canteen items: if the commissary sells tobacco products and lighters/matches, frequent cell searches can prevent stockpiling;
- electrical lighting, wiring, appliances: correctional officers should know the locations of electrical panels in their areas. The condition and wiring of all appliances should be checked;

- fire safety equipment, fire doors, fire corridors and stairwells, evacuation routes: all equipment (hoses, extinguishers, air packs) must be checked daily.

[Catanese, 1988]

There are certain high risk areas in the facility. Disciplinary housing areas where problem inmates are located should be checked for flammable materials. Cells housing mentally disordered inmates or juveniles should also be checked. An easy way to start trouble is to start a fire. Another high risk area is the kitchen where clean-up procedures should be followed at all times. [Catanese, 1988] Any area housing computers, audio-visual equipment or fans should be monitored as well as the use of food warmer carts which can blow circuit breakers.

The American Correctional Association (ACA) recommends these concepts be part of a well-developed fire plan: [ACA, 1997]

- prevention: training in fire hazards and diligent inspections of all fire equipment and alarms;
- staff training: besides prevention, training in evacuation routes, alarms, use of equipment, etc. Training should be joint between the agency and local fire department, including quarterly fire drills and exercises and refresher training;
- inmate awareness: through the initial orientation, inmates should be aware of fire hazards and the dangers of carelessly handling smoking materials;
- control and storage of flammable materials: chemicals, cleaning agents, paper materials should be stored properly;
- notification: a general order should specify a sequence of who is to be notified and respond from the line officer/staff who discovers a fire all the way up to the local fire department;
- evacuation procedures: evacuation plans should be known by all staff, *including* civilian and support staff. Evacuation routes should be posted;
- response procedures: a fire plan should specify where local firefighters should respond and by whom they will be escorted to the fire; also included should be procedures for conducting searches for missing inmates and staff;
- post-fire procedures: included here are procedures for caring for injured staff and inmates, moving and housing displaced inmates and the determination of the fire's cause by trained investigators. The final report should be used as a staff training tool.

ACA recommends the usage of well-trained inmate fire crews. However, there are correctional staff who feel that this may breach security.

Summary

The correctional facility is more than a mere building to house inmates. It consists of several key areas: staff and inmate entry/exit points, perimeter, administration areas, control centers, visiting areas and service areas. Other key areas are reserved for inmate housing. The custody level or housing is determined by classification procedures: intake, housing decisions and handling of disciplinary cases. Also crucial to the security of the physical plant is fire safety which must be practiced by all staff.

Review Questions

1. What are some security concerns concerning visiting?
2. What are the three important objectives of classification?
3. What should be asked of inmates in an in-depth classification interview?
4. What areas/items should be inspected in a fire safety inspection?

Terms/Concepts

Classification   Perimeter
Administrative segregation   Administration areas
Disciplinary segregation   Control centers
Entry/exit points   Visiting areas
Control centers   Receiving/intake
General population housing

References

Bales, Don (ed.), *Correctional Officer Resource Guide*, 3rd Ed., ACA, Lanham, MD, 1997.

Catanese, Robert, "Fire Safety," *Jail Operations Bulletin*, Vol. 1, No. 3, American Jail Association, 1988.

Cornelius, Gary, *Jails in America: An Overview of Issues*, 2nd Ed., American Correctional Association, Lanham, MD 1996.

Henderson, James D.; W. Harvey Rauch and Richard L. Phillips, *Guidelines for the Development of a Security Program*, 2nd Ed., Lanham, MD, ACA, 1997.

Chapter 9

Key and Tool Control, Headcounts, Searches and Transportation

Security is a term that is used very frequently in a correctional facility. Officers might hear that the warden's new directive "improves security" or that an inmate was moved to segregation to "maintain the security of the institution."

Security is defined by Webster as "freedom from danger, fear or anxiety; a place of safety" and has two main principles: (1) the prevention of escapes by inmates; and (2) the maintenance of peace and order in the facility. It requires constant vigilance. [Newcomb, 1989] All people who live and work in the facility must be protected from harm as is the public.

This chapter will explore the basic security duties of the correctional officer: key and took control, headcounts, searches for contraband and the transporting of inmates. These duties are an integral part of officers' daily responsibilities in the institution.

Key and Tool Control: Correctional facilities are locked facilities. Cellblock doors, security gates, staff area doors, food slots on cellblock doors all require keys. While some large doors may be opened electronically from a control booth, the backup system in case of power failure is a key. Keys include the old fashioned metal kind *and* the newer computer lock "proximity cards" or "prox cards" that open a door by swiping it across a computer lock. Keys also include handcuff keys which could be a prized possession for an inmate if stolen or lost.

Key control is basically common sense and accountability. Basically, besides post or housing keys used by the officer inside the facility, there are emergency keys and restricted keys. *Emergency keys* allow the staff rapid access to every part of the facility in case of riot, fire, power outage or other emergencies. A master key that opens *all* security gates is an emergency key. *Restricted keys* are for certain areas such as commissary, staff offices, gyms, laundry, etc. They are issued only to staff who work in those areas. [ACA, 1997]

In some large facilities, administrators have established *keyed zones* or areas that require only certain keys. If the inmates, for example, seize an officer, they cannot get to another area. In no case, however, should officers working in inmate housing areas or with inmates be issued keys to external doors or doors that lead to the outside of the facility. [Newcomb, 1989]

The following key control procedures are recommended by the American Correctional Association: [ACA, 1997]

- Keys must be cross-indexed and numbered. Records should show where the keys fit, what keys are on what ring, who handles that ring, etc. Also keys must be checked out from a secure control area.
- Keys never should be tossed or left in a lock. Keys should be physically *handed* from one staff member to another.
- Keys to such areas as the armory or tool storage areas should never come into contact with inmates, *ever*.
- Entrance keys, external door keys or grand master keys should not be in circulation in the institution.
- Employees should *never* take institution keys home.
- If appropriate, such as in minimum security institutions, inmates may possess keys for lockers, rooms or work assignments. Inmates should never see security keys or be allowed to handle them.

Homemade Keys

Hardware stores are not the only places where keys are made — inmates can make them, too! Take the case of a prisoner in the Florida Department of Corrections where officers conducting a strip search discovered a homemade key which could open doors throughout the institution. A subsequent investigation discovered more hiding places where several dozen weapons were found. When the officers conducted a body cavity search, they found in the inmate's rectum seven hacksaw blades, thirty-four razor blades, $2,000.00 in cash and six homemade handcuff keys.

Adapted from: *Law and Disorder, Weird News of Crime and Punishment,* by Roland Sweet, N.W., Signet, 1994.

Tool Control: Tools in the hands of inmates become weapons or instruments of escape. Correctional facilities, like other buildings that are heavily used, frequently are in need of repair: door locks, elevators, etc, can wear out. All maintenance workers should be escorted and be responsible for safeguarding their tools when working in the facility. Upon leaving, the entire work area must be inspected to make sure no tools or discarded material is left behind that could be fashioned into weapons.

All tools used by facility staff must be accounted for, either by a tool control officer who signs tools in/out to staff and supervised inmate workers or by a check in/out system where staff logs out tools for use and logs in returns. Inventories are a must, preferably in the form of a daily check. Some institutions use shadow boards where officers can see quickly at a glance if any tools are missing. Tool control can also cover kitchen utensils and janitorial equipment. [ACA, 1997]

Headcounts: One of the most important duties that the correctional officer performs is the headcount. Inmates must be accounted for *at all times* even when out of the facility on a transport, a doctor's appointment or while in court. Corrections facilities are bound legally to know where inmates are.

There are three types of counts that are performed. They are:

1. *Formal count*: a regular count required by staff at certain times such as at shift change, before lockdowns and at meal times. Formal counts may be counted five or six times per day or as often as two hours in maximum security institutions.
2. *Census counts*: verification of inmate presence at a program, work detail or activity (i.e., recreation).
3. *Emergency count*: count taken because of an emergency such as a fire, riot, disturbance, power outage, escape, etc.

[ACA, 1997]

If an inmate wishes to escape, he/she needs to successfully thwart the count. Such methods may include having another inmate be counted twice, using a dummy in a bed (for night counts) or convincing staff by forged pass or verbal manipulation that they are supposed to be in an area, program or activity, but in reality, they are not. [ACA, 1997]

In reality, officers can conduct counts anytime they feel it is necessary. In fact, the inmates should be well aware that they are subject to a count at any time.

Guidelines for Effective Headcounts

Concerning headcounts in any type of correctional facility, officers should:

- be aware that they, not inmates, control the count. If necessary, inmate movement can be stopped. Inmates may be required to stand in front of their cells or stand in line. Two officers may be necessary to conduct counts of large numbers of inmates;

- counts only should be conducted by officers, and never by inmates. Inmates should never be permitted to assist in a count;
- if the count is interrupted, start over;
- all inmates should be checked by physical observation in their living/work/programs areas at least every thirty minutes;
- when conducting a headcount, the officer should see skin. Inmates have escaped using life- like heads and lumps under bed clothes to fool officers;
- inmates should be observed for changes in morale or mood. Emotional changes in inmates can "tip" the officer off that something is wrong such as violence, escape attempts/plans, sexual assaults or suicides;
- all counts — formal, informal, census or emergency — must be documented in a log or on a form. In training, it must be stressed that when an officer signs for a count, he/she is signing an official record that he/she physically accounted for that inmate;
- if the officers' count cannot be verified by the official roster, the count must be retaken.

Sources: Walter Newcomb, "Basic Security Principles," Jail Operations Bulletin, Vol 1, No. 7, 1989, American Jail Association; *Correctional Officer Correspondence Course, Book III, Security Issues,* ACA, 1997.

Searches: Besides headcounts, another crucial duty of the correctional officer is searching: searching common areas, living areas, incoming mail, vehicles entering and leaving the facility, and inmates themselves. Thorough searches are very instrumental in maintaining tight security in the institution.

The goal of any good search is to ascertain if the inmate has *contraband* or items not authorized by the facility administration such as illegal drug, weapons (including homemade weapons), etc. Contraband can also include excess authorized items such as an inmate having two extra blankets when inmates are only issued one. [Cornelius, 1996] Contraband covers a broad range of items and its definition can include anything that correctional officers feel is a threat to institutional security.

Generally, contraband is defined differently in each correctional facility, other general guidelines parallel the above definition. Contraband can be any item not permitted to be received by inmates, sold inside the facility, received from the outside, or if approved, changed or modified. [ACA,

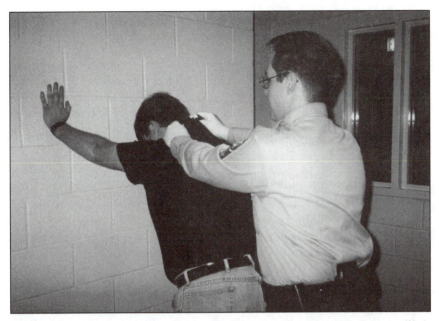

Jail officer searching an inmate. Note that the officer places the inmate at a safe distance, off balance. The officer proceeds to check the inmates body for contraband or weapons. Note the gloves.

1997] Possession or trafficking in contraband is a disciplinary offense. Also, an inmate selling illegal drugs within the institution can be charged with an in-house disciplinary offense and a criminal or "street" charge.

Searches in correctional systems fall into three categories: individual inmate searches, housing unit/work area searches, and vehicle searches. [ACA, 1997]

Individual inmate searches: There are three types:

1. *Frisk or "patdown"*: This is the most general type of search. It encompasses inspection of the inmate's clothing and body through the clothing (see illustration). Officers run hands over clothing to ascertain if anything is hidden in cuffs, under arms, etc. (see photo).

2. *Body or "strip" search*: Strip searches examine the skin surface of the inmate, including hiding places in hair, behind the ears, under breasts (females), armpits, genitals (male), behind the knees, on the soles and between toes, and between the buttocks. Dentures and prostheses are removed and inspected.

3. *Body cavity search*: This type of search should be done due to a reasonable suspicion that the inmate has concealed contraband inside a body opening. It should be performed *only*

upon authorization of the warden, staff duty officer, etc. Also, it *must* be performed manually or by instrument by trained medical personnel.

Patdowns do not have to be in private, but strip and body cavity searches must be in private and performed in a way not to offend the dignity of the inmate. Officers should be behind inmates for safety. All searches should be documented, pat searches on a log or shift report, strip and body searches on an incident report.

Housing unit/work area searches: These searches of dayrooms, cells, kitchens, closets, classrooms, libraries, etc., should follow the principle of being "systematically unsystematic." This means that the staff should have a plan where to search, but make it appear random to keep the inmates off guard. Inmates refer to these types of searches as "shakedowns."

All things in the area should be searched, including bedding, furniture, wall cracks, holes, books, magazines, newspapers, large cans (for false bottoms), window bars, frames, ventilators, shelves, drawers, cabinets,

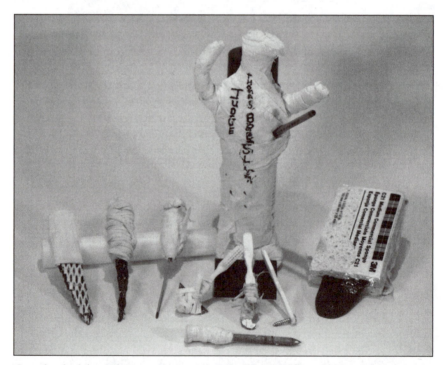

Contraband—left to right: two wire screens, handmade ice pick, three weapons made from toothbrushes and sharpened metal, sponge with sharpened metal from a radio speaker; bottom: sharpened bolt; top: "voodoo" doll made from toilet paper with a judge's name printed on the doll.

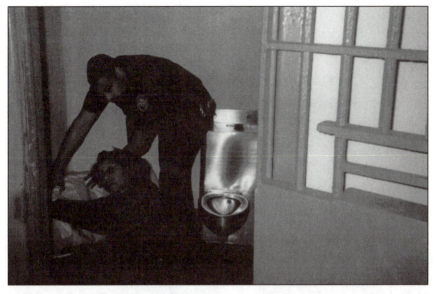

No matter what type of correctional institution, *any areas* where inmates have access should be searched frequently and thoroughly.

etc. However, in this era of AIDS, officers should look *before* they search. Inmates do secretly hide needles for tattooing or IV drug usage and an officer searching "blindly" can get stuck. [ACA, 1997]

Vehicle Searches: All commercial vehicles such as delivery trucks, trash trucks, etc., should be searched when entering the perimeter. Some institutions use mirrors, mechanics, "creepers" or inspection pits to check underneath for contraband. Narcotics or pharmaceuticals should be unloaded in a secure area away from inmates. Also, the contents list must be checked against the payload, particularly paying close attention to boxes partially opened, damaged or marked in an unusual way. [ACA, 1997]

Staff must remember that inmate workers (trusties) are the "movers and shakers" of contraband in the facility. Trusties also have access to materials that other inmates do not. When inmate labor, including trusties, is used, there is a strong possibility that security will be breached. [Newcomb, 1989]

Transportation: Transporting inmates, even for short distances, is one of the most dangerous tasks for a correctional officer. When transporting an inmate, the inmate, who is always to be considered an escape risk, is out of the secure environment of the institution. Inmates have escaped while on a transport and some of these escapes have been very daring. For example, a convicted murderer brought to a Massachusetts hospital emergency room for puncture wounds escaped when a woman masquerading as a

Good security mandates that all visitors and vehicles entering the facility should be identified, logged, and searched if necessary.

nurse held the guard at bay with a handgun. The "nurse" was believed to be the inmate's wife. [*Washington Post*, 9/7/86]

Contraband in its many forms is a testament to *inmate ingenuity*. Inmate ingenuity is defined as the unlimited imagination and ideas inmates exhibit in terms of contraband, manipulation (see Chapter 11) and escape attempts.

The Albany County, New York, Correctional Facility has experienced first hand "inmate ingenuity" like many institutions with a variety of contraband (see Appendix). [Szostak, 1998]

Inmates have made shanks from the metal arches in shoes [Szostak, 1998] and have even sharpened toothbrushes. One jail officer reported that an inmate took a hollow plastic pen barrel and glued (by melting plastic) a sharpened coin on the end for an arrow! Inmates have placed razor blades upright in deodorant sticks. There is no end to "inmate ingenuity." [Cornelius, 1996]

To have as safe a transport as possible, the American Correctional Association (ACA) recommends the followings steps:

1. *Planning*: Officer should plan the basic route of travel *and* an alternative route in case of emergencies. Transporting officers

should check the inmate's file for security violations and behavioral problems. The inmate's identity must be verified before transporting.

2. *Preparing*: Officers should never assume that an inmate and his/her belongings have been searched by another officer. The inmate may complain that a search has already been done; this could be a ploy to throw the officer off. Inmates should be strip searched before transporting and after the inmate returns to the facility. Inmates' belongings must be thoroughly searched. The transporting vehicle must be checked for contraband left by an inmate or worker and to see if the vehicle is operable.

[ACA, 1997]

Every inmate, through appearing to abide by the rules, may attempt to escape if an opportunity presents itself. Restraining devices must be used. The most common are:

- handcuffs: two connected metal rings, locked, placed around the wrists. They should be double locked with the holes fac-

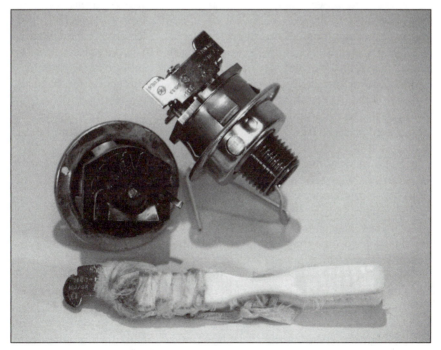

Contraband — standard sprinkler head modified into a weapon at the end of a toothbrush.

ing the inmate's body or head. Inmate's hands should be facing in opposite directions. Handcuff keys are small as are paper clips and can be used to escape if inmates have them hidden on their person.

- waist chain: effective because it lowers mobility of inmate's hands. It is placed through the inmate's belt loops and attached to handcuffs.
- ankle shackles: larger and sturdier, they act like handcuffs, but around the ankles.

Other guidelines are that transporting officers should follow procedures at all times and *always* be cognizant of the fact that *any* inmate may seize an opportunity to escape. Inmates should be visible at all times, seated away from officers' weapons and not be allowed to change seats or come into contact with the public.

Patrol Techniques

Correctional officers, like their counterparts on the street (police officers), must patrol their "beats." That beat could be the facility perimeter, a dormitory, a housing unit, a floor of cellblocks, etc. Each inmate housing area is a community just like each street or subdivision in an outside community. Each "community" has its security flaws and different inmate personalities.

Officers on patrol should be aware of security breaches, fire hazards, etc. Also, the officer should know as much as he can about inmates in his/her area, activities going on and the whereabouts of all inmates in the designated area. He/she should know who comes, who goes, and who is authorized to be in an area.

Checks of areas and unusual occurrences must be logged. The elements of security discussed in this chapter—counting, key/tool control and searches—all interact during the officer's shift.

The officer's worst enemy besides the inmates is complacency. Complacency resulting in boredom can be an ally to the inmate. Officers working the same routine for a long period of time can become complacent, especially when a false sense of security sets in because serious incidents rarely occur. Examples of officer complacency include: failure to check identification of inmates, poor searches, sleeping on post, inadequate control of tools and keys, watching television on post, playing computer games on post, poor inspections, sloppy work habits, poorly written reports, etc. In one institution, the command staff, as a drill, planted a laminated card along the perimeter. The card read: "Bring this to the Chief of Security."

Officer checking perimeter fence, Maryland House of Correction.

At least seventeen officers walked by this card over a six-day period before it was discovered! [Zzerniak and Upchurch, 1996, Cornelius, 1996] Rotation of personnel, training exercises and close supervision can combat complacency.

The use of informants to aid law enforcement officers is as old as the law enforcement profession itself. Police officers get the information needed to solve crimes from those close to or are engaging in criminal activity.

The corrections officer, as part of his/her daily patrol duties, uses confidential informants. Simply defined, a *confidential informant* is an inmate who gives information to a correctional officer on the condition that his/her identity will remain anonymous. [ACA, 1997]

Inmates who act as informants usually want something and what they want may not be entirely clear to the officer. However, some motives of an inmate informant are as follows:

- *fear*: the inmate feels threatened by other inmates' activities *or* planned activities such as an escape plot. The informant wants no part of them.
- *revenge*: the inmate believes that he/she has been treated unfairly or harshly by other inmates.
- *animosity*: to eliminate competition from other inmates, such as in trafficking contraband or making a "power play," the inmate may turn informant.

- *egotism*: the inmate wants the staff to think well of him/her.
- *reward or favor*: the inmate may relate information to an officer in hopes of receiving a reward or favor such as a trustie job, special visit, etc.
- *desire to reform*: an inmate may become an informant because they feel remorse for their crime and wish to do a "good deed" for society.
- *playing a game*: an inmate may give false information to confuse officers, especially new, inexperienced officers.

[ACA, 1997]

Officers must use common sense when dealing with confidential informants. The inmate should never be promised any type of reward and all information should be relayed up the chain of command to the officer's supervisors for discussion and follow up. The officer should *never* reveal the identity of the inmate, either verbally or in writing. [ACA, 1997] Many officers use the terms "confidential source," "reliable source," or "anonymous source/inmate" all which mean confidential informant.

Correctional officers realize the value of inmates giving up information to the staff—being a "snitch." Inmates are snitches in one way or another and are in prison because they were informed on, according to an officer at the Lebanon (Ohio) Correctional Institution. The trait is brought into the prison. One ten year veteran of Lebanon says that snitching "stops a lot of things...it prevents drug deals...escapes...and it prevents people from getting hurt." [Wojda, Wojda, Smith, Jones, 1991]

Escapes

A fundamental goal of a good correctional security system is the prevention of escapes. Every inmate thinks of escape at one time or another. Some dismiss the thought while others try. To the correctional officer, *every* inmate is an escape risk, no matter what his/her charge or demeanor.

The term *escape* can be defined as "an inmate's criminal absence from the confines of the institution or extended confinement area" with the intent to remain at large." [Camp & Camp, 1997] The absence is unauthorized and the inmate is subject to criminal prosecution as well as in-house disciplinary action. The extended confinement area could be the community, program or work detail outside the facility if the inmate is legally permitted access such as work release. An inmate could be charged with escape if he/she was on work release and did not report to a job. An inmate can be charged with escape from a work detail or transport.

Inmate Escapes

In 1996, escape statistics broke down into the following:

Work release/Furlough walkaways	10,570	89.8%
Low/Minimum custody	1,035	8.8%
High/Medium Custody	168	1.4%
Total	11,773	100.0%
Total Captures*	6,297	53.4%

*Includes all inmates captured or returned to custody *regardless* of when they escaped.

> Source: "Inmate Escapes and Captures During 1996," *1997 Correctional Yearbook*, p. 18

Some escapes are daring such as the first helicopter escape where an inmate was lifted from the yard of a Michigan prison in 1975. [Fox & Stinchcombe, 1994] A desperate escape occurred in 1983 in Alabama where eleven inmates ran through holes hacked in fences under a barrage of shotgun fire. Within forty-five minutes, nine were recaptured. [*Washington Post*, 8/29/83]

Women inmates desperately try for freedom, too. In 1984, five inmates, including two convicted killers, escaped from maximum security by squeezing through steel bars covering a window. The women, ranging in size from 5'2", 110 lbs, to 5'6", 150 lbs., squeezed through bars fifteen inches high and less than eight inches apart. [*Washington Post*, 12/17/84]

Staff mistakes can make an escape easy. For example, in 1982, two Pennsylvania county prison employees were suspended after one left his post to get coffee, leaving his keys on his desk and two doors unlocked. An inmate charged with rape and kidnapping escaped. A few months before, the same inmate escaped from a West Virginia jail by crawling through a ventilation system to the jail roof! [*Pittsburgh Press*, 12/31/82]

Two inmates from a Southern jail used a piece of light fixture to open a jail door latch. It was easy because the door installer hung the door *upside down*! [*Detroit News*, 1996]

Inmate Ingenuity: Escapes

How far will inmates go in devising escape plans and carrying them out? Here is a sampling:

- a Florida convicted murderer on a medical transport confined to a wheelchair for seven years got out of the wheelchair, and commandeered a van by getting the officer's gun and uniform. He escaped and an official said that the staff had never seen the inmate walking.

- A Maine inmate escaped from a jail in a garbage can and eluded capture for three days.
- Three Utah inmates pried open three security doors and walked out of a prison dressed in civilian clothes.
- In 1984, Florida's famous death row inmate, Theodore Bundy, and another inmate had sawed through cell bars with hacksaw blades. The plot and hacksaw blades were discovered before the inmates could escape.
- Three Texas inmates purchased hundreds of yards of dental floss at the jail's canteen (commissary). Authorities discovered that they braided it into a rope and used cardboard salt and pepper containers for stirrups on a ladder.
- In 1993, two convicted killers escaped from a Southern U.S. prison by using a makeshift sixteen-foot ladder to get over a razor wire topped fence. While helicopters, SWAT teams and dogs searched, the next day a convicted armed robber escaped by stowing away in a departing delivery vehicle. Authorities believe he took advantage of the diversion created by the first escape.

Sources: *Law and Disorder: Weird News of Crime and Punishment* by Roland Sweet; *Washington Post*: 11/14/93, 7/20/84, 2/17/87; USA Today, 11/1/93.

Jail correctional officers' duties extend frequently to the courthouse. Inmates must be escorted from the jail to court and defendants appearing in court are often remanded to custody. In 1985, a prisoner hit a deputy U.S. Marshal in the face and grabbed her service weapon after she had removed her handcuffs to put him in a cell. Fortunately, he was subdued and no one was killed. [Murphy, *Washington Post*, 6/22/85]

In 1986, a prisoner escaped from two separate courthouses by: (1) forcing a wire mesh security screen; and (2) punching a hole in a bullet-proof glass dividing screen. [Murphy, *Washington Post*, 4/4/86]

While escape policies and procedures vary from facility to facility, certain items are basic in nature. To prevent escapes, policies should include these measures:

1. Reporting unrest, tension, changes in inmate behavior or conduct;

2. Basic security accountability: tool and key control, counts, searches, inspections, etc.;
3. Classification review of all inmates including designating high risk inmates;
4. Proper work and living assignments;
5. Prompt correction/repair of security breaches and plans to cover breaches until repairs are completed.

[ACA, 1997]

A functional escape plan provides procedures for maintaining security, notifying law enforcement agencies, and strategies for capturing the escapee. The American Correctional Association (ACA) recommends eighteen points (see Appendix).

One thing that law enforcement agencies must have in order to successfully recapture an escapee is escape intelligence. *Escape intelligence* is defined as a comprehensive package of information that lets agencies know as much information as possible about the escape, safety concerns and who should be contacted in case of apprehension. The following information should be in this summary: [Henderson, Rauch & Phillips, 1997]

- name of escapee, including all known aliases or nicknames;
- escapee's sex, race, nationality/ethnic origin, birthdate, age, height, weight, hair/eye color, scars, marks, tattoos, state of residence and social security number or numbers, if the inmate uses more than one;
- recent photos of escapee;
- escapee's crime, sentence and any detainers (detainers are charges pending from another jurisdiction);
- Federal Bureau of Investigation numbers, state police numbers and/or local police case numbers;
- fingerprint classification;
- last known residence, past associates, likely places, residences, groups, etc., to which he/she could return;
- driver's license and vehicle information, if available;
- information as to whether the escapee is considered violent, dangerous or armed;
- name and title of the agency staff person who should be contacted if another agency captures the escapee.

Intelligence must be gathered when an escape occurs. No only do staff have to file a detailed report, other information must be gathered from inmate informants, staff observations, the family of the escapee (if cooperative, etc.) The incident must be analyzed for causative factors, security breakdowns, etc., for use in training and revising procedures. One key part of an escape investigation is the gathering of information from the inmate's file, visiting lists, property and mail. [Henderson, Rauch, and Phillips, 1997]

Summary

Security in a correctional institution is an ongoing process involving observation of inmates through key and tool control, headcounts, proper searches, safe transportation of procedures and escape prevention and apprehension. The basic definition of security is "freedom from danger" for staff, inmates and the public. Lack of control can cause assaults, escapes and security breakdowns. Procedures must be in place and followed.

Keys and tools can become serious security problems if placed in the hands of inmates. Common sense methods of control, such as logs, etc., can help in their control.

Headcounts are crucial to security and must be conducted properly, either formally or informally. Searches of inmates and facility areas reduce the risk of contraband.

Transporting inmates safely takes careful planning and preparation. Inmates in desperate bids for freedom can escape during transports or by "inmate ingenuity"—schemes and daring plans, sometimes involving contraband.

Inmate informants can pass along information to the officer, but an informant's motive may be self-serving.

Review Questions

1. Why is the control of keys and tools important?

2. Name four guidelines for successful headcounts.

3. Define contraband and describe several examples.

4. Describe the three types of inmate searches.

5. How should a correctional officer prepare for a safe transport?

6. What motives could a confidential informant have in supplying information to staff?

7. Name four points of a good escape plan.

Terms/Concepts

Security

Emergency keys

Restricted keys

Keyed zones

Formal count

Inmate ingenuity

Confidential informant

Escape

Census count

Emergency count

Contraband

Frisk or "patdown"

Body or "strip" search

Body cavity search

Escape intelligence

References

Bales, Don, ed., *Correctional Officer Resource Guide*, 3rd Ed., American Correctional Association, Lanham, MD, 1997.

Camp, George and Camille, *The Corrections Yearbook*, 1997, South Salem, N.Y. Criminal Justice Institute, 1997.

Cornelius, Gary, "Complacency: Our Own Worse Enemy," *Journal of Correctional Training*, IACTP, Winter 1996, pp. 28-29.

Cornelius, Gary, *Jails in America: An Overview of Issues*, 2nd Ed., American Correctional Association, Lanham, MD 1996.

Correctional Officer Correspondence Course Book III: Security Issues, ACA, Lanham, 1997.

Czerniak, Stan W. and James R. Upchurch, "If it Ain't Broke, Break It: Continuous Improvement in Prison Security," *Corrections Today*, July 1996, pp. 62-64.

Fox, Vernon & Jeanne Stinchcombe, *Introduction to Corrections*, 4th Ed., Englewood Cliffs, Prentice Hall, 1994.

Henderson, James D., W. Hardy Rauch, and Richard L. Phillips, *Guidelines for the Development of a Security Program*, 2nd Ed., Lanham, MD, American Correctional Association, 1997.

Newcomb, Walter, "Basic Security Principles," *Jail Operations Bulletin*, Vol. 1, No. 7, American Jail Association, 1989.

Sweet, Roland, *Law and Disorder - Weird News of Crime and Punishment*, N.Y., Signet, 1994.

Szostak, Edward, "Maintaining Safety and Security by Managing Contraband," *American Jails*, American Jail Association, July-Aug, 1998.

"The Lighter Side," *Detroit News*, Home Page, 1/11/96, http://www.det news.com/menu/stories/31707.htm

"Two Suspended After Jail Escape," *Pittsburgh Press*, 12/31/82, p. A-5.

USA Today, 11/1/93.

Washington Post, "Around the Nation: 11 Escape Top Security Prison in Alabama," 8/29/83.

Washington Post, "Third Florida Inmate Missing After Two Murderers Escape," p. A4, 11/14/93.

Washington Post, "Paraplegic Escapes," 2/17/87.

Washington Post, "5 Inmates Escape," 12/17/84.

Washington Post, 8/22/84.

Wojda, Grace; Raymond Wojda; Norman E. Smith; Richard Jones, *Behind Bars*, Waldorf, ACA/St. Mary's Press, 1991.

Chapter 10

Interacting with Inmates

Correctional officers are locked into a controlled environment just as the inmates are. However, correctional officers can leave after their shift and the inmates stay. During that shift, whether it be eight, ten or twelve hours, the correctional officer must be able to effectively: (1) communicate with inmates in a two-way or reciprocal fashion; and (2) give instructions in a way that the inmates willingly comply. In other words, inmates and staff must "get along."

Correctional officers do not carry weapons while around inmates in the institution. Their primary means of not allowing tensions to escalate are their brains and the communications which they speak. Good communication with inmates means much more than just talking with them; it means interaction and effective interpersonal communications.

One basic rule that officers should keep in mind is that inmates must be viewed as people. An officer who stereotypes inmates into "slang" categories such as slugs, scumbags and a few more colorful terms will find his/her job difficult. These prejudices will be felt by the inmate. Interacting with inmates is only part of the whole being of the officer. This "being" or "makeup" is called *officer comportment.*

Officer comportment simply means how an officer presents himself/herself in doing the job or carrying out his/her duties. [Halford, 1990] While the duties, both formal and informal, of the correctional officer have been discussed in Chapter 2, how correctional officers carry themselves shape opinions by other staff and inmates. Not only do these opinions shape views about the officer, but also about the agency. If the correctional officer presents a negative demeanor and appearance to inmates and staff, two-way communications and a positive work climate where inmates obey rules and get along with officers will not occur.

Realistically, how a correctional officer presents himself/herself depends on three key components: professionalism, ethics and mental outlook on the job. In turn, these three affect these forms of communication with inmates: non-verbal communications, verbal communications and correct assertiveness. Officer comportment means that the officer follows a code of ethics and good work standards. Good officer comportment permits the officer to deal with stress, enhance a sense of self-esteem and job satisfaction and contribute to the corrections profession and his/her agency. [Halford, 1990]

Professionalism

Professionalism is a word that is used often in society today. Officers and staff are told to look and act "professional." The term is based on a professional occupation having standards and requiring special skills. In 1978, Rudoni, Baker and Meyer examined the basis upon which professionalism in any job or occupation is defined or structured.

- public recognition: citizens know that pre-trail detainees and convicted offenders are kept securely in our nation's correctional facilities by correctional staff;
- production of a valued or highly regarded social function: safe custody, rehabilitation of criminals and returning the criminal to society as a law abiding citizen. We, as a nation, pride ourselves on not having a cruel, barbaric and biased correctional system;
- special knowledge and job skills: to be a correctional worker, one must possess special knowledge about the inmates in their care. Special job skills include communication skills, interpersonal relations and correct assertiveness;
- special education or training: to obtain the above knowledge and skills, officers undergo specialized training: law, weapons, self-defense, security procedures, etc.;
- discretion and autonomy in performing duties: officers have discretion in many cases of whether to charge inmates (in-house or criminal) with infractions; he/she also have a wide leeway in dealing with inmates and their problems in ways that benefit the security of the facility and often the well being of the inmate;
- performance in accordance with minimum standards: duties and actions must be in compliance with Federal/state statutes, court decisions, Federal/state correctional standards, and organizations such as the American Correctional Association;
- peer review: to enforce performance standards for acceptable professional conduct and job performance: this is accomplished through review boards, promotional exams and promotional processes.

[Gilbert, 1989]

Other views of professionalism echo the view of officers having a high degree of competency. James A. Gondles, the Executive Director of the American Correctional Association, states that "professionalism is achieved through programs of recruitment and enhancement of the employees' skills, knowledge, insight and understanding of the correctional process." [Gondles in Hutton, 1998]

To break this down further, a professional employee possesses skills such as proficiency at security procedures; knowledge of the facility rules, polices and inmate population; insight in discretion in dealing with inmates; and understanding of the process: legal issues, etc. For the purposes of this chapter, dealing with inmates in a mature way through clear communication is a professional job skill.

The Honorable Helen G. Corrothers, former ACA president and a former commissioner of the U.S. Sentencing Commission, writes that "... corrections' rehabilitative objective can only be accomplished in the appropriate environment...in which inmates feel safe and where rehabilitation is encouraged and supported. The correctional officer's attitude and degree of professionalism contribute to this type of environment." [Corrothers, 1992]

To be professional around inmates who have an underlying mistrust and disdain towards the officer, a correctional officer must have a professional appearance exhibiting self pride and confidence. Clean uniforms, shined shoes and a proper bearing tells inmates that this officer must care about his/her appearance and will pay attention to details on his/her posts.

Along with a professional appearance, another key factor is knowledge of policies and procedures. A professional officer knows the policies and procedures of the facility or how things are supposed to be done.

Policies and procedures are important to enhancement of the professionalism of the correctional officer. They perform these key functions: [Hutton, 1998]

- policies and procedures enable the facility to meet standards: state, Federal or by professional organization such as ACA;
- state what the mission of the facility is and what is to be done. For example, policy might state that all inmates will be treated humanely;
- procedures state how the policies will be carried out such as all inmates will be given a medical screening upon entry;
- policies and procedures supply employees with guidelines on how to do the job and ensure uniformity among all shifts;
- policies and procedures protect the employee against (1) inmate lawsuits and (2) unfair actions and evaluations from supervisors;

- policies and procedures are tools that aid supervisors in managing and directing employees;
- policies and procedures are a guide that inform employees what they can/cannot do and serve as references in case of a question.

To be effective, policies and procedures must change with the help of staff review and employee input. [Hutton, 1998] Professional officers should be thinkers and make suggestions to supervisors in writing.

Ethics

Closely related to the professionalism of an officer is his/her adherence to ethical conduct. Like the word professionalism, ethics is a term used in describing the ideal officer.

Ethics is defined as the "study of what constitutes good or bad conduct." [Pollock, 1994] If an officer treats all inmates fairly and in a dignified manner, his conduct is ethical. If he subjects them to ridicule and brutality, he is behaving in an unethical manner.

While the above definition is rather simple and direct, a more detailed definition of the term is promulgated by the FBI National Academy. Ethics in policing and which could include corrections are the "standards of conduct that govern behavior." Also, the philosophy of ethics raises such questions as:

- What is a good person?
- What is it that an officer should and should *not* do?
- What actions are right and what actions are wrong?
- What principles guide good behavior?
- What are officers' obligations and rights?

[Sirene, Kelly and Malone, 1994]

An officer who practices good ethics has a good moral foundation. He/she applies the basic definition of ethics to the agency and institution's policies, rules and regulations and the laws/codes of the government. [Sirene, Kelly and Malone, 1994] While this philosophy has been recognized as *police ethics*, it can be applied to the discipline of corrections.

Lack of Ethics

Unethical behavior by correctional officers is embarrassing to the agency and has a definite impact on staff morale.

In 1993, one corrections agency experienced about forty employees being arrested and charged with bribery or drug violations inside a correctional facility. Eight were convicted and twelve pleaded guilty. One officer agreed to smuggle cocaine into the facility for only $300.00. The undercover police and FBI operations also resulted in employees being charged with introduction of contraband into an institution. An arraigning judge asked "If we can't trust the guards, who can we trust?"

Source: *Washington Post*, 4/8/94
and "Corrections Officers Held in
Smuggling" by Ruben Castaneda,
The Washington Post, 11/5/93.

The above true example illustrates an example of severe lack of ethics. To officers and staff doing their utmost to do a professional job, the public example of bad officers can discourage them, especially when citizens may think that all the officers in the agency are bad.

Surveys that have been conducted of good work performers state that they exhibit themes based on the following:

- discipline and obedience;
- working;
- religion;
- doing the "right" thing in the face of unpopularity or difficulty;
- frugality not wasteful;
- makes an individual effort in achieving success.

[Black, 1996]

Most supervisors would agree that these are desirable traits for correctional officers, especially doing the right thing even if other staff thinks the action unpopular.

How do these philosophic views apply to corrections? The best answer is by Harold W. Clarke, Director, Department of Correctional Services, Lincoln, Nebraska, and clear behavioral guidelines (see Appendix).

Informal Ethics: The Correctional Subculture

In a perfect world, correctional officers would adhere to policies and procedures to the letter. In reality, correctional officers have to survive and get along with their peers. Kauffmann in 1988 listed the rules of the correctional officer's subculture:

1. Always go to the aid of another officer.
2. Don't buy [smuggle] drugs. This action puts all correctional officers in danger.
3. Don't inform or "rat" on another correctional officer.

4. Never make another officer look bad in front of inmates no matter what the correctional officer did.
5. In an inmate/officer dispute, always side with the officer.
6. Always support officer sanctions against an inmate (including illegal use of force).
7. Don't be a "white hat" or good guy. This could be seen as being "buddies" with the inmates.
8. Maintain officer solidarity against outside groups, public, administration or the media.
9. Show positive concern for fellow correctional officers. Don't dump problems, help them out.

Adapted from: Ethics in Crime and Justice: Dilemmas and Decisions, 2nd ed., Jocyleyn Pollack, Wadsworth, 1994.

Mental Outlook on the Job

The view that an officer has towards the job can determine his/her ethics and the degree of professionalism exhibited. In a perfect world, the ideal correctional officer knows all of the general orders, his/her uniform is "spit and polish" and mistakes are never made.

In reality, a serious threat to a correctional officer's sense of ethics and professionalism are relations with inmates. In dealing with them day after day, officers find that it is easier to overlook infractions, operate with some favoritism, and be "easy" in order to get inmates to comply with orders and the running of the post. This may contribute to officers crossing into a hazily defined gray area resulting in getting *too* friendly or personal with inmates. [Crouch, 1980; Pollock, 1994]

How officers view their jobs or functions as a correctional officer has a direct bearing on how ethical and professional they are around inmates. If the view is negative against supervisors and the agency, correctional officers may feel that they and the inmates have more in common with each other. If that occurs, infractions are overlooked and the practice of good security practices may suffer as well as the start of unethical conduct and possibly corruption. [Pollock, 1996; McCarthy, 1991]

In the most simple terms, correctional officers have a choice in how they feel about their jobs. According to Robert Johnson of American University, officers can be either "hacks" or "human services officers." On a positive to negative line in terms of how inmates are treated, hacks represent the negative while the human service officers represent the positive. [Johnson, 1996]

Smug Hacks

As Johnson explains this type of officer, the public image of the prison officer is one of a "mindless and brutal custodian." Toch and Klofas in 1982 labeled these officers as *smug hacks* or "subcultural custodians." [Johnson, 1996] A summary definition of hacks could be:

> An officer who is alienated from the positive aspects or goals of corrections; an officer who uses violence and negative communication to keep order.

Alienation is a key part of the definition. The hack may feel that he/she is a "uniformed prisoner" or one who has a lot in common with inmates. Both are locked in, both have to go by rules that are at times unrealistic and both get reprimanded by supervisors and the officers. The stress that these negative feelings cause are not dealt with in a positive way and are often taken out on the inmates. [Johnson, 1996]

This model of working can be described as a war-like "us versus them" philosophy where the officers are the "good guys" and the inmates are the "bad guys." Naturally, the good guys are always right. Hacks do not want to hear the inmate's side of an issue. Non-compliant inmates are forcibly coerced into submission by threats, intimidation or *goon squad* tactics.

Bowker, in 1980, defined goon squads as "groups of physically powerful correctional officers who 'enjoy a good fight' and are used to restore the status quo by muscle power." [Johnson, 1996] Hacks may respect the goon squad members as their kind of officers who do not waste time talking to inmates. They use force and the job gets done.

Other research in this area, especially by Kauffmann, illustrate the negative effects of being a smug hack and looking upon the job in a negative way. According to her research in the 1970's at the Walpole, Massachusetts State prison, smug hacks can create a clique which promotes a subculture of violence. Inmates are not seen as human beings in distress or who have problems, but as "dehumanized creatures beyond the reach of care or compassion." [Johnson, 1996]

The following are examples of the behavior of "smug hacks." Often their actions were underhanded or indirect and at times served them as ways to "mentally get to them," aggravate them or punish them: [Kauffmann, 1988]

- withholding toilet paper, matches or food;
- playing "head games" or as one officer said: "guy wants to make a phone call? You can make him wait ten, twenty min-

utes. Guy wants some writing paper? Tell him you don't have
any;"

• adapting the "Hard Ass" role where the officer becomes coldly
  indifferent to inmates and the surrounding violence.

Crouch and Marquart in their research in Texas prisons found that
some officers had similar beliefs: to cow or deceive convicts so as to gain
their compliance. Commonly referred to "messing up their minds" and
"keep them off balance," these methods involved making the inmates feel
uncertain. One officer asked an inmate several times if he "slumbered" in
bed. Confused, the inmate asked "do I sno?" [snore]. Everyone but the
inmate knew what "slumber" meant. Other officers starred at selected inmates for long periods in order to make them uncomfortable and worried. [Crouch and Marquart, 1980 Johnson, 1996]

In an institution where everyday dealings with inmates are governed by
the hack mentality, the inmates learn to resent the officers and distrust
them, feeling that their welfare is not important. As a result, positive, two-
way communication between correctional officer and inmates is not firmly
established.

Human Services Officers

Correctional officers can look at their jobs in another way: where as
corrections is an important function of the criminal justice system and
some inmates can be changed if they encounter staff who not only act pos-
itively, but communicate to them in a mature, caring way. According to
one prison officer, in order to be a professional, an officer's conscience
should be his/her guide. The officers should care enough about inmates
and themselves to do the job in a responsive way without violence and the
use of force is a last resort. [Johnson, 1996]

Human service officers can achieve control in their areas without dis-
playing a hostile or superior attitude. Influence over inmates and positive
leadership can be attained with a minimum of friendliness and respect.
Officers who are known to be friendly and fair are obeyed most readily as
well as being liked. [Glaser, 1969, Johnson, 1996]

The human service officer is the opposite of the smug hack. Instead of
isolating themselves in their jobs, human service officers try to foster positive relationships with inmates and try to make a difference. The actions
of these officers are based on these three themes:

1. Providers of goods and services: inmates' needs of food, cloth-
    ing, medication, etc., are met. The officer uses positive com-

munication skills to persuade dirty inmates to bathe, sloppy inmates to clean up, etc. Inmates will respect the officer as one who makes sure things run right. Officers report that if a promise is made to an inmate to take care of a problem, that promise should be kept, even in routine problems like getting a towel. Unkept promises lower the inmates' respect for the officer and he/she is marked.

2. Referral agent or advocate: cutting through the facility's "red tape" is important. For example, an inmate is desperately requesting placement in a drug program. He has written requests, but has not heard anything. An officer calls the counseling office and finds out information for the inmate. The inmate calms down and the officer has defused a frustrated inmate. Officers know, however, that they cannot do this all the time, but occasionally it is beneficial.

3. Institutional adjustment: this may be one of the most important aspects of the human service mentality. Many corrections workers report seeing themselves in different roles: psychiatrists, doctors, social workers, parental figures, etc. Also, many officers say that when they interact with an inmate experiencing a personal problem, they would listen and offer advice. Others say that they would approach such an inmate and offer help.

[Lombardo, 1988]

In the daily world of the correctional institution, human service officers are given opportunities to assist inmates and inmates respect them as staff who will listen. Being able to empathize, not overly sympathize, with the inmates secures their cooperation. [Lombardo, 1988] As one corrections officer says:

Sure, we can sit at our posts all day, but these inmates are people with problems. Recently, an inmate was worried about his paycheck. He needed someone to get it, bring it to the jail so he could sign it over and get it cashed. His family needed the money. The work place would not take collect calls, so I gave him a call after verifying the number. He went back to the block relieved and a lot less tense.

[Cornelius, 1998]

The attitude of the officer will translate into low he/she communicates with inmates either verbally or non-verbally. An officer practicing good, professional communication skills will maintain good, direct eye contact with the inmate, stand facing him/her and not slouch or appear disinterested. In making rounds or conducting business on the post, the officer should be dressed neatly and be well groomed.

Verbal communication, to be effective, depends on the officer practicing good listening and speaking skills. An officer has to realize that in the correctional environment, they are the first persons that inmates will go to with requests, problems and questions. Secondly, the officer must realize that each inmate has his/her own unique way of speaking: some speak clearly, some are somewhat abrasive, some speak mostly in street slang, etc.

Many agencies instruct new personnel in the Interpersonal Communication model of communications which has been a main staple of communications training in corrections for almost the past twenty years. It is a detailed model of communication, but for brevity, the National Institute of Corrections identifies these basic components:

- positioning: the officer is close enough to the inmate, still maintains a safe distance, and is alert to the inmates' presence;
- posturing: the officer stands erect and maintains direct eye contact with the inmate. The officer may lean forward a little. Distinctive mannerisms such as pen clicking, foot tapping, etc., are avoided;
- observing: the officer is careful to see, hear and interpret what is happening, while watching verbal and non-verbal clues in the inmate such as voice tremors, agitation or nervousness. What is important here is that the officer makes inferences on what facts are observed: a calm inmate is nervous, the inmate is agitated, etc.
- listening: the officer hears out the inmate and suspends judgment. He/she concentrates on key words and determines the inmate's mood and/or intensity of the message. Listening is one of the most critical aspects of good inmate/staff communication.

[Fox & Stinchcombe, 1994]

While these aspects are the ideal forms of good interpersonal communication, the reality is that in a busy institution, staff must order inmates about quickly to ensure compliance with regulations or defuse emergencies. For example, an officer trying to defuse a possible fight between two inmates tells them to quickly move apart — NOW! However, later, and if the inmates have complied, the officer can practice positive communication skills to hear their problems.

Over time, correctional officers learn to balance personal concern for the inmate with professional caution. By doing so, objective judgments and rational decision making occur. This is called detached commitment. [Fox and Stinchcombe, 1994] As one veteran officer recalls:

> One Sunday morning an inmate, who I knew quite well, told me that he had tried the night before to kill himself with a shoe lace noose, which had broken. I listened to the guy's problems: drinking, debts, unfaithful wife, etc. I felt sorry for him and thought that if I was in his shoes, I might be suicidal, too. But, I moved him to a high observation receiving cell on restricted issue until the psychologist could check him out. This was on Super Bowl Sunday. He swore that he was over his crisis and wanted to see the game. I stuck to my decision. After listening to him and offering advice, I just felt that I could not take the chance.

[Cornelius, 1998]

According to Daniel Stieneke, Director of the North Carolina Department of Corrections, Office of Staff Development and Training, effective communication skills with inmates is one of a correctional employee's most important tools. Effective communication starts by the officer *listening* to the inmate, to their problems, fears, concerns, emotions, etc. They have them, like staff members do. While many inmates may not open up at first, if they see that the officer is trustworthy and concerned, that may change. Not only is listening crucial, so is speaking. Verbal messages to inmates should be in clear, respectful tones. [Bayse, 1995]

All of these positive ways of dealing with inmates and effectively communicating with them come together for the officer in work tool called positive assertiveness or *correct assertiveness.*

This term means simply that the officer gets his/her point across without causing arguments, tension or stress. [Cornelius, 1994] It incorporates common sense communication as well as calmness, seeing the other's point of view, looking at the whole situation and respect and consideration for other people. [Cheek, 1984, Cornelius, 1994]

True, at times, especially during emergencies, orders must be given and complied with immediately with no time for debate. However, most daily communication with inmates is non-emergency and routine, but may include disagreements, denials and resistance. Officers must remember in overcrowded institutions that even the routine can escalate into the dangerous. There are seven components to correct assertiveness: [Cheek, 1984; Cornelius, 1994]

Components of Correct Assertiveness

In using correct assertiveness in communicating with inmates, the correctional officer should strive to balance the communication with what he/she and the inmate both want to say and what they both want heard. In a situation when interacting with inmates, the officer should:

- Consider the context: What is the environment? Are other inmates present? Good communication should be away from noise, interruptions, distractions, etc. Also, how is your mindset? Are you both tired, tense, upset? Don't criticize in front of other inmates.
- Maintain calm: good communication is enhanced if all parties are not upset; understanding and cooperation increase.
- Consider the other's point of view: in good two-way communication, each party should try to see the other's viewpoint. Listening is important. Both officer and inmate should explain his/her side. The officer may disagree, but will be looked upon as a staff person who will listen and try to understand.
- Explain your side: it is important that inmates receive an answer to a request or question. They may not like it, but they will feel that at least they are being treated as people. They will respect officers for explaining the situation. If a reason can be given without violating security, it should be, instead of a curt "NO!"
- Come to a solution: both parties should work together to come to a solution. At times with resistant inmates, an officer may have to say that both sides have been heard and the inmate has several choices. Compromise is important.
- Consider the consequences: after hearing both sides and all factual information, officers make decisions. An officer must weigh the consequences or what may or may not happen.
- Don't run hot and cold: inmates respect an officer who is even tempered and not moody. Communication style can be affected by moods.

Adapted from: *Stress Management for Correctional Officers and Their Families* by Frances Cheek, Ph.D., ACA, Laurel, MD, 1984; *Stressed Out! Strategies for Living and Working with Stress in Corrections* by Gary F. Cornelius, ACA, Lanham, MD, 1994.

Staff Stress

One thing that can affect the way that staff members deal with inmates is how well stress is managed. Whereas twenty years ago, scant, if any, attention was paid to corrections officers' stress. Corrections officers were supposed to "hold it in," do not show any signs that the job is getting to you, etc.

Corrections has come a long way in the 80's and 90's, similar to the progress made in suicide prevention. However, if correctional officers allow themselves to be "burned out," positive interactions with inmates will suffer.

Stress is the reaction of our bodies and minds to demands (called stressors) made upon us. For correctional officers, uncooperative inmates, shift work, staff shortages, excessive noise, manipulative inmates and escapes are all stressors. Some research has indicated that correctional officers consider lack of input into decision making and poor management contributes greatly to their stress. [Cornelius, 1994]

Burned out employees exhibit a bitter, sour, apathetic attitude towards their work, and may forget that corrections is a human service, caring profession. Techniques such as mental relaxation, healthy diet, exercise and interests outside of the institution can result in a worker who is properly focused and positive in his/her job. [Cornelius, 1994]

Summary

Interacting with inmates has generally been regarded as staff having good communication skills. In reality, it combines professionalism, ethics, how staff look at their jobs and good non verbalized and verbal communication.

Officers must view inmates as people as this shapes how positive communications can be. Professionalism in corrections means the job has special standards and skills; ethics means to know what must be done correctly and not incorrectly. A tool of the corrections professional is adherence to policies and procedures.

Officers can either be smug hacks, whereby they hate their jobs and act accordingly or can be human service officers trying to get the most positive results from their jobs. A tool for this officer is correct assertiveness, which provides for balanced communications.

Review Questions

1. What is the basis of professionalism in an occupation?

2. What are ethics?

3. Discuss the rules of informal ethics in the correctional officer subculture.

4. Discuss the differences between smug hacks and the human services officer.

5. What is correct assertiveness?

Terms/Concepts

Officer comportment	Smug hacks
Professionalism	Goon squad
Ethics	Human services officers
Police ethics	Correct assertiveness

References

Bayse, Daniel, *Working in Jails and Prisons: Becoming Part of the Team*, ACA, Lanham, Md, 1995.

Black, Lee Roy, Ph.D., "Development of a Strong Work Ethic, *The State of Corrections 1996 Proceedings*, ACA, Lanham, MD, 1997.

Bowker, L., *Prison Victimization*, Elsevier, NY, 1980.

Castaneda, Ruben, "Corrections Officers Held in Smuggling," *Washington Post*, 4/8/94.

Cheek, Frances, Ph.D., *Stress Management for Corrections Officers and Their Families*, ACA, Laurel, MD, 1984.

Clarke, Harold W., "Examining the Role of Ethics in Corrections," *The State of Corrections 1992*, ACA, Lanham, MD, 1993.

Cornelius, Gary F., *Stressed Out! Strategies for Living and Working with Stress in Corrections*, ACA, Lanham, MD, 1994.

Corrothers, Hon. Helen G., excerpt: "Career v. Job: Why Become a Correctional Officer?" *The Effective Correctional Officer*, ACA, Lanham, MD, 1992, pp. 1-10.

Crouch, Ben, ed., *Keepers: Prison Guards and Contemporary Corrections*, Springfield, Ill., Chas-Thomas, 1980.

Fox, Vernon & Jeanne Stinchcombe, *Introduction to Corrections*, 4th Ed., Englewood Cliffs, Prentice Hall, 1994.

Gilbert, Michael J., "The Challenge of Professionalism in Correctional Training," *Journal of Correctional Training*, July, 1989, pp. 13-26.

Glaser, D., *The Effectiveness of a Prison and Parole System*, Indianapolis, Bobbs-Merrill, 1969.

Halford, Sally Chandler, "Officer Comportment," Jail Operations Bulletin, Vol II, No. 8, American Jail Association, 1990.

Hutton, Scott D., Ph.D., *Staff Supervision Made Easy*, Lanham, MD, ACA, 1998.

Johnson, Robert, *Hard Time: Understanding and Reforming the Prison*, Wadsworth, 1996.

Kauffmann, Kelsey, *Prison Officers and Their World*, Cambridge, Harvard Univ. Press, 1988.

Lombardo, Lucien X., *Guards Imprisoned: Correctional Officers at Work*, 2nd Ed., Cincinnati, Anderson, 1989.

McCarthy, Bernard, "Keeping an Eye on the Keeper: Prison Corruption and its Control," in *Justice, Crime, and Ethics*, ed. M. Braswell, B. McCarthy and B. McCarthy, pp. 239-253, Cincinatti, Ohio, Anderson, 1991.

Pollock, Joycelyn M., *Ethics in Crime and Justice, Dilemmas and Decisions*, 2nd Ed., Wadsworth, Belmont, Cal., 1994.

Sirene, Walt; James M. Kelly, and Marita Malone, *Leadership in Developing the Organizational Ethic: Ethics in Policing*, 3rd Ed., FBI Academy, Quantico, VA, 1995.

Toch, H. and J. Klofas, "Alienation and desire for job enrichment among correctional officers," *Federal Probation*, 46(1982), pp. 35-44.

Washington Post, 11/5/93.

Chapter 11

Avoiding Manipulation

Staff in correctional facilities deal with many different types of inmates: large/small in size, varying degrees of criminal backgrounds, substance abuse, etc., and different personalities. The same is true for staff: some are hacks, some practice human service, some are weak, some are strong willed and "by the book."

There is one common denominator running through the above—staff by their positions and authority—control the environment in the facility and the inmates would like to gain a significant amount of that control for themselves. The inmates attempt to gain control by the practice of manipulation.

When a staff member falls victim to inmate manipulation, a small but *significant* crack opens up in the facility's security network. The result can be the injury or death of staff/inmates/visitors, escape, introduction of contraband, etc. The list can go on. Ultimately, the inmate gains power and stature over the staff.

Resisting inmate manipulation is a skill that should be learned and practiced by *all* staff members who interact with inmates on a daily basis. Also, volunteers who come into the institution to assist programs should also have this training.

To successfully resist inmate manipulators, staff should have knowledge in three areas:

1. The personality of the inmate;
2. How inmates do time; and
3. The process of manipulation.

The Personality of the Inmate

Offenders are not born inmates, they *become* inmates through prisonization and the development of niches (see Chapter 6). While much research has been done concerning the personalities of inmates, this section will focus on observations from Bayse, Samenow and Bennett. Veteran staff are aware of the distinct personalities and behaviors of street-wise criminals in terms of manipulation.

175

1. *Bayse*: According to Daniel Bayse, author of *Helping Hands: A Handbook for Volunteers in Prisons and Jails* (see references) and a corrections counselor, inmates exhibit the following traits:
    *   *Inmate masks*: inmates will wear different personalities to suit the environment and their needs, like masks. For example, to a volunteer or counselor, they may seem attentive, contrite and remorseful, if it gains them sympathy. Back in the unit, they brag about "fooling" people. Before a parole board hearing, an inmate may brag about his criminal record and how he will not get caught next time. In front of the board, he is sorry and swears to stay out of trouble.
    *   *Narcissism*: many inmates feel that they are "number one" and the world has to suit them.
    *   *Need for power and control*: criminals like the excitement that comes with wielding power over victims: drug dealers having addicts beg, sex offenders forcing people to have sex with them, etc.
    *   *Lying*: lying is fundamental in the criminal lifestyle. Denials that they were involved in a crime are common.
    *   *Frustration*: the theme of "I want what I want when I want it" could be the inmates' theme song. Many are impatient and do not have the self-discipline to complete treatment programs. They may blame others: the police, correctional officers, counselors, etc., for their shortcomings.
    *   *Lack of remorse or guilt*: inmates often convince themselves of their innocence—they blame the victim. For example, an inmate serving life for the murder of a state police officer implied that it was the trooper's fault because he reached for his gun when the inmate went for his.
    *   *Lack of empathy*: inmates have little or no concern about the impact of their acts on victims. They may say: "He [she] wasn't *really* hurt when I stabbed him [her]. He [she] only spent an hour in the hospital and will be fine in no time." [Bayse, 1993]
2. *Samenow*: Dr. Stanton Samenow is a respected psychologist in Alexandria, Virginia. In his book, *Inside the Criminal Mind* (see references), he observes that being incarcerated does not change the inmate's view that he is "top dog." Their motto is "If you serve time, let time serve you." Manipulation schemes continue and obeying rules is due to wanting the staff to look at him/her as being a "good" inmate, not due to rehabilita-

tion. The life-long attitude of the criminal is to do as he pleases and this continues behind the walls. [Samenow, 1984]

3. *Bennett*: James Bennett served as Director of the U.S. Bureau of Prisons from 1937 to 1964. He observed that the niche (see Chapter 6) is important to the inmate as is the manipulation process. He wrote that "one of the first challenges for new prisoners...is to try to make a place for themselves with the other men...Sometimes the 'snow' job is crucial...how to impress everybody with one's potential importance." [Bennett, 1970, Leinwand, 1972]

The above three views represent observations of inmates' behavior by three professionals. Other traits have been observed, such as changes in inmates that are dangerous and must be viewed by staff with concern. Many inmates now have less remorse and conscience than inmates in years past.

One of the best illustrations of this is reporter Miles Corwin's (Los Angeles Times) interviews with older inmates incarcerated in California's Tehachapi State Prison. The article appearing in 1993 revealed that newer inmates were more violent and exhibited little or no remorse for hurting their victims. A Los Angeles police psychiatrist, Dr. Michael Zona, said that this behavior can be attributed to sociopaths — people who have no feelings or concerns and have an anti-social personality. [Cornelius, 1995]

How Inmates Do Time

The reader should review Chapter 6 to gain insight into how inmates do time. Underlying the aspect of having needs met and the development of a niche is the idea of comfort. Inmates want to do their time as comfortable and "hassle free" as possible and avoid the pains of imprisonment.

To meet the needs of activity, privacy, emotional feedback and safety, inmates may lie. Lies and concocted stories may get them a transfer to protective custody, for example. To obtain a sense of emotional feedback, inmates may "warm up" to staff, trying to portray themselves as "regular people."

The Process of Manipulation

To inmates who have lived a lifestyle of lying and using people, manipulating others is a way of life. In fact, *manipulation* has been described

A complacent, sloppy officer will be a target for inmate manipulators.

as the "name of the game" in prison as well as on the street. In these environments, people are expected to be "cagey" and naive persons tell the truth. The criminal victimizes weak people in and out of prison; they are "fair game." While the law-abiding citizen is honest, truthful and solves life's problems using legitimate means, the criminal/inmate will deceive and use lying and violence to cope. The result of living like this is that inmates who survive prison life become tougher and less able to feel for themselves and others. [Johnson, 1996]

Using people, finding niches, wanting things their way all exhibit a need for control. To understand inmate manipulation, staff must understand the definition of the word which has three components:

1. Attempt to control another person or persons;
2. By subtle means;
3. To get something that is wanted or needed.

[ACA, 1992]

For correctional staff, manipulation follows these components, but with the attempts to control comes attempts to change staff by subtle means that can be very artistic. The result is to get something that is wanted, needed or achieved.

To properly guard against manipulation, correctional staff must ask themselves, "What do the inmates want to control? What might they really want? Are they telling the truth?"

Inmates' Views of Manipulation

Inmates also have, like corrections professionals, an opinion about manipulating others. Here is a sampling:

... "the working code" of a convict is at bottom to best the man, the pig [officer].—Jack Henry Abbott

[Manipulation] It's called a jailhouse wise. It was effective in my individual case...but it's totally no good...you can manipulate the prison better than they can manipulate you...In prison you learn to con and control, to master everyone, to control your facial expression."—James Brodie

> Sources: *In the Belly of the Beast, Letters from Prisons,* by Jack Henry Abbott, NY, Vintage, 1981.
>
> *The Shame of the Prisons,* by Ben Bagdikian and Leon Dash, NY Pocket Books, 1972.

Inmates often practice *verbal deception* or lying. A competent officer can check things out and uncover the lie. Also, inmates engage in *situational deception*—misleading without lying. For example, an inmate going by a cellblock wants to pass in contraband. Two inmate friends distract the officer. [Knowles, 1992]

The manipulation schemes may be either small scale, one-time requests by inmates to staff or larger, more elaborate schemes. Short term or small schemes require very little planning and is one on one. Also, the inmate will see how "easy" the officer is. [Knowles, 1992] Smaller versions may be something like an inmate asks an officer on post if he can go to a certain block to pay a friend back some cigarettes. The officer says yes, thinking "what's the harm?" A larger scale version could be several inmates each asking an officer for favors that involve bending or breaking the rules over a long period. At the appropriate moment, the officer is threatened with exposure to supervisors if he/she does not do a big favor for the inmates such as bringing in drugs. [Knowles, 1992]

Like understanding what the term manipulation actually means, the best method to learn about it is to examine each component:

1. attempt to control another person or persons: the facility staff controls the environment: the housing assignments, mail, television, phone, food, etc. The inmate wants to control the environment and get contraband in, get into a housing unit that he/she likes, etc.

Inmates will target a staff person. A staff target is not the ethical, professional officer, but more like a sloppy, lazy, inattentive officer. Studies of con games in jails indicate target officers who are:

- naive or are too trusting of inmates;
- too friendly or familiar with inmates — they want to be "friends;"
- lacking professionalism and ethics;
- exhibiting low self esteem;
- apparently isolated or divided from colleagues.

[Knowles, 1992]

An officer or staff member who is a target may turn to inmates for conversation and company, forgetting that *the inmate is an inmate.* When staff become too familiar with inmates, a threat arises to the staff's professionalism. According to Sykes, staff are dependent on inmates to obey rules and complete tasks. Staff may overlook inmate rules, infractions, and can be dangerous if staff members feel more comfortable around inmates than staff; they get too personal. [Pollock, 1994]

2. by subtle means

Inmates may categorize staff into soft, hard and mellow categories of supervisory style. *Soft employees* are generally very trusting, overly familiar with inmates and naive. *Hard employees* are those who go by the book and pay strict attention to policies and procedures. *Mellow employees* are those who are soft and hard at the appropriate times. Manipulators tend to go after soft employees because they hesitate to say no or take command and hard staff because inmates believe that the exterior hardness hides a weakness. Inmates feel that the mellow employee would take too much time to work on by subtle means. [Ariz. DOC, 1984]

Inmates also may engage in either individually or as a group processes such as the "test of limits" or *fish testing.* The test of limits is as it says, the manipulator asks or pushes the employee into bending or breaking the rules. In other words, to see how far the manipulator will go before the employee says no, takes action or makes a decision in line with policy. [Ariz. DOC, 1984] The test of limits and fish testing does not usually happen quickly. Inmates may work on the officer for weeks or months, all the while doing favors for the officer such as getting coffee, running errands as a trusty, etc. The idea is to get the staff member to see the inmate(s) as nice, friendly, a "buddy" and not an inmate.

Other methods include inmates over complimenting the staff member, saying things like "you care, not like the other officers," "we can talk to you," etc. The goal is to befriend the staff member, especially a weak one, who will find it hard to say no. [Ariz. DOC, 1984]

Many of these processes overlap. For example, Officer Jones works a general housing unit in the prison. He is new and has been on for about eight months. Trusty Smith notices Jones does not move around his area too much and seems rather shy. Over the next few weeks, he offers to get Jones coffee, run messages to other officers, etc. He compliments Jones repeatedly saying that he really cares about the inmates, more than officers on the other shifts. Jones finds Smith welcome company and talks to him more frequently. On day, Smith asks Jones if he could go to the far end of the tier and say hello to an old friend, for "just a minute." Jones says sure, why not, not knowing that Smith is delivering some contraband.

Empathy v. Sympathy

When inmates manipulate, they are hoping the officer or staff member is sympathetic instead of empathetic. *Empathy* is shared understanding and/or experience of feelings, thoughts or attitudes. A staff member can empathize with an inmate's problems *without* feeling sorry for him/her. *Sympathy* is defined as sameness of feelings with pity and compassion. [Ariz. DOC, 1984] Sympathy is less objective than empathy. For example, an inmate manipulator approaches an officer supervising visiting about getting more visiting time with his girlfriend. He tells the officer he misses her, as been locked up for a while, etc. An empathetic officer understands the pains of incarceration and tells the inmate that he understands and the inmate will have to request it in writing through channels. A sympathetic officer will pity the inmate and give him extra time right away.

There appears to be no end to the mind games that the inmate manipulator will use on the staff; so the staff see them as other people, friends, etc., and not strictly inmates. These methods may range from the inmate saying "only you [staff person] can help me" to sexual references and touching. [Ariz. DOC, 1984] If the staff person does not correct the inmate firmly when "brushed," lightly touched or flirting, this may be a green light to the inmate to go ahead further and press the manipulation.

Staff weakness and manipulation by inmates may result in what is called the *"set up,"* a process where the staff member unknowingly plays into the inmates' hands. Selecting a victim, eliciting sympathy, testing the limits are steps to court and mislead the staff person. Inmates will then get a handle or *lever*—an act by the staff person, viewed as kind and thoughtful, that the inmates may use to wield to pressure. It could be bending the rules, allowing some minor infraction to go unnoticed or letting a minor piece of contraband slip by. The last stage of a set up is presenting the staff person with a "*shopping list*" or list of demands from the inmates. Refusal is now difficult. The employee may fear exposure or dismissal and sometimes he/she does what the inmates want. This final wrap up of the set up where the employee is forced to comply is called the "*sting.*" [Ariz. DOC, 1984]

Not every game or manipulative act by inmates is part of an elaborate set up. Frequently, it involves acts to "seduce" the staff into thinking that "inmates are okay," "they mostly are good," etc. The tools that the manipulator uses, besides the aforementioned over friendliness, etc., can involve luring staff into sexual, romantic-appearing relationships.

Examples of Inmate Manipulation

The boundaries of inmate manipulation are only limited by the boundaries of imagination and daring, sometimes involving others. Consider these examples of subtle means:

- An inmate in a maximum security prison ran a drug ring using drugs received from visitors and guards. He also attempted to entice a corrections employee to change his release date in his prison record to make it appear that he was close to release.
- In 1992, a criminal justice professor gave two prison inmates a cutting tool and helped them break out because "he was in love with one of them."
- Two officers lost their jobs because they were convinced to put $1,500.00 into an outside bank account to purchase a motorcycle from an inmate. The trouble was, the motorcycle never existed.
- An inmate persuaded three correctional employees to head an investment scheme to raise money for a treasure recovery from a sunken Spanish galleon. The inmates even printed stock certificates in the prison print shop and sold them to their friends. What was recovered from their $50,000.00 investment? Nothing.
- An inmate being transported back to a jail from a psychiatrist appointment persuaded his guards to stop at a hotel for dinner. He went unescorted into the restroom and escaped out the back door. Officials described the inmate as "...so glib and

friendly that they [officers] said it was easy to forget he is a prisoner."

Sources: Bayse, Daniel, J.,
*Working in Jails and Prisons:
Becoming Part of the Team,*
Lanham, ACA, 1995; "Million-
aire Convict Gives His Guards
the Slip," by Mary Jordan,
Washington Post, 4/25/96; "DC
Jail Escape—A Clean Get-
away," by Paul Duggan, *Wash-
ington Post,* 1/25/95.

3. to get something that is wanted or needed: sex, money, escape, power over other, drugs and weapons smuggled in, etc.

One of the most difficult things for staff in working in a correctional facility is knowing when an inmate is trying to manipulate them. Not all inmates are schemers and engage in deceit. The safest practice is to keep a guard up all the time and assume that no matter how friendly the inmate or how apparently sincere, a manipulation may be in the works. All staff members are always targets to get something that is wanted or needed:sex, money, escape, power, etc.

Guidelines to Resist Inmate Manipulators

The following are "common sense" rules that staff should follow to keep their guard up against manipulators. [Knowles, 1992]

1. When informed of a situation by an inmate, a personal problem requiring action, a request, etc., check it out before taking action.
2. There is a line between staff and inmate. Never share personal information such as social life, significant others, children, etc., with an inmate.
3. Always look and act professional. Follow policies and procedures and keep supervisors informed, especially when an apparent manipulation is attempted. Use body language and posture to present an image of self confidence.
4. Be decisive. Never appear to be indecisive or at odds with colleagues in front of inmates. Inmates will use these as a wedge to separate a staff "target" from other staff. Say no and mean it.

5. Be aware of where you are, what you are saying, and who may be listening. As one jail officer said: "The inmate grapevine is better than AT&T." Control rumors; inmates love them.

6. Documentation is important. Incident reports, memos, etc., being written informs staff of inmates' actions and makes it more difficult for the inmate to keep a secret.

Summary

To be an effective part of the correctional facility's security network, staff must be trained in resisting inmate manipulation. To accomplish this, staff must be trained in the personality of the inmate, review how inmates do time, and the process of manipulation. The inmates' personality is one often of wearing masks and lying to hide their real intentions. Manipulation is basically an attempt to control someone by subtle means, which sometimes are well planned. Officers and staff must be empathetic and not sympathetic. There are common sense approaches for staff to guard against manipulation.

Review Questions

1. To successfully resist manipulation, staff should have knowledge in what three areas?

2. What does it mean when it is said that inmates wear masks?

3. What are the three components of the act of manipulation?

4. Inmate manipulators target staff who exhibit what traits?

5. Explain the differences between empathy and sympathy.

6. Name four protectors against manipulation.

Terms/Concepts

Inmate masks	Sympathy
Manipulation	Fish testing
Verbal deception	Set up
Situational deception	Shopping list
Soft employees	Lever
Hard employees	Sting
Mellow employees	Empathy

References

Abbot, Jack Henry, *In the Belly of the Beast: Letters From Prison*, NY Vantage, 1981.

Arizona Department of Corrections, Academy Core, Inmate Games and Set Ups, 5/84.

Bagdikian, Ben and Leon Dask, *The Shame of the Prisons*, NY Pocket Books, 1972.

Bayse, Daniel J., *Helping Hands: A Handbook for Volunteers in Prisons and Jails*, Lanham, Md, ACA, 1993.

Bayse, Daniel J., *Working in Jails and Prisons: Becoming Part of the Team*, Lanham, Md, ACA, 1995.

Bennett, James V., *I Chose Prison*, NY, Alfred K. Knopf, 1970.

Cornelius, Gary F., "The Changing Inmate," *The Twenty Minute Trainer*, IACTP, Fall '95, pp. 8-9.*

Duggan, Paul, "D.C. Jail Escape: A Clean Getaway," *The Washington Post*, 1/25/95.

Johnson, Robert, *Hard Time: Understanding and Reforming the Prison*, Wadsworth, 1996.

Jordan, Mary, "Millionaire Convict Gives Guards the Slip," *Washington Post*, 4/25/96.

Knowles, Sgt. F.E., "Con Games and Inmates: What the Line Officer Needs to Know," *Jail Operations Bulletin*, Vol. IV, No. 7, American Jail Association, 1992.

Leinwand, Gerald, Ed., *Prisons*, N.Y. Pocket Books, 1972.

Pollock, Joycelyn M., *Ethics in Crime and Justice, Dilemmas and Decisions*, 2nd Ed., Wadsworth, Belmont, Cal., 1994.

Samenow, Stanton, Ph.D., *Inside the Criminal Mind*, N.Y., Times, 1984.

Working With Manipulative Inmates Correspondence Course, Book I, ACA, Lanham, MD, 1992.

See also "Recent Crimes Shock Old-Timers Doing Time," by Miles Corwin, *Washington Post*, 12/26/93, p. A19.

Chapter 12

Inmate Violence

When anyone is locked up against their will, especially in overcrowded conditions, it is logical to assume that violence—inmate on inmate and inmate on staff—will occur.

Corrections staff must be concerned with the daily possibility that they will either be victims of violence or have to intervene or defuse a violent situation. The concerns are many: fear of death, serious injury and disease (exposure to HIV, etc.). Every facility, no matter how well operated and secure, is prone to violence.

Violent acts in corrections facilities range from isolated incidents such as fights, assaults, etc., to larger, more serious incidents such as homicides and riots. This chapter will give the reader an overview into violence and the inmate; the next chapter will discuss riots and disturbances.

The reason for inmate violence has been a subject of much research. Prisons and jails have an appearance and a reputation of being tough places with emphasis on security: walls, barbed wire, towers, etc. Even with strict security procedures and state-of-the-art hardware, highly volatile inmates continue acts of stabbing, raping, gang warfare and rioting. New inmates must learn that to survive, he or she must look and act as tough as other inmates. The highest priority of an inmate is survival. [Samenow, 1984]

An inmate who is locked up expects to do as he pleases and to maintain status among his or her peers, will choose disciplinary punishment rather than obey orders or give in to the staff. This quest for status may cause a physically aggressive inmate to use profanity or hit or punch an inmate or staff member when feeling threatened or infringed upon. An inmate switches TV channels and is punched. A staff member may be attacked unaware with a flying chair after denying an inmate's request. One inmate did not like the vegetable soup at lunch, demanding another portion to replace "the dregs of the pot" or "slop." The worker ignored him and the inmate threw soup in his face. [Samenow, 1984]

The roots of inmate violence could possibly be traced back to deviant acts on the street. According to Katz, many young offenders are *bad asses* or become persons who overtly take on symptoms of deviance and that is regarded as good. An offender who is "real bad" is described as tough and not easily influenced. He is not yielding. A "bad ass" axiom to live by is that others do not know who he is or where he is coming from and

Inmate being escorted in restraints at Maryland House of Correction. A safe escort technique is to have two officers walk behind the inmate.

quickly he can cross the distance and destroy the others. They might say: "I"ll jump you on the street good; I'll come upside your head; I'll fuck you up good." [Katz, 1988]

Correctional institutions, especially prisons, are places of unrest and frustration for inmates. Many inmates are frustrated. Some inmates seethe inwardly. They may "mouth" words of disobedience or defiance, but know where to stop. Others have less self restraint, they verbally insult staff, defy orders and try to assert their individuality. Others act aggressively by physical attacks on property, staff and other inmates. Many staff members see inmate violence as routine or as a built-in component in corrections. The reasons are possibly overcrowding, under staffing, where the safety of inmates is jeopardized, and changes in good time and parole policies. From 1990 to 1995, 410 inmates were killed by other inmates in federal and state prisons. [Fox and Stinchcombe, 1999, Bureau of Justice Statistics, 1997]

How Violent Are Our Corrections Facilities?

- Between 1990 and 1996, the percentage of violent offenders (based on offense) remained at almost half: 46% in 1990; 47% in 1996.

- During 1996, 68.3% of assaults committed by inmates were against other inmates; 31.7% were against staff members.
- In 1997, 67 inmates were killed by other inmates in federal and state prisons. Two inmates were killed by staff. Two staff/officers were killed and 14,283 were assaulted by inmates. The number of inmates injured by staff totaled 1,172. From 1996 to 1997, the number of inmates killed by other inmates fell from 73 to 67 respectively.

Source: BJS Bulletin: Prisoners in 1997, 8/98; *Correctional Yearbook 1997*, by George and Camille Camp, p. 37; *Corrections Compendium*, ACA, June, 1998, Vol. 23, No. 6, p.9.

Inmates do not cope with life and its problems in a mature fashion. Whereas the moral citizen addresses problems without deception or violence except for self defense, inmates use deception (see Chapter 11) and violence as coping mechanisms. People become devalued and become "fair game." Inmates live in a social jungle where "the weak versus the strong." One factor in the development of a violent lifestyle in the inmate is the absence of nurturing, loving relationships early in life. Self hatred develops and can propel the person into a life of violent crime. [Johnson, 1996]

The culture of inmate violence can be symbolized by the type of inmate known as the *state raised convict*. This type of inmate is defined by Johnson as "men [women] reared on rejection and abuse in orphanages, detention centers, training schools and youth prisons." In other words, they were raised by the staff in tough state institutions and find themselves locked up for long periods in prison or other correctional facilities. One inmate called prison the *"belly of the beast."* [Johnson, 1996]

These hard core convicts have many interpersonal failures in life and view violence as their only way of being taken seriously as a person of importance. In predatory groups or cliques, singly or as gang members, they victimize weak and defenseless inmates while maintaining a cool, hard manliness over emotions that are impulsive and raw. [Johnson, 1996] Other researchers describe this world in similar terms.

The prison world is the only world with which he [the state raised convict] is familiar…This is a world where disputes with a pipe or a knife and the individual must form tight cliques for protection.

[From: *The Felon* by John Irwin, Prentice Hall, 1970.]

Extremely reduced life options, meager material existence and limited experience with formal and polite urban social organization results in in-

Superintendent Ed Szostak with Secretary Amy Comproski examines a metal weapon fashioned from parts of a sprinkler head.

mates being distrustful and suspicious of people different from them. [Irwin, 1980] In this world, violence is not thought of as bad behavior, but as a means to cope and survive.

The negative image of prisoners or convicts in society can lead to inmates taking on an *"outlaw identity"* as a reaction to society's view. These inmates scorn society's disapproval of them, engage in violent activities of gangs, feel no mercy or compassion for others and are ready to use violence to protect themselves or achieve their desired ends. Values are looked upon as weaknesses. [Irwin and Snedeker, 1989]

This is a frightening climate in which all staff have to be on their guard. A journalist touring a prison mentioned to an inmate that the male inmates were in such great physical shape. His answer was that an inmate has to be in good shape and can get killed if he does not have a group to protect him. [Kosof, 1984]

It is not uncommon for fights, rapes and murders to occur in prison. Fights happen daily; rapes and murders are reported less frequently. Some fights involve homosexual activity, but almost anything could spark an argument, like a cigarette, for example. [Kosof, 1984]

Inmates may fight over a television program, food on a tray, a perceived insult about a girlfriend or boyfriend—the reasons may vary.

Inmates' Views on Violence

Polite guys [inmates] are never rude. They'll always say "excuse me" before burying a knife in another man's chest.

"Stories from the Yard" from
Iron House, Jerome Washington,
Vintage, NY, 1991

An inmate released from a maximum security prison dreams of knifing victims screaming in shock, of fights involving himself pounding relentlessly on a faceless prisoner. He used to wake up angry in prison and not talk to anyone until noon. In his sleep he still remembers where he kept his shank.

Source: "Readjusting to Life on
the Bricks" by Courtland Milloy,
The Washington Post, 2/17/83.

To a prisoner it is an insult to grapple hand to hand with anyone. If someone ever strikes him with his hand (another prisoner), he has to kill him with a knife...All the violence in prison is geared for murder, nothing else. You can't have someone with ill feelings for you walking around. He could drop a knife in you any day.

Source: *In the Belly of the Beast,
Letters from Prison* by Jack
Henry Abbott, N.Y. Vintage,
1981.

Attacks by inmates on inmates and on staff can be swift and savage. In 1995, in an eastern U.S. prison, a 45-year-old inmate was stabbed by a fellow inmate and was pronounced dead twenty minutes later. [Metzzler, 1995] A correctional officer, age 34, was fatally stabbed while securing inmates in their cells after dinner. [IACO, 1995]

Whenever a correctional officer gives a hostile inmate a direct order or attempts to gain compliance with rules and regulations, underlying anger and resentment in the inmate can spill over and explode. Sometimes the violence is unleashed instantly; sometimes officers are later ambushed.

Chief Criscone (left) of the Albany County Correctional Facility inspects a metal knife (shank) fashioned from a sneaker's arch support; Superintendent Ed Szostak (right) examines a new type of contraband resistant sneaker which does not contain metal arches.

Staff Countermeasures

Control of inmate violence in a correctional facility is the job of everyone who works there. While the main brunt of this task falls upon the line correctional officer, counselors, service staff, etc., can all help by reporting inmate behavior and keeping classification and custody staff informed of unusual occurrences or information about inmates. It is a never ending battle.

Probably the best defense against inmate violence is for staff, anyone who works around inmates, to remember at all times that they can be a target for an inmate assault. Also, staff in inmate housing, work and program areas must realize that fights between inmates or an assault on an inmate can happen at any time.

Many officers fear the kind of violence which is unprovoked by them, unpredictable and spontaneous. As one Massachusetts prison officer said, this type of violence "...could happen any time, any day, any minute. In this business, you just don't know." [Kauffman, 1988]

While violence among inmates could be a result of personality conflicts, gang warfare, arguments over the television, etc., the reasons that inmates turn on officers can also vary. According to one veteran jail officer:

> Inmates may act violently due to the influence of drugs, alcohol (including homemade brew) or due to a mental disorder. Also, you never know if the inmate has just received bad news about court, his girlfriend or wife is dumping him, etc. Some inmates act "macho" and will fight officers trying to move him or conduct a search. I've seen inmates fight officers over taking a shower...one guy challenged officers to come in and get him because he was creating a disturbance. You *always* have to be on your guard."

[Cornelius, 1998]

Unprofessional officers who lack maturity and ethics can provoke violence. Calling inmates names, using racial slurs, or embarrassing inmates in front of other inmates can turn up the heat on a boiling pot, causing the inmate to lose his temper. One Massachusetts prison officer said that other officers can get hurt because of an officer using insults on inmates such as "maggot." He said that "...I can get hurt because this [officer] is acting non-professional or stupid, out and out dumb." [Kauffman, 1988]

How does staff deal with violence and/or the threat of it? Several methods are:

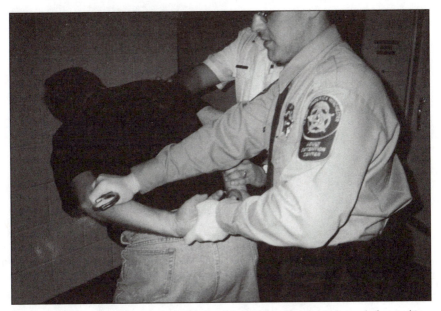

Some inmates object to being searched, and "break bad." The officer has to be ready for anything.

- *Physical control*: Simply hands on use of force by staff to protect inmates from each other or staff from assault. For example, an officer strikes an inmate who is assaulting another officer or a fight is physically broken up by restraining inmates. An inmate or inmates may be destroying property and legally can be restrained.

Officers can use *non-lethal use of force* or physical force (holds, restraints, blocks, etc.) that overcome resistance, ensure compliance and does not cause death. *Use of deadly force* means that the officer can use force "likely to cause death or great bodily harm," generally as a last resort to protect someone's life or the officer's own life. The use of deadly force should be regulated by agency policy and state or local law. [ACA, 1998]

Firearms are usually thought of when discussing deadly force. For non-lethal force, items such as pepper spray, batons, and "stun guns" can be used. Officers should document all uses of force on an inmate. Also, the inmate upon which the force is used must receive immediate medical attention. This includes inspecting restraint devices used on an inmate such as handcuffs, etc.

CERT Team members prepare to subdue an inmate.

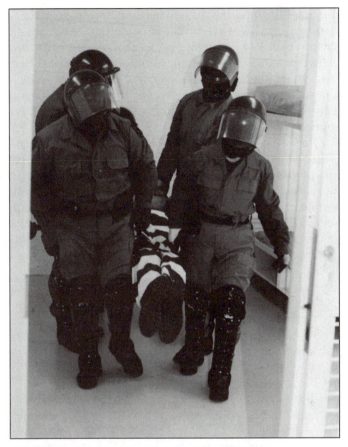

CERT Team transporting inmate to secure housing.

Physical force also includes the "hardware" of the facility: perimeter walls, gun towers, electrified fences, security gates, doors, locks, cameras, etc. These can serve to limit violence by controlling inmate movement and keeping them under observation. Also, the physical presence of officers in uniform — the *uniform presence* — can limit violence. Large numbers of staff in uniform (custody, classification, recreation, etc.) can remind the inmate constantly of staff physical presence and line of sight observation by officers. [Bowker, 1985]

• *Legal and administrative sanctions*: Inmates want out, to be released as quickly as possible. Violent inmates run the risk of having time added to their sentences by disciplinary committees taking good time or the time off an inmate's sentence for attending programs, good behavior, working in the institution, etc. Also, a classification committee can increase the custody level of an inmate because of violent behavior. Finally, the inmate population should realize that if they commit crimes such as homicide, sexual assaults, assaults, etc., they will be charged with a *street charge* or inmate jargon for getting charged with another crime while incarcerated. A conviction could mean more time. [Bowker, 1985]

- *Strategies to manage the behaviorally disordered offenders*: These are potentially violent inmates who have serious cognitive or emotional deterioration and are dangerous to themselves or others due to poor impulse control. Recommended treatment would involve qualified mental health staff treating the problem in these areas: social climate/environment, interpersonal communication, multi-disciplinary treatment planning, and taking a non-violent crisis intervention approach. [Maestas, 1993]
- Re-examine correction's approach to inmate violence: This is perhaps the most logical solution which encompasses the staff, environment and policies.

  According to Joseph D. Lehman, Commissioner of the Pennsylvania Department of Corrections, writing in 1992, these steps can be effective in dealing with inmate violence: [Lehman, 1992]

1. Recognition of the stresses of prison environment: Inmates feel little or no control over situations. Changes such as changes in goods, services and policies may provoke violence if perceived as harassment. The environment has an undercurrent of violence between inmates and inmates on staff, especially where primary contact with staff is over rules enforcement.

2. Separation of violence into categories based on victims' identification and the motivation of the aggressors: Inmate protest, an officer's command, searches finding contraband, disciplinary actions, cellblock/institution transfer, etc. The aforementioned categories are generally reasons for inmate on staff assaults.

   Concerning inmate on inmate assaults, the reasons could be gang related, drug related or sexually motivated.

   Staff must track violent incidents relative to security, inmate classification level, the number of inmate assailants per incident and number of incidents per each inmate. Also, factors must be noted as to location of the incidents,

Restrained inmate being placed in a cell.

time of occurrence, type of weapon(s), including fists, and the severity of the injuries.

3. Identification of potential intervention points and development of a strategy: Once data on violence is collected, staff must develop a strategy for the reduction of incident frequency and severity. Questions must be asked: Is more staff presence needed? What is going on with potentially violent inmates?

4. Evaluation of inmate activities and programs: Based on information gained, classification procedures, contraband deterrence policies and inmate programs must be evaluated. Are classification decisions such as housing assignments objective and consider inmate behavior? Are strong predatory inmates placed with weak ones? Should certain inmates be segregated? Is the staff doing enough to counteract the flow and/or manufacture of drugs and weapons? Are inmates offered programs in skills training such as anger management, impulse control and cognitive skills?

5. Strategies for staff: Staff should be trained in interpersonal skills training, with emphasis on the best places and times to resolve inmate conflicts. This may improve officers' skills in dealing with inmates and by defusing tense situ-

ations, assaults on staff may decrease in number. Training should include information gained from officers who keep things calm—the "level headed" ones. Also, the "hot heads" in the staff should be observed. Training should incorporate how each do their jobs and the positive and negative results of their actions. Mature inmates could be questioned as to what they think of staff/inmate interactions and if anything can be improved.

Lehman concludes by stating that changing the prison culture is not easy, but it can be done. He advocates the implementation of policies that advocate a *zero tolerance* of violent behavior. Simply, this means that the institution staff will not tolerate violence by inmates on other inmates or staff for any reason; no exceptions will be made. Conflicts and disagreements will be resolved in a mature, adult manner.

Related to this strategy will be the use of alternative strategies of conflict resolution: trouble shooters, mediators and arbitrators. These methods can supplement the inmate grievance procedures.

Communications must be improved: from the staff to the inmates and the inmates to the staff. Both groups should feel free to talk to one another without negative reactions or behaviors. Also, staff should conduct audits and assessments to monitor the communications and *institutional climate*. The "climate" is the mood of the institution: tense, frustrated, non-communicative, etc. Since violence may be born of frustration, the frequent examination of the inmates' mood and then taking positive steps to improve the situation are beneficial. [Lehman, 1992]

Summary

Violence is inherent to the field of corrections. Often, among inmates, it is a result of deviant backgrounds and life on the street, where conflicts are settled with violence. Many inmates are frustrated and have not learned mature coping skills.

State raised inmates use violence as a symbol of importance and being taken seriously. Staff must remember that they are targets at all times. Staff who are immature and unprofessional open themselves as targets.

Countermeasures include the use of physical control, legal/administrative sanctions, and strategies to manage behaviorally disordered inmates. A proactive strategy is needed, such as recognition of prison stress, examining violent occurrences, adapting zero tolerance policies, and improved staff training.

Review Questions

1. What is meant by an inmate being a "state raised convict?"

2. Define "bad ass."

3. Explain three methods of staff control of inmate violence.

4. How can staff re-examine correction's approach to violence?

Terms/Concepts

Bad asses

State-raised convict

Belly of the beast

Outlaw identity

Uniform presence

Behaviorally disordered offender

Institutional climate

Physical control

Non-lethal use of force

Use of deadly force

Legal and administrative sanctions

Street charge

Zero tolerance

References

Abbott, Jack, *In the Belly of the Beast: Letters From Prison*, NY, Vintage, 1981.

Bender, David and Bruno Leone (Senior Editors), *America's Prisons: Opposing Viewpoints*, San Diego: Greenhaven Press, 1991, articled used: "Prisons are Violent and Dehumanizing," by John Irwin and Michael Snedecker, Ch. 3.

Braswell, Michael, Steven Dillingham & Reid Montgomery, Jr. (Editors), *Prison Violence in America*, Anderson, Cincinnati, 1985.

Bureau of Justice Statistics Bulletin, CJ 170014, *Prisoners in 1997*, August, 1998.

Bureau of Justice Statistics, *Correctional Populations in the United States 1995*, U.S. Justice Dept., 1997.

Camp, George and Camille, *The Corrections Yearbook*, South Salem, N.Y., The Criminal Justice Institute, 1997.

Corrections Compendium, Vol. 23, No. 6, American Correctional Association, June 1998.

Dictionary of Criminal Justice Terms, American Correctional Association, Lanham, MD, 1998.

Irwin, John, *The Felon*, Englewood Cliffs, NJ, Prentice Hall, 1970.

Irwin, John, *Prisons in Turmoil*, Canada, Little Brown, 1980.

Johnson, Robert, *Hard Time: Understanding and Reforming the Prison*, Wadsworth, 1996.

Katz, Jack, *Seduction of Crime*, Basic Books, 1988.

Kauffman, Kelsey, *Prison Officers and Their World*, Cambridge, Mass, Harvard University Press, 1988.

Kosof, Anna, *Prison Life in America*, Franklin Watts, 1984.

Lehman, Joseph, "A Vision for Dealing with Violence in the '90's," *The State of Corrections*, ACA, Lanham, MD, 1992.

Maestas, Michael G., M.S., "Potentially Violent Offender Management Model," in *The State of Corrections Proceedings 1993*, Lanham, MD, 1993.

Metzler, Kristin, "Lorton Inmate Stabs Prisoner, 45 to Death," *The Washington Times*, 2/7/95.

Milloy, Courtland, "Readjusting to Life on the Bricks," *The Washington Post*, 2/17/83.

The Keeper's Voice, Winter 1995, "In Memoriam Officer Philip K. Curry 1960-1994 He Served," pp. 36-37.

Washington, Jerome, *Iron House,* N.Y. Vintage, 1991.

Chapter 13

Riots and Disturbances

Riots and disturbances are nightmares to the correctional staff—from the warden down to the line officer. Riots and disturbances can result in injury or death to staff members and inmates, property damage and a complete breakdown of authority.

Every correctional officer must keep alert to the fact that in a facility where people are being held against their will, riots and disturbances can occur. The key to their prevention is to not only understand what they are, but how they can be prevented.

Riots and disturbances are similar, but not exactly the same. The American Correctional Association (ACA) Dictionary of Criminal Justice Terms gives a practical, clear definition of each:

Riot: coming together of a group of persons [inmates] who engage in violent and tumultuous conduct. Their actions create a serious risk of causing injury, property damage and public alarm. In a correctional institution, rioting inmates control a significant part of the facility for a significant period of time.

Disturbance: not as large in scope or seriousness as a riot. Fewer inmates are involved, the duration is shorter in time, and there is no control or minimum control of a part of the institution.

A step down from a disturbance is an *incident*, where only one or two inmates are involved and there is no control over any part of the facility.

In correctional history, large scale events at Attica and Santa Fe prisons were riots and became notorious for death and destruction. However, there are countless lower scale disturbances and incidents annually in correctional facilities throughout the United States. [ACA, 1998]

Riots and disturbances are very serious, as illustrated by the following examples:

- *December, 1974*: Approximately 100 inmates arm themselves and take over the maximum security section of the Lorton Reformatory (DC Prison). Ten guards are taken as hostages and after twenty hours of negotiations over grievances, the hostages are freed. Related to this incident is an escape by four inmates in a prison guard's car; an inmate's body is later found inside. [*Washington Post*, 7/11/86]

- *January, 1983*: At Ossining, N.Y. Correctional Facility (Sing-Sing), seventeen hostages were seized and held by over 600 inmates for fifty-three hours. The inmates were protesting their status as "transients," or awaiting transfers to other prisons. The guards (hostages) were treated well and some were protected from assault by other prisoners. [*Washington Post,* 1/12/83]
- *November, 1994*: A suburban Washington D.C. jail erupted in violence when eleven inmates attacked an inmate and trashed a dayroom. [*Washington Times,* 11/3/94]
- *February, 1978*: A fight between a Mexican-American inmate and a black inmate over who owned a pair of trousers hanging in a washroom erupted into a riot involving over 300 inmates. Six barracks were smashed and the infirmary burned down at a minimum security honor ranch in California. [*Washington Post,* 2/22/78]
- *December, 1982*: A thirty-minute disturbance involving fifty inmates fighting left a maintenance foreman dead from stab wounds when he rushed to help staff in a Virginia maximum security federal prison. The fight involved rival inmate groups. [Gregg, 1982]

Since 1970, several notorious riots have occurred in our nation's prisons, namely at Attica, New York, in 1971; at Santa Fe, New Mexico, in 1980, and at Lucasville, Ohio, in 1993.

Attica: Synonym for Riot

The Attica Correctional Facility is a maximum security state prison located in upstate New York. In September, 1971, Attica held 2,243 inmates; many were recidivists convicted of violent crimes. Most of the inmate population were young, black or Puerto Rican inmates from urban areas. This background contrasted with the makeup of the 380 correctional officers, who were mostly white and were hired from the surrounding rural area. They had little or no training and because of post bidding per a union contract, the officers who had the most contact with the inmates were young and inexperienced. Due to budget constraints, employees' salaries were low and inmate programs or rehabilitation activities were almost nonexistent.

Differences in the inmate population and the officer corps led to the officers' feeling that they were losing control. It was difficult to deal with inmates from New York City spewing revolutionary speeches and rhetoric. Some officers only communicated by banging clubs on the wall, signaling move, line up, etc.

A group of inmates formed the "Attica Liberation Faction," labeling Attica as a "classic institution of authoritative inhumanity upon men." Rumors of brutality were common.

The facility was a pressure cooker waiting to boil over and on September 9, 1971, it did. Speculation exists to this day if the riot was "sparked" or was planned. Some inmate calendars had September 9 circled. At 8:30 a.m., a group of inmates refused to line up for a work detail and an inmate fight with the officers resulted. Another incident involved a lieutenant being assaulted. Two inmates involved in the incident were assigned to disciplinary housing and rumors abounded that officers were retaliating violently on the inmates. One of the officers involved in the incident was attacked while returning a group of inmates to their cells after breakfast. The riot had started.

The riot spread quickly. A gate was defective, the staff had too few officers and the communication system was outdated. There was no riot control plan, which caused confusion. Over 1,200 inmates took over four cellblocks and over forty hostages. Officers were outnumbered—there were under 100 to supervise 2,243 inmates over fifty-five acres. Homemade weapons surfaced among the inmates: knives, pipes, baseball bats and spears fashioned from scissor blades and broom handles.

With tear gas, part of the prison was regained by officers. However, some 1,200 inmates held cellblock D and the yard it faces. Ingenious inmates, using captured equipment, welded gates shut and shredded prison fire hoses.

The inmates released twelve hostages so they could get medical help. One later died. The other hostages were stripped, dressed in inmate clothing and blindfolded.

State Corrections Commissioner Russell G. Oswald met with the inmate leaders in the yard and agreed to a demand to let in the news media. He also agreed to let in outsiders such as newspaper columnist Tom Wicker, Congressman Herman Badillo, attorney William Kunstler among them, to "oversee" negotiations. As a result, there were over thirty negotiators.

The negotiators and inmates compromised on a list of twenty-eight demands, many for improved procedures and conditions. However, the inmates refused to accept any plan which did not include unconditional amnesty and transportation for inmates wishing to go to a "nonimperialist country" and the removal of the Attica superintendent.

Meanwhile, pressure from officials and the hostages' families was building to retake the prison. Following the inmates' refusal to release the hostages in exchange for the twenty-eight points, New York State Police and the National Guard attacked. In the confusion, there were inadequate advance planning, uncoordinated leadership, the use of weapons (shotguns) not conducive to precision firing, and the lack of adequate medical personnel; thirty-nine people died (including ten hostages) and eighty were wounded.

Officials learned much from Attica. The Attica Commission investigated and recommended that:

* the possibility of negotiated settlement should be explored before using lethal force.
* authorities should retake the facility without lethal force, if possible.
* negotiations will not be productive if conducted in the presence of hundreds of inmates.
* negotiations must be private, on neutral ground, without the press, and if outsiders are admitted, limitations on their function must be set.

> Source: "War at Attica: Was There No Other Way?" Time, 9/27/71, in *Prisons*, Gerald Leinwand, Ed., N.Y. Pocket Books, 1972 and *Introduction to Corrections: Fifth Edition*, by Jeanne Stinchcomb and Vernon Fox, Prentice Hall, Upper Saddle River, NJ, 1999.

The Attica riot became the mental image in contemporary times of a prison riot and public awareness of the brutality of prison riots was reinforced by the riot at the New Mexico State Penitentiary at Santa Fe.

The Santa Fe riot occurred in February, 1980. It ranks as one of the most brutal in United States penal history: thirty-three inmates were killed at the hands of fellow inmates. Death occurred by beheading, hanging and blow-torching. Inmates were raped. Many of the prison buildings were burned and trashed. [Press, et al., *Newsweek*, 1980]

Santa Fe was overcrowded and undermanned. In a prison where the capacity was 900, 1,136 inmates were housed at the time of the riot. Programs were few; most inmates were idle. Officers lacked training, especially in prison violence. Most were trained "on the job." [Mahan, 1985] On the night of the riot, only twenty-two officers were on duty. [Press, et al., *Newsweek*, 1980]

When an officer attempted to confiscate some homemade alcohol, or *raisinjack*, he was jumped by drunken prisoners. His keys were taken and inmates subsequently seized control of most of the prison. Several officers were taken hostage. The worst brutality occurred in Cellblock 4 where inmate informers were housed. Rioters cut through doors with acetylene torches and seared informers' faces and genitals. One informer had a steel rod driven ear to ear through his head. One was trussed in a hanging noose and thrown off a second tier catwalk. The jerking almost decapitated him. Another inmate beheaded a victim with a shovel. [Press, et al., *Newsweek*, 1980]

In the end, the inmates gave up and the prison was surrounded by state police and National Guard troops. The inmates did ask for media coverage. [Press, et al., *Newsweek*, 1980; Mahan, 1985] The power of the media is well known to rioters.

These two notoriously brutal riots illustrate that the possibility of a riot in a correctional facility cannot be ignored. Riots are nothing new: the first took place in 1774 at the Newgate Prison built over an abandoned mine in Simsburg, Connecticut. [Fox & Stinchcomb, 1999] Even the Walnut Street Jail experienced riots in the early 1800's and Alcatraz experienced a riot in 1946. Since 1774, over 300 prison riots have occurred and 90% of these took place during the last four decades. [Allen & Simonsen, 1998]

How do riots start? Some researchers think that an event, such as a fight, staff/inmate confrontation, inmate transfer, etc., serves as a *riot spark* and ignites an already volatile atmosphere. Others think that inmate leaders plan a riot in advance.

Sometimes, just staff enforcing rules can touch off a riot. A 1986 riot in a Florida detention center started when guards tried to stop inmates from taking the inmates' shoes and renting them back at $1.00 a day. [Barber, 1986]

The vulnerability of a facility to the occurrence of a riot or disturbance is determined by the presence of *pre-disposing factors* or factors of corrections institutions that can reinforce the potential for trouble. [Fox & Stinchcombe, 1999] These underlying causative factors are:

- institutional environment regimentation, lack of privacy, sexual deprivation, separation from loved ones and friends, gang activity, brutality, poor food, etc.;
- substandard facilities: aging institutions that are old, in need of repair and overcrowded;

CERT Team approaches scene of inmate disturbance.

- inadequate funding: lack of funding and deficit financing leads to lack of repairs, lack of programs, etc.;
- overcrowding: results in tension, anger, predatory inmates, taxing services beyond reasonable limits. As one inmate said after a 1986 riot: "they made us sleep eight inches apart... Lord, it is hot. That's why were did it [riot]." [Anderson & Lewis, 1986];
- inadequate staffing levels: increasing number of inmates being supervised by too few staff results in lack of proper supervision, lack of responses to requests and grievances, etc., and a climate of depersonalization where inmates are not treated like humans, but more like numbers or crowds;
- idleness/lack of programs: idleness and tension can be reduced through positive programs such as education, vocation and recreation. Satisfying activities can maintain emotional stability and enhance self-esteem;
- public apathy: the public's lack of concern over prison conditions and rehabilitation can result in staff taking the same attitude;
- punitive attitude: society can demand retribution and harsh punishments, and these are dangerous attitudes to take in a

tense, riot-prone facility. Supervisors must oversee staff who are positive towards their jobs and the treatment of inmates;
- inequities in the criminal justice system: tensions and frustrations increase when inmates see disparity in court sentences and what they perceive are unfair practices by the parole boards.

[Henderson, American Correctional Association, 1990]

In this environment are a variety of inmate groups: the sociopathic inmate who is anti-social and who schemes against facility staff, racial and ethnic minorities, gangs, radical organizations and inmates who are mentally disordered whose behavior can be unpredictable and bizarre. [ACA, 1990] A type of inmate, the *political prisoner*, may emerge. Not to be confused with the noted political prisoners in other countries who are imprisoned for their political beliefs, the correctional "political prisoner" is an inmate, usually in a minority group, who blames society, the rich, prejudicial courts, etc., for his incarceration. In a riot situation, this type of inmate could act as a leader for a radical or racial group.

In a flammable mix of the institution environment, overcrowding and different types of inmates living in a facility, one might ask what brings different inmates together to cause a riot or disturbance *and* what keeps this cohesiveness going?

Principles of Collective Behavior

To understand inmate unity in a riot or disturbance, facility staff must understand the *Principles of Collective Behavior*:

1. Unity: inmates are likely to unite over *common* issues: issues that affect all or most of the inmate population. Common issues could be: visiting, food, medical care, etc. An example is the 1987 disturbances in the Federal prisons at Oakdale, Louisiana, and Atlanta, Georgia. Cuban inmates/detainees held 125 hostages without harm and negotiated a uniform agreement. The central issue binding them together was the possibility of repatriation to Cuba which affected them all.
2. Frustration: agitators have an easier time recruiting inmates to their cause if inmates are angry, fearful, frustrated and feel that they have grievances. This was illustrated at Attica, where the inmates' list of demands showed frustration and anger about how the institution was run.
3. Highly charged atmosphere: when a riot or disturbance is imminent or has started, the atmosphere is ripe for rumors which

can turn a group of inmates into a mob. Police, sirens, fire equipment, news media, etc, can result in the inmates banding more tightly together.

[Henderson, ACA, 1990]

Causes of Inmate Riots: 1980-1995

The fifteen years from 1980 to 1995 are significant in the study of prison riots. There were 919 incidents; from 1900 - 1979, there were 415. Most of the prison riots in the United States since 1900 have happened in these recent fifteen years.

Out of the 919 incidents, the causes reported most were:

	Number	Percent
Confrontation with other inmates (possibly race related)	389	42.33%
Unknown causes (no clear cause reported)	140	15.23%
Rules/regulations violations	97	10.56%
Racial tension	81	8.81%
Gang related	52	5.66%

Other factors, such as confrontation with staff, security issues, food, combination of factors, etc., each accounted for less than 5%.

Source: Reid Montgomery, Jr., Ph.D., and Gordon Crews, Ph.D., *A History of Correctional Violence: An Examination of Reported Causes of Riots and Disturbances*, Lanham, MD, American Correctional Association, 1998.

Warning Signs

The inmates will be the first to know if something is about to occur and may behave in certain ways that could be noticed by any staff member. [Montgomery, Jr., and Crews, 1998] Observation of these behaviors should be documented by "information only" reports or by memorandum. These documents should be sent up the facility chain of command to upper level supervisors. All facilities should have an intelligence officer or committee whose function is to analyze the *institutional climate*. To simplify in weathercasting terms, information received about inmate behaviors could act as a barometer on the atmosphere of the inmate population: Tense? Apprehensive? Prone to violence?

Different researchers have devised different lists of warning signs. However, the underlying theme is that inmates are acting abnormally in their interactions with staff and each other.

Riot/Disturbance Warning Signs

The following list is a compendium of warning signs that a riot or disturbance may be imminent:

- Increases in:
  - — contraband found
  - — reports on misbehavior/incidents
  - — requests for cell change
  - — assaults on staff
  - — verbal defiance of staff members
  - — purchases of food from canteen/hoarding
  - — smuggling of contraband by visitors
  - — manufacture/possession of weapons
  - — sick call attendance
  - — protective custody requests/admissions
  - — thefts of food from kitchen
  - — requests for anti-anxiety or anti-depression medications
  - — requests to go to infirmary or outside hospital
  - — excessive or specific demands from inmates
  - — number of calls from family or friends about institution conditions
  - — number of grievances, especially about an unpopular policy change, called *grievance flooding*
  - — suicide attempts
  - — employee resignations

- Warnings:
  - — to family and friends not to visit
  - — to well liked staff to take leave or a sick day
  - — anonymous warnings that something is going to happen

- Decreases in:
  - — attendance at movies, meals, recreation
  - — number of inmate workers

Inmates may also avoid staff with whom they had been friendly, separate into groups along racial/ethnic lines, cluster in groups with "lookouts" posted or even change the seating arrangements in the dining hall by race, or changes in the recreation yard by designating gang/race/ethnic "territory" may occur.

Silence could be a key, especially silence in the dining hall, movies or recreation. Inmates may also mail out to family or friends personal belongings. Inflammatory or anti-authority written materials may appear.

In summary, there usually are signs that something may happen. The correctional staff has to be alert for them or anything that frequently appears out of the ordinary, especially with a large number of inmates.

Sources: "Strategic Planning for Correctional Emergencies," Lanham, MD, ACA, 1996, appearing in *A History of Correctional Violence: An Examination of Reported Causes of Riots and Disturbances*, by Reid Montgomery, Jr., Ph.D., and Gordon A. Crews, Ph.D., Lanham, MD, 1998; *A History of Correctional Violence: An Examination of Reported Causes of Riots and Disturbances*, by Reid Montgomery, Jr., Ph.D., and Gordon A. Crews, Ph.D., Lanham, MD, 1998; Henderson, James D., *Riots & Disturbances in Correctional Institutions*, Laurel, MD, ACA, 1990; Fox, Vernon and Stinchcombe, Jeanne, *Introduction to Corrections, 5th Edition*, Upper Saddle River, NJ, Prentice Hall, 1999.

Authorities believe that the best time to intervene in a riot is before strong leaders organize the inmates. However, due to the confusion and speed of these events, this may be the time where staff is disorganized and trying to mount a response. Riot control/response plans must be in place with the following goals:

- locate the disturbance;
- isolate the disturbance;
- evacuate unsafe areas of staff and non-involved inmates;
- resolution of the situation.

[Fox & Stinchcomb, 1999)

Riots should be ended by negotiation and not by use of force, if at all possible. Sadly, this is not always the case. Sometimes inmates listen to reason; sometimes force has to be shown or used. Consider these examples:

- Camp Hill Correctional Institution (PA), October, 1989: In a two-day riot, inmate complaints were overcrowding, sub-standard staff training, medical care and changes in visitation. Seventeen staff members were taken hostage; damages totaled $3 million. Through negotiation, inmates surrendered, but rioted again the next day. The second riot was ended by force.
- Montana State Prison, September, 1991: Nine inmates involved in disturbance, complaints included lack of programs, confinement to cells twenty-three hours a day, staff abuse, poor food, limited phone access, and a poor grievance system. Five staff were taken hostage; five protective custody inmates were killed. Damages totaled about $100,000.00. The event ended by use of pyrotechnic tear gas canisters by the Disturbance Control Team.
- Southern Ohio Correctional Facility (Lucasville), April, 1993: Riot lasted eleven days and nine inmates and one officer died. Complaints included resistance on religious grounds to a TB skin test, crowding, lack of programs and tighter security procedures. Damages totaled $26 million. Riot ended by negotiation.

[Montgomery, Jr., and Crews, 1998]

An increasing trend in U.S. jails and prisons has been the development of *Emergency Response Teams (ERT)*, sometimes called Disturbance Control Teams or by similar names.

An ERT is trained to respond to serious incidents, such as fights, riots, disturbances, forced cell moves, hostage situations, shakedowns, etc. Team members are trained in squad tactics, crowd control, use of force, non-lethal weapons, special weapons and emergency reaction strategies. [Henderson, 1990]

The American Correctional Association recommends that ERT members be in good standing in their agency, including being in excellent physical shape and demonstrating proficiencies in weapons, riot control techniques, use of force procedures, repelling, tactical response, and facility emergency

Correctional Emergency Response Team, Manatee County Sheriff's Office.

plans. They should be reliable, stable and of sound judgment in emergencies. Other specialized training, such as security hardware, is undertaken. [Henderson, 1990]

Correctional Emergency Response Team (CERT) and Tactical Apprehension and Control Team (TACT)

The Manatee County, Florida, Sheriff's Office has developed an effective response to inmate disturbances and other emergencies. This response is in the form of highly trained, well equipped law enforcement officers in the CERT and TACT teams.

Over fifty deputies are assigned to the CERT and TACT teams, drawing from a pool of correctional and law enforcement deputies. CERT can take care of problems inside the institution and TACT can handle outside problems.

CERT team members receive specialized training in:

- cell extractions
- riot control
- high risk transports
- shakedown (searches)
- perimeters for hostage situations.
  TACT team members are trained in these areas:
- protests or marches

- mass arrests
- riots
- parades
- general crowd control

On September 16, 1996, illegal immigrant detainees trashed POD G-1 in a protest for better food, television and sneakers. Some ninety inmates were locked down. Warnings from staff went unheeded and the trashing was repeated on the following day. CERT and TACT were called in and the inmates got quiet due to a show of force. Order was maintained and each inmate was interviewed by immigration authorities. Without the show of force and discipline of CERT and TACT, the situation could have escalated into a riot.

"A professional approach by a professional agency—ready to respond, prepared for the worst, with a single mission of maintaining peace." That is the view of the teams.

Source: Videotape: "Correctional Emergency Response Team and Tactical Apprehension Control Team, Manatee County Sheriff's Office, c. 1997. Special Thanks: Lt. Jim Conway.

Prison riots can end or be terminated by a variety of means. Available data from U.S. prison riots and disturbances from 1990-1995 indicated the following ways the events ended, in descending order of frequency:

- Use of force/assault   28.23%
- Show of force   24.70%
- Negotiation with inmates   21.56%
- Use of chemical agents   11.37%
- Voluntary surrender by inmates   9.41%
- Threats by prison administration   4.70%

(Due to rounding, total may not equal 100%.)

Source: *A History of Correctional Violence: An Examination of Reported Causes of Riots and Disturbances*, by Reid Montgomery, Jr., Ph.D., and Gordon A. Crews, Ph.D., ACA, Lanham, MD 1998.

CERT members approach the inmate.

While negotiation with inmates without the use of force or the show of force is always hoped for as a way to end the event peacefully, it is not always the case. Statistically, using and showing force have been the main factors.

All staff should be aware of the workings of the facility's riot response plan. The American Correctional Association recommends that a *riot/disturbance response plan* incorporate these elements:

- prevention techniques and recognition of signs of tension: good inmate/staff communications, staff recognition of the warning signs, proactive responses.
- chain of command: who is in charge until the regular command staff arrives is important, as is delegation of functions in the plan to personnel.

- notification and call up procedures: policies must be in place for shift supervisors, command staff and outside authorities (police, fire, etc.) to be contacted. Also, other sections in the facility such as counselors, food service, programs, etc., must be contacted and given instructions for evacuation if necessary.
- command center operations: two command centers are needed —a primary one in a totally secure area in the facility and an auxiliary or backup outside the facility in case the first is overrun. Communications to and from the command post must be established by radio, phone or intercom.
- intelligence gathering: information as to the event's location, who (inmate and staff) are involved, any injuries, etc., has to be gathered quickly *and* on an ongoing basis.
- selection/assignment of emergency squads and options for action: the plan should specify what response teams do what; ERT members have been pre-selected. Options for action must be thoroughly discussed: assault, utility cut off, negotiate, etc. If outside assistance such as police and National Guard are to be used, they must be trained personnel and know under whose authority they act and exactly what will they do.
- equipment: selection, use, accountability: the issue of batons, riot helmets, gas equipment, shotguns, etc., must be worked out in advance: who gets what. Weapons must be pre-prepared, loaded and ready. Also, since riots and disturbances are confusing and hectic, there must be a plan in place for the return and accountability of all equipment.
- follow up: after the event is resolved, the riot/disturbance should be thoroughly examined, noting good points of response and action and areas needing improvement. This information is helpful for recruit and in-service training.

[Henderson, 1990]

As each facility is different, so are the nature of riots and disturbances. No two events are exactly alike. However, there are certain basic rules of dealing with the rioting inmates. They are:

- Inmates who are rioting will not be granted illegal freedom;
- Authorities will not grant immunity or amnesty from prosecution. Prosecution will be pursued whenever possible;
- Persons under strain and duress, such as hostages, lose all authority and status. For example, if a prison shift supervisor is taken hostage, he is "no longer a shift supervisor."

View from tower #2 at Maryland House of Correction.

- Keys and weapons are never to be surrendered to inmates. Authorities shall not provide drugs or alcoholic beverages to inmates.
- Authorities will not provide transportation to assist inmates in leaving the facility.

[Henderson, 1990]

Every facility, no matter how old, how constructed, or how big, should have a plan to deal with riots and disturbances. Even a county jail holding only fifty inmates could erupt in a disturbance.

In terms of prevention, the better the facility is operated, the less riot/disturbance prone the facility is. One of the best proactive strategies is staff simply being mobile and walking around. Staff presence meets the inmate need of safety. Also, inmates can ask the staff questions and a well-informed staff workforce can dispel rumors, look into inmates' concerns, etc. By walking around, staff can also spot inmate troublemakers and the signs of possible unrest discussed previously in this chapter.

There are a variety of methods that staff can use to build a positive institutional climate and reduce inmate tension. They are:

- *Grievance process.* A method for resolving inmate complaints in a mature and reasonable manner, this mechanism gives inmates a forum for their complaints. Complaints are filed in writing and are either investigated by staff and a reply given to the inmate or a hearing with staff and inmate takes place.

- *Ombudsperson.* This is a staff person who will resolve problems and give satisfactory solutions to inmates' problems. In the military, a similar position is inspector general.
- *Inmate councils*: The inmates elect representatives, who then discuss with the inmate population their problems, concerns, and anxieties. The representatives then bring this information to the council and subsequently the warden.
- *Inmate inventories.* Based on Likert's scale of measurement, the staff can measure how tense and riot prone the climate is. Questions are asked of the inmates and the responses contain the terms "easy" and "difficult" at each end of a scale having spaces from 1 to 5. Items could be:
  — opportunity to see the medical staff;
  — chance to speak to officer in housing unit;
  — opportunity to sign up for programs.
  — Inmates mark their feelings using the easy to difficult five point scale. Random surveys are taken periodically and the responses measured. If the staff, for example, see that 90% of inmates surveyed indicated that it is difficult to speak to an officer in their housing area, frustration may be building.

[Montgomery, Jr. & Crews, 1998]

- Staff training: staff training on riot prevention must be ongoing, emphasizing techniques to reduce tension and enhance security.
- Programs: positive programs that promote self-help and self-esteem are healthy outlets for inmates instead of idleness. Recreation programs are always beneficial in reducing built-up tension.

Anti-Violence Programs

It is possible to teach inmates how to deal with life's problems (including incarceration) without violence. At New York's Elmira Correctional Facility, inmates can participate in a twenty-two hour workshop called the Alternative to Violence Project (AVP) where they learn how to deal with prison violence. Subjects that are taught include examination of self-violence, breaking down barriers, relaxation and fun, building community spirit and proper intervention techniques. Inmates learn that there are other ways to deal with problems other than assaults. [Montgomery, Jr. and Crews, 1998]

In the Pennsylvania Department of Corrections, a conflict resolution training program for inmates was developed prior to 1980. Originally designed as a program resource for aggressive inmates, the program now trains inmates and officers in conflict resolution and positive communications. Conflict resolution training teaches listening, problem solving and mediation. Items of emphasis include anger management/control, forgiveness and nonviolence. Officers give the training high praise and inmates have noticed positive changes in formerly "by the book" disciplinarian-type officers. From 1980 to 1994, over 1,500 staff and inmates in the Pennsylvania Department of Corrections took the training. During the 1989 riot at Pennsylvania's Camp Hill state prison, inmates in the New Values substance abuse program who had gone through the training were the only inmates who did not take part in the riot. Also, they helped officers so that they would not be assaulted. [Love, 1994]

Summary

All correctional facilities are prone to riots and/or disturbances. Riots and disturbances are not interchangeable — riots are more large scale and deadly. Notorious riots in U.S. history include riots at Attica, New York, and Santa Fe, New Mexico.

Pre-disposing factors such as negative aspects of the institutional environment and punitive attitudes by staff can help to cause a riot. Inmates will come together through the Principles of Collective Behavior. There are usually warning indicators to a riot or disturbance that staff must be aware of. Riots may be either planned or "sparked." Most events end by a use of or show of force. Every facility should have a riot plan and engage in pro-active activities such as inmate programs, grievance procedures, etc., which are designed to head off inmate frustration and solve problems.

Review Questions

1. What are the differences between a riot, a disturbance and an incident?

2. What recommendations came from the Attica Commission?

3. Name five pre-disposing factors of a riot.

4. What are the Principles of Collective Behavior?

5. What was the leading cause of prison riots from 1980-1995?

6. Name five warning signs of a riot.

7. What are several components of an effective riot/disturbance response plan?

Terms/Concepts

Riot

Disturbance

Incident

Attica

Raisinjack

Grievance process

Ombudsperson

Anti-violence programs

Riot Spark

Pre-disposing factors

Political prisoner

Principles of Collective Behavior

Institutional climate

Emergency response teams

Inmate councils

Inmate inventories

Grievance flooding

Riot/disturbance response plans

References

Allen, Harry and Clifford Simonsen, *Corrections in America: An Introduction*, 8th Ed., Upper Saddle River, NJ, Prentice Hall, 1998.

Anderson, John and Nancy Lewis, "D.C. Trying to Move Hundreds of Inmates," *Washington Post*, 7/11/86.

Barber, Ben, "Inmates shipped out after riot," *USA Today*, 5/30/86.

"California Prison Riot," *Washington Post*, 2/22/78.

"Chronology of Major Incidents at Lorton," *Washington Post*, 7/11/86.

"Correctional Emergency Response Team and Tactical Apprehension Response Team," videotape, Manatee County Sheriff's Office, c. 1997.

Dictionary of Criminal Justice Terms, American Correctional Association, Lanham, MD, 1998.

Freeman, R., "Strategic Planning for Correctional Emergencies," (appearing in Montgomery & Crews), ACA, Lanham, MD, 1996.

Gregg, Sandra, "Va. Jail Aide Killed, 1 Hurt in Disturbance," *Washington Post*, 12/26/82.

Henderson, James D., *Riots and Disturbances in Correctional Institutions*, Lanham, MD, ACA, 1990 (3rd Ed.).

Leinwand, Gerald, *Prisons*, "War at Attica: Was There No Other Way?" from *Time*, 9/27/71, N.Y. Pocket Books, 1972.

Love, Bill, "Program Curbs Prison Violence Through Conflict Resolution," *Corrections Today*, ACA, 8/94.

Mahan, Sue, "An 'Orgy of Brutality' at Attica and the 'Killing Ground' at Santa Fe: A Comparison of Prison Riots," in *Prison Violence in America*, Brasswell, Michael, *et al.* (Editors), Cincinnati, Anderson, 1985.

Montgomery, Reid, Jr., Ph.D., and Gordon Crews, Ph.D., *A History of Correctional Violence: An Examination of Reported Causes of Riots and Disturbances*, Lanham, MD, ACA, 1998.

"Ossining Prison is Secured as 2-Day Siege is Ended," *Washington Post*, 1/12/83.

Press, Aric, *et al.*, "The Killing Ground," *Newsweek*, 2/18/80.

Stinchcombe, Jeanne and Vernon Fox, *Introduction to Corrections*, 5th Ed., Upper Saddle River, NJ, Prentice Hall, 1999.

Wagner, Arle, "9 Named in Montgomery Jail Melee," *Washington Times* (Metropolitan Times), 11/3/94.

Chapter 14

The History of the Courts and the Rights of Inmates

This chapter and the next will discuss the issue of inmate rights. This is a complicated issue—dealing with a wide range of subjects from inmate rights under the Constitution to frivolous lawsuits to recent Court decisions that dictate how correctional staff will ensure that inmates have certain rights.

Although the subject of inmates' rights can also be technical, these two chapters will present a practical, line staff approach to inmate rights discussing these areas:

- history of the courts concerning the rights of inmates;
- emergence of the jailhouse lawyer and law libraries;
- liability of staff and negligence;
- tests: clear and present danger, compelling state need;
- synopsis of inmate rights;
- how staff can protect themselves from inmate suits.

The whole subject of inmate suits and litigation is a changing one, involving state courts, the federal courts, the Supreme Court and the U.S. Congress. Due to this changing nature, the discussions in these two chapters will serve as a general guide. All corrections facilities should have access to a legal resource —an attorney—who can keep the staff advised and assist with training.

Another reason for access to attorneys is that the issue of inmates' civil rights is a complex one involving procedures, court rules and documentation. These areas involve forms, deadlines and procedures for inmates to follow and qualified legal help can advise facility staff what inmate's rights are and how they can exercise them.

For correctional staff, the first step in learning the civil rights of inmates is acceptance of these facts:

1. Inmates do not lose all civil rights when they become incarcerated;
2. The courts have granted certain civil rights to inmates and they can exercise them, whether correctional staff agree or not;

225

3. Under certain circumstances or conditions, if staff cause these rights to be violated, they can be held liable and consequences may include loss of job and/or paying monetary damages.

Acceptance of all of these points is crucial to understanding inmates' rights. Concerning number 2, common phrases among corrections officers are that "inmates have too many rights," and "inmates have more rights than officers." These phrases are the result of frustration and lack of understanding.

The granting of inmate rights by the courts have resulted in better treatment for inmates resulting in higher professional standards for facilities and better training, as will be made clear in this chapter.

It is not surprising that surveys of correctional officers reflect these attitudes. This may be the result of court decisions that compel administrators to implement policies and procedures consistent with inmate rights, while working conditions and rights of employees take secondary priority. In a survey of 254 officers in four different prisons conducted in 1996, the following responses were given to the statement: "Inmates have more rights than officers."

Strongly agree	78%
Agree	14%
Strongly disagree	1%
Disagree	7%
Not sure	0%
	100%

[Stevens, 1998]

Evolution of Inmates' Rights

Inmates did not always enjoy civil rights as compared with the state of inmate litigation today. Some researchers say that we are in the midst of an *inmate litigation explosion*, or more simply, inmates are filing suits more frequently and correctly than in past decades. For clarification, consider that in 1962, only 1,500 lawsuits alleging various complaints against correctional administrators and staff were filed by federal prisoners. This number had tripled by 1987. In the state prisons, over 12,000 legal actions (petitions and suits) were filed by inmates in 1971. By 1987, the annual number of filings by state inmates was almost 33,000. [Thomas,

1988, Champion, 1990] In 1996, BJS statistics said federal and state inmates filed more than 42,215 civil rights actions; in 1995, the federal district courts disposed of almost 38,000 civil rights complaints filed by state inmates. Not surprisingly, approximately 1% were resolved in the inmate's favor. [Collins & Grant, 1998]

Correctional staff have gotten better in defending themselves from inmate litigators. Through recordkeeping, training and awareness of inmates' civil rights, a well-managed institution has an excellent chance of successfully defending itself against inmate litigation. Significant changes in staff training, hiring and correctional management have resulted from the courts and corrections officials trying to "head off" inmate lawsuits. [Hopper, 1985, Champion, 1990]

Unlike other citizens, prisoners have not always enjoyed the protection of the Constitution and especially the Bill of Rights. For many years, inmates were looked upon as human beings who were always to be considered sub-standard. In fact, in the 1871 Virginia Case of *Ruffin v. Commonwealth,* the judge stated that "prisoners have no more rights than slaves," reflecting public opinion at the time that not only was punishment to be harsh, but without certain rights. [Bronstein, 1980, Champion, 1990] The Thirteenth Amendment protected this, forbidding slavery "except as punishment for crime whereof the party shall have been duly convicted." [Lund, *et al.,* 1995]

Prisoners have been "guinea pigs" in various social experiments and medical research projects. During World War I, for example, prisoners were used to test the physical effects of a variety of gases and wartime products. In 1980, prisoners in several prisons were used in experimental drug research. Until the early 1940's, sterilization of certain prisoners was practiced in some state prisons because it was believed at the time that criminal behavior was hereditary. [Champion, 1990] The National Commission for the Protection of Human Subjects has recommended a ban on on-therapeutic drug research using inmates and the U.S. Food and Drug Administration has extended to inmates the right to voluntarily participate in such experiments based on informed consent. [Schroeder, 1983, Champion, 1990]

To put inmate rights in perspective, the evolution of inmate rights can be sectioned into three periods or eras: the hands off, the hands on and the one hand on/one hand off eras. [Collins, 1997]

The *hands off era* lasted for most of the history of corrections in the United States, ending by 1970. During this time, the courts did not get involved with inmate litigation. The reasoning by jurists was that they knew nothing about correctional administration and the guiding concept of *federalism* which means that federal courts should avoid interfering with the activities of state and local government wherever possible. [Collins, 1997]

During this era, correctional authorities wielded much power and enjoyed freedom from court inquiry; public opinion was basically apathetic with little concern for the welfare of those incarcerated. Training was minimal, if conducted at all.

Inmate complaints went unheeded in this era. The following cases are examples of conditions in U.S. prisons and jails at that time as well as the courts' response:

- In 1951, a case involving a federal jail in Alaska was examined by an Alaskan court. The jail was old, built of wood frame and up to forty inmates were housed in a room so small that less than nineteen square feet per inmate was allowed. Only twenty bunk beds were in the room, there was only one shower and one toilet and heat was provided by an unsafe wood stove. There was only one exit. Young inmates (age sixteen) were housed there. The judge agreed that the facility was a "fabulous obscenity," and stated that it was not fit for human habitation. However, no Eighth Amendment (cruel and unusual punishment) finding was concluded; the judge, while noting the poor conditions, said that the inmates' living conditions were better than U.S. soldiers fighting in Korea. The only possible relief was to release prisoners. [Collins, 1997, *Ex Parte Pickens,* 101 F. Supp. 285 (D. Alas., 1951)].
- An Alabama case dealt with inadequate medical care. Inmates handled both treatment and records. Examples included a maggot infested wound that went untreated for twenty days; an incontinent inmate patient was forced to sit on a bench as not to stain his bedding and as a result, he frequently fell and his leg was eventually amputated. [Collins, 1997, *Newman v. Alabama,* 503 F.2d 1320 (5th Circuit, 1974)].
- The state of Arkansas was the site of an infamous controversy concerning the brutal conditions in the state prison system. Inmates were subjected to horrible barbaric acts and forced by torture to comply to prison rules. Torture methods included starvation, flogging and shoving needles under inmates' fingernails. [See box.] In 1970, the U.S. Supreme Court said that the Arkansas state prison system was guilty of committing barbarous acts against inmates in the case of *Holt v. Sarver,* 302 F. Supp. 362 (E.D. Arkansas, 1970). This case signaled a new approach by the courts to prison reform, calling the prison system at the Cummins Prison Farm "to be not only

shocking to 'standards of decency' but immoral and criminal as well." [Champion, 1990; Lund, *et al.*, 1995]

The Tucker Telephone

The device called the Tucker Telephone symbolizes the inhuman conditions of the Arkansas prison system in the late 1960's which led to the *Arkansas prison scandal.*

Named for the Tucker Prison Farm, the "telephone" consisted of an electrical generator taken from an old crank-type telephone. The "problem" inmate [in the opinion of the staff] was strapped to a table by physicians and officers. Electrodes were fastened to the penis, testicles and toes. Electrical charges were sent into the body when the crank was turned. The resulting shocks were unbearable and if an inmate was deemed especially unruly, he suffered "long distance calls." Some prisoners suffered psychological disorders and irreparable testicle damage. Some inmates were, according to Murton and Hyams, "literally driven out of their minds."

The "telephone" was also used by the staff to extract information from inmates. The device was designed by one of the prison superintendents. Besides the telephone, there were other poor conditions — inmates appeared about forty pounds underweight, underwear was not issued, mattresses and bedding were filthy and rotten. Shoes were not issued and inmates had three choices: go barefoot, wear rubber boots or buy shoes. Two pairs of socks were issued twice a year. Shower and toilet areas were filthy and stank.

In an effort to clean up the prison system, the governor appointed Tom Murton to head the prisons. Murton, a former criminology professor at Southern Illinois University, uncovered the hell of the Arkansas prisons. It was an uphill battle. State officials were skeptical: one said that he didn't believe that "stuff" because "ninety-five percent of the complaints of convicts are lies." Another said that "Arkansas had the best prison system in the United States." Fearing political embarrassment, Murton was fired by the administration in 1968. With the case of *Holt v. Sarver* in 1970, the scandal finally ended when the Supreme Court agreed with inmate complaints.

Sources: Insiardi, James A., 1987: *Criminal Justice, 2nd Ed.*, N.W.: Hartcourt, Brace and Jovanovich*; Murton, Thomas O. And Joe Hyams, 1976, *Accomplices to Crime: The*

Arkansas Prison Scandal, N.Y. Grove Press*; Schroeder, Kathleen, 1983, "A Recommendation to the FDA Concerning Drug Research on Prisoners," *Southern California Law Review*, 56: 969-1000*; Champion, Dean, *Corrections in the United States: A Contemporary Perspective, 1990*: Prentice Hall, Englewood Cliffs, NJ; and Murton, Tom and Joe Hyams, *Inside Prison USA*, 1969, NY Grove Press.
*cited in Champion.

With the attention to substandard prison conditions that these cases generated and the advent of the civil rights cases of the 1960's, the hands off period started to end. More attention was being given to the rights of minorities and the underprivileged. Lawsuits by inmates started finding their way into the courts, sometimes with or without attorneys.

With the courts beginning to pay attention to inmate litigation, the *hands on era* began and lasted through the 1970's. The courts began to respond to conditions cases, disciplinary due process issues, religious freedoms and many issues under the Bill of Rights. Due to these cases, inmates gained new rights, the opinion of which are still being debated today. [Collins, 1997]

A serious problem with the hands off era was that for many years, the courts did not interfere in corrections and now the trend was reversed. In the confusion that followed, in some cases, the courts became very detailed in their decisions on how correctional facilities should be operated — from food, prison uniforms, double celling, etc. However, courts began to notice and rely on professional standards from organizations such as the American Correctional Association. [Collins, 1997]

During this period, the media became a method to which the public could see conditions in prisons and the cases which were addressing them. For example, the case of *Ruiz v. Estelle*, 1980 F. 2d 115, was profiled in *Newsweek* in 1979. This case concerned the lack of medical care in the Texas Department of Corrections. The suit combined eight inmates' complaints, alleging that an inmate whose arms were amputated in a farm machinery accident went without prompt medical care and was raped at the hospital by another patient at the prison hospital. Other complaints included brutal conditions in solitary confinement; suturing without anesthesia an inmate who had mutilated himself; and an inmate, a former truck driver, performing surgery. [Bonventre and Marbach, 1979]

Inmates took advantage of the courts' empathy during the hands on era. Between 1966 and 1996, the number of lawsuits filed by inmates in federal courts rose from 218 to 68,235. [Fox & Stinchcomb, 1999]

The last era, the *one hand on/one hand off era* represents a compromise between the first two eras. Sometimes called the *restrained-hands approach*, courts sought to balance the rights of the inmates against the security needs of the correctional facility. Courts are not as quick to impose their own solutions to problems; they give correctional staff and administrators an opportunity to correct the problem. [Fox & Stinchcomb, 1999]

The restrained hands approach era is where corrections has been since the early 1980's. [Collins, 1997] It is a realistic approach: the courts are not getting too involved so as to hamper the legitimate efforts of correctional staff. Courts look to see if restrictions on an inmate's perceived constitutional rights meet a *legitimate penological interest* or a function or need promoting the safety and security of the facility. [Fox & Stinchcomb, 1999]

Another way to look at the balancing test is to state that no one, citizen or inmate, has an absolute right to constitutional protection and can do anything he/she wants. The *balancing test* weights the competing interest of the state (usually security) against the individual constitutional rights of the inmate. In these types of cases, no one is right or wrong, just one side is more right than the other and that is the direction scales tip. [Lund, *et al.*, 1995]

So, how right or correct is the corrections side? Legal experts recognize the following legitimate concerns that represent the "state's" interest in detention.

- Security: policies and procedures that prevent escapes, injury, death, riots, the introduction/manufacture of contraband and promote the safety and welfare of inmates and staff;
- Management and custody: Utilization of space and facility resources, including manpower;
- Order: procedures and policies to maintain order and discipline, such as inmate compliance with rules and regulations;
- Punishment: permits the abridgement or denial of privileges so as to maintain order or to deter wrongdoing;
- Rehabilitation: concerns the treatment of the inmate for institutional adjustments and/or the future reintegration into society; the positive and constructive influence over the inmate population must be maintained;

- Resource limitations: this is considered by the courts to be the weakest of all justifications when balanced against inmate rights. Some courts will not consider resource limitations such as lack of funding, for example. Courts want to know how a constitutional right will be met, instead of whether it will be met, especially concerning budget.

[Lund, *et al.*, 1995]:

These concerns, in the courts' eyes, allow correctional administrators to enforce disciplinary rules, provide programs, use resources to meet the space demands of a growing inmate population and to conduct searches and screen mail for contraband.

The balancing test takes these concerns and balances them against the inmate request (through litigation) that a constitutional right be granted to him. The balancing test has four basic parts:

1. Is there a rational, valid or reasonable connection between the restriction (Rule, policy, etc.) and the "legitimate penological interests" of the facility? For example, in one case, a group of Muslims sued over a rule that prohibited them from attending an Islamic service. The inmates were in a "gang minimum" and were required to work outside the facility. This conflicted with the time of the service. The Supreme Court found that there was a valid connection between the restriction and the security of the facility.
2. Are there alternative ways available to the inmate to exercise his rights in question? In the above case, the Supreme Court found there were: other Muslim services, access to an Imam (Muslim religious leader) and permission to have special religious diets.
3. If the request is granted or the right is accommodated, will it have a "ripple effect" on staff, resources, and so forth? In this case, the Supreme Court said it did not.
4. The reasonableness of the rule or restriction will be shown if there is no obvious or easy alternatives to meet the inmates' interest at a minimal cost to the facility.

[Collins, 1997] [*O'Lone v. Shabazz*, 107 S.Ct. 2400 (1987)]

Besides the *Shabazz* case, a second case, *Turner v. Safley*, 107 S.Ct. 2254 (1987), further clarified the balancing test. In *Turner*, inmates sued, challenging the rules prohibiting inmate to inmate mail and inmate marriages. The Supreme Court agreed with the mail restriction, but not to the marriage rule. The balancing test became known as the *Turner* test. [Collins, 1997]

Although the term "legitimate penological interest" is vague and can include a lot, another term is related. It is: *compelling government interest*: anything that represents a serious threat to a facility's security, order or discipline. For example, contraband would be included under this definition. [ACA, 1998]

Realistically, for correctional staff, the restrained hands approach is common sense. Inmates have limited rights; limitations are imposed by correctional staff pursuant to an important goal—security of the facility and the safety of all who live and work there. Inmates, through court actions, have tried to get some of these limitations lifted, as we will see in Chapter 15.

Also, inmate lawsuits have exposed wrongful conditions and actions by staff, such as in the *Holt* and *Ruiz* cases which were discussed previously.

Correctional staff encounter many inmates who state that they will file suit. Some inmates are quiet and sincere; otherwise are more threatening and try to intimidate staff, especially new officers. Inmates can sue if they want, like any other citizen, but filing suit and winning are too different things.

With the emergence of inmates' civil rights and their demands to be heard, there came into prominence the political prisoner (see Chapter 13) and the *jailhouse lawyer* or, as some staff say, the "writ writer."

A jailhouse lawyer is an inmate who is proficient in writing writs, briefs and filing court actions. He/she has no formal training in the law. The action of a jailhouse lawyer include violation of inmates' rights, representation of inmates in disciplinary cases, appeals of disciplinary cases and other legal matters such as assisting in their own defense in court. [ACA, 1998]

Jailhouse lawyers often assist inmates in these matters and the courts have allowed such assistance. Jailhouse lawyers are not to be underestimated. Many know what forms to file, what cases to research and what procedures to follow in getting their case—civil rights lawsuit or criminal—into court. Correctional officers have found themselves in federal courts facing inmates' lawsuits accusing them of using excessive force, denying them religious freedoms, using too many restrictions on mail, denying them medical care and so on. Just because an officer is sued does not make the inmate's case valid, but care and caution should be taken towards inmates who know their way around a law library.

According to legal experts, inmates generally file litigation which are in these categories:

- *habeas corpus actions*: the inmate claims that he/she is incarcerated illegally or in custody in violation of a constitutional right. A habeas corpus action usually attacks a court action or agency which is responsible for holding the inmate in custody. Because a habeas corpus petition names the custodian as a defendant, such as the sheriff, warden, etc., a corrections staff name may appear on the document. An inmate sometimes will challenge a disciplinary hearing and may name an individual employee.

- *torts*: usually filed in state court, a tort action seeks damages when the plaintiff (inmate) is owed some duty by the defendant (corrections staff). The tort claims negligence [see box] on part of the defendant. Claims in tort actions include medical malpractice, failure to protect the inmate from harm and improper supervision, training and assignment of staff resulting in harm to the inmate.

[Collins, 1997]

Negligence

The term negligence is widely used in inmate legal actions. Basically, the inmate telling the court that the corrections staff owed a duty to protect, the treatment of a medical problem, etc., and it was not performed.

Perhaps the best definition is by Dean Champion:

Tort [action] involving a duty from one person [staff] to another [inmate], to act as a reasonable person might be expected to act, or the failure to act when the action is appropriate; failure to exercise reasonable care toward another. Gross negligence includes willful, wanton and reckless acts, without regard for consequences and are totally unreasonable.

Negligence can take three forms—negligence itself is failure to act as a reasonable person would. For example, an officer pulling inmates for programs forgets to check the "keep separate list." Two inmate enemies come into contact and one assaults the other. *Gross negligence* are actions of reckless disregard of the consequences. For example, two inmates are known enemies and officers fail to keep them apart at the scene. They later fight and one suffers serious injuries. *Willful negligence* is when a staff member intentionally does something to cause harm. For example, an officer is angry at an inmate who cursed at him the day before. The next day, the inmate slips on a wet floor and breaks his arm. The officer waits two hours to call for a medical officer.

All correctional staff should receive training in negligence and how failing to do a proper job may lead to an inmate lawsuit.

Sources: Champion, Dean,
*Corrections in The United
States: A Contemporary*

Perspective, 1990, Englewood
Cliffs, N.J., Prentice Hall; Sutty,
Thomas, et al., *Legal Issues for
Correctional Staff Correspon-
dence Course*, 1994, Lanham,
MD, American Correctional
Association.

- *civil rights actions*: Most inmate lawsuits which involve correctional staff are civil rights lawsuits brought under a federal
  law, Title 42 United States Code § 1983 (42 USC 1983) or
  known as the Civil Rights Act of 1871, or more commonly,
  § 1983. This law was interpreted in the 1960's by the U.S.
  Supreme Court as a legal remedy that allowed citizens to sue
  state and local officials when their policies, practices and specific acts were below the standards of the United States Constitution. Later, the Supreme Court decided that inmates in
  our nation's jails and prisons could challenge conditions of
  their confinement on the premise that such conditions violated
  their constitutional rights. [Hanson & Daley, 1995]

42 USC 1983

Every person who, under color of any statute, ordinance, regulation, custom or usage of any state or territory or the District of Columbia, subjects or causes to be subjected, any citizen of the United
States or any person within the jurisdiction thereof to the deprivation of any rights, privileges or immunities secured by the Constitution
and laws, shall be liable to the party injured in an action at law, suit
in equity or other proper proceeding for redress.

Source: Roger A. Hanson and
Henry W.K. Daley, *Challenging
the Conditions of Prisons and
Jails*: A Report on § 1983 Litigation, NCJ 151652, Discussion
Paper: Bureau of Justice Statistics, January, 1995.

Basically, § 1983, as inmates call it, says that if a government official
(like a correctional officer) deny inmates' protection of their constitutional
rights, they (the inmates) can sue and collect damages (money).

Inmates like to file civil rights suits or 1983 actions rather than tort suits
for several reasons. Historically, civil rights suits are brought before federal courts because federal courts have shown more sympathy to inmate

claims than state courts, where torts are filed. Also, the scope of relief is broader in a civil rights case than in a tort. There is no injunctive relief in a tort and state law sometimes limits damages. State law may also immunize officials from damages or may not allow punitive damages. Finally, tort suits do not provide for attorneys' fee awards, which are allowed in civil rights cases. [Collins, 1997]

Inmates file federal civil rights cases in federal district courts. Each federal district court is located in a larger area called a circuit. The district courts are the lowest level of the federal court system. Within each circuit are several districts and there are thirteen federal court circuits in the United States, dividing up ninety-six federal district courts. Circuit courts are also called the United States Courts of Appeals, the second level of the federal judiciary. The third and final level is the United States Supreme Court. The Supreme Courts hears selected cases on appeal from the lower courts; its ruling is binding on all federal and state courts. [ACA, 1994]

Nature of Complaints: § 1983 Suits

Recent research has given corrections professionals insight on the nature of complaints of § 1983 litigation. The National Center for State Courts, in conjunction with the United States Bureau of Justice Statistics (BJS), studied § 1983 cases disposed of in 1992 by U.S. District Courts located in Alabama, California, Florida, Indiana, Louisiana, Missouri, New York, Pennsylvania and Texas. These states have nearly 50% of U.S. § 1983 litigation and are representative of the entire range of § 1983 nationwide.

In an examination of the subjects of corrections activities being challenged, the study found the following issues and corresponding rates of frequency:

- Medical treatment: failure to provide back braces,   17%
  corrective shoes, dentures, necessary surgeries, etc.

- Physical security: excessive force by officers, failure   21%
  to protect from assaults and rapes by other inmates,
  harassments and threats by staff, no prevention of
  inmate property theft, unreasonable body cavity
  searches.

- Due process issues: improper procedures in   13%
  administrative segregation placement, intra-prison
  transfers, disciplinary actions, classification.

- Living conditions: diets that are not nutritionally   4%
  adequate, inadequate clothing, denial/limitations
  of exercise.

- Physical conditions: overcrowding, inadequate   9%
  toilets/showers and sanitation, excessive noise,
  fail to protect against AIDS exposure and tobacco
  smoke.
- Denial of religious expression, assembly, visitation   4%
  and racial discrimination.
- Denial of access to courts, law libraries, lawyers,   7%
  plus interferences with telephone calls and mail.
- Harassment and assault by arresting officer.   3%
- Invalid conviction or sentence.   12%
- Other: denial of trial, denial of parole, etc.   11%

  TOTAL   100%

Source: Roger A. Hanson and
Henry W.K. Daley, *Challenging
the Conditions of Prisons and
Jails*: A Report on § 1983
Litigation, NCJ 151652, Bureau
of Justice Statistics, January,
1995.

Most § 1983 cases end in court dismissal (74%). Motions by the defendant (correctional staff) account for 20% of dismissals. [Hanson & Daley, 1995]

To keep the burden of inmates' lawsuits manageable, courts attempt to weed out frivolous lawsuits. A *frivolous lawsuit* is litigation that has been filed, but lacks legal merit. [ACA, 1998] An inmate can threaten to sue or may even file suit, but that *does not* mean that the court sees merit in the case.

Frivolous Lawsuits

Inmates, including some who have considered themselves jailhouse lawyers, have sued correctional staffs for a variety of reasons. Here are some examples from Virginia, Florida and Ohio:

Virginia

- One inmate sued for a court order which would direct prison officials to provide him with Rockport shoes instead of the brand issued by the prison system.

- One inmate sued three times, claiming that he is too embarrassed to use the toilet in front of his cellmate; he demanded a single cell.
- One inmate set fire to his cell, then filed suit, alleging that the prison staff had failed to protect him from himself and demanded $250,000 in damages! Further investigation revealed that when his request to immediately meet with the staff psychologist was not met, he set fire to himself to gain correctional officers' attention.

Florida

- An inmate sued the state because he was not allowed to have soap on a rope.
- An inmate sued the state because he preferred wood floors when playing basketball and the prison gym had a concrete floor.
- An inmate wolfed down his Thanksgiving turkey dinner. He then sued the state on religious grounds claiming that the stuffing served had bits of turkey in it and that violated his religion.

One jailhouse lawyer in Virginia has filed more than 120 lawsuits. He told a newspaper that the filing of frivolous lawsuits is "part of the game." He claims that since becoming incarcerated in the early 1970's, he is the victim of a continuing campaign by unknown "hit inmates." He claims that the "hit inmates" are ordered by the Department of Corrections because he is a "writ writer."

Some states have taken action to cut down on frivolous lawsuits. In 1996, Ohio enacted a law that has provisions to make inmates reconsider the filing of frivolous litigation. Inmates are required to pay at least part of the filing fee. Also, courts have procedures by which a lawsuit could be declared invalid. What led to this action was that 800 inmate lawsuits were filed in Ohio in 1995; 95% of these were dismissed. According to Ohio's Attorney General, the defense against these suits cost $1.7 million. In 1997, Virginia began taking similar steps to curb nonsense lawsuits, after the Attorney General stated that his office spends over $28,000 annually defending the Commonwealth.

Sources: Fugate, Larry, "New law cracks down on frivolous inmate lawsuits," *Columbus*

Daily Reporter, 7/19/96, http://
sddtsvn.sddt.com/Columbus/
files3/9607193; "Florida's
Attorney General Bob
Butterworth's Top 10 Frivolous
Prison Inmate Lawsuits," http://
www.mindsprng.com/~iam392/
lawsuit.htm; James S. Gilmore,
III, Virginia Attorney General
News Release: "Attorney General Gilmore Seeks Limits on
Frivolous Inmate Lawsuits; Releases 'Top 10' List," 1/29/97,
http://www.state.va.us/~oag/
pres/frivsuit.htm

Inmate lawsuits look for two things from corrections officials: liability and damages.

To clarify, there are fundamental differences between criminal law and civil law. Criminal law actions are initiated by the state because of harm to society and seeks punishment. Civil law actions are started by a victim, due to harm to a particular person and seeks compensation. [Fox & Stinchcomb, 1999]

In the simplest terms, *liability* means "the responsibility for one's own behavior," based on the term liable which means "obligated or responsible according to law." [ACA, 1998] To be liable in a civil rights case, a defendant (correctional staff) must have caused the constitutional violation on the inmates or have caused the injury. Under § 1983, liability is imposed when someone such as a corrections officer "causes a constitutional violation" [such as denial of religious freedom]. Courts will focus on this aspect of the suit. [Collins, 1997]

While corrections officers and staff can be subject to *criminal liability* if litigation proves that an employee on the job broke a specific law or criminal statute, most inmate litigation involves *civil liability*—the violation of civil rights resulting in the payment of monetary damages or compensation. [Fox and Stinchcomb, 1999]

Inmates know that the average line staff member has limited ability to pay damages so they file suits that challenge policies and procedures set forth by agency heads and supervisors. In other words, the agency who hires and supervises the employee can also be held liable. This concept is known as indirect liability or *vicarious liability* which goes beyond the actions of the line staff. [Fox and Stinchcomb, 1999]

Vicarious Liability

The responsibility for another's actions or failures to act [omissions]. Correctional supervisors are held responsible for the actions of employees under their supervision.

Source: *Dictionary of Criminal Justice Terms*, American Correctional Association, 1998, Lanham, MD.

Vicarious liability is a result of a situation where someone other than an employee, such as a supervisor, knew or should have known what was happening or about to happen, but did nothing to prevent the situation. As a result, the lack of action was the proximate cause of harm, injury or death to the inmate. [Fox and Stinchcomb, 1999]

For example, a shift supervisor knows that a certain housing unit holds hard core inmates that frequently fight and security must be maintained at all times. A new officer, a rookie, reports for duty and tells the supervisor that he has not gone through training. The supervisor assigns him to the housing unit, saying that he needs a "warm body" on that post. No instructions or pass on information are given. The rookie officer leaves his post for an hour to take a break. One inmate then attacks another, who suffers a broken jaw and concussion. Is the shift supervisor subject to vicarious liability? *Yes.* He knew of a potentially harmful situation and by putting an untrained officer in that unit, the situation was a proximate cause of the assault. Perhaps the inmate would not have assaulted the other if a seasoned veteran officer (or maybe two) had been assigned to the unit.

Three key elements of vicarious liability are basically three critical jobs performed by corrections supervisors:

1. Failure to train: the employing agency could be held liable if the employee being sued could prove that he/she was not properly training in their job.
2. Negligent supervision: a supervisor would be liable if he/she knew of a situation where an employee was doing something wrong and this was not corrected.
3. Negligent employment or retention: closely linked to negligent supervision, a problem employee is hired and/or retained on the job. For example, an employee with a poor performance record for sleeping on the job is hired. One night, he falls asleep on post and an inmate suffers a fall and is not immediately treated, resulting in complications. Another employee

has a record of ignoring inmates' complaints. He ignores an inmate's request to move and as a result, the inmate is assaulted. In both cases, the supervisors, as well as the employees could be held liable, especially if it can be proven that these problems were known and supervisors did nothing.
[Fox and Stinchcomb, 1999]

A recent case of vicarious liability occurred in Boston in 1998, where a federal court jury awarded $37,500 to an inmate who claimed he was harassed by a prison officer who he had shot in the head in 1991. The shooting victim later became a prison officer. The inmate said supervisors did nothing while the officer kept the inmate awake at night and beat him twice in the shower. The case is being appealed. [*Chicago Tribune*, October 1998 in *Keeper's Voice*, Fall, 1998]

In civil rights cases, an inmate or plaintiff may ask for the following types of relief from the courts:

- *Injunctive relief or injunction*: a court order that orders the defendant (corrections agency) to stop doing something or to do something. For example, an inmate sues and wins, claiming that the jail staff had inadequate medical treatment due to short staffing. The court, by issuing an injunction, orders the sheriff to immediately hire more medical officers and implement a new staffing/coverage plan.
- *Declaratory relief*: the court issues a statement declaring that inmates have certain rights. For example, an inmate sues and wins over the issue that his/her religious rights under Judaism were violated because the prison has no provisions for Jewish services or access to a rabbi. The court declares that Jewish inmates have the same rights as Christian and Muslim inmates.
- *Monetary damages*: monetary damages paid in civil rights cases are the same as paid out in tort suits: nominal, compensatory and punitive.

  — *Nominal damages* means that the defendant pays the plaintiff a "token" sum because the harm done is very minor. The sum may be $1.00.
  — *Compensatory damages* means that the defendant or agency pays out-of- pocket expenses incurred by the plaintiff. These expenses can include lost wages, medical bills, money for pain and suffering and attorneys' fees. These expenses can be short term (i.e., to cover an existing medical bill) and long term (i.e., in an injury case, the loss of health or use of a part of the body over time).

— *Punitive damages* are what correctional staff fear the most. If an officer has to pay punitive damages, he/she has to pay out of their own pocket, similar to a fine or a criminal case. Punitive damages have two goals: punish staff and deter other staff from similar behavior.

[ACA, 1994]

In Chapter 15, the issue of inmate rights will continue to be explored with a current synopsis of inmate rights and a discussion of several key cases in recent years. At the conclusion of this topic, there will be guidelines on how correctional staff can protect themselves from inmate litigation.

Summary

Correctional staff must accept the fact that inmates do not lose all civil rights and constitutional protections when incarcerated. While most officers tend to say that inmates have more rights than staff, the state and federal courts see differently. Inmates are allowed to sue in torts and civil rights cases especially under § 1983. Historically, inmates have been viewed as little better than slaves and after periods of non-involvement and detailed involvement (hands on and hands off eras), corrections is now in a period where the courts will intervene in a restrained way, balancing inmate rights versus security. Inmates seek money damages and liability from staff, and these each take several forms. The courts frown upon frivolous inmate lawsuits or legal actions without merit, and states are taking steps to combat them.

Review Questions

1. Explain the differences between the "hands off/hands on," and "one hand off/one hand on" era.

2. Describe conditions in jails and prisons before intervention from the courts.

3. What are the states' legitimate concerns concerning detention?

4. Describe the four parts of the balancing test.

5. Concerning § 1983 suits, what are the reasons that inmates file the most suits?

6. Discuss the three elements of vicarious liability.

Terms/Concepts

Inmate litigation explosion
Hands off era
Hands on era
Tucker Telephone
Restrained hands approach
Legitimate penological interest
Balancing test
O'Lone v. Shabazz
Turner v. Saffley
Compelling government interest
Jailhouse lawyer
Habeas corpus actions
Frivolous lawsuit
Liability
Criminal liability
Civil liability

One hand on/one hand off era
Federalism
Arkansas prison scandal
Torts
Negligence
Gross negligence
Willful negligence
Civil rights actions
42 USC 1983
Injunctive relief
Nominal damages
Compensatory damages
Punitive damages
Declaratory relief
Monetary damages
Vicarious liability

References

Bonventre, Peter and William D. Marbach, "Hell in Texas," *Newsweek*, 1/15/79.

Bronstein, Alvin J., "Prisoners' Rights: A History," in *Legal Rights of Prisoners*, Beverly Hills, CA: Sage, 1980.

Champion, Dean, *Corrections in the United States: A Contemporary Perspective*, Englewood Cliffs, NJ, Prentice Hall, 1990.

Collins, William J.D., *Correctional Law for the Correctional Officer*, 2nd Ed., Lanham, MD, ACA, 1997.

Collins, William C. and Darlene C. Grant, "The Prison Litigation Reform Act," *Corrections Today*, August, 1998.

Dictionary of Criminal Justice Terms, American Correctional Association, Lanham, MD, 1998.

Fox, Vernon & Jeanne Stinchcomb, *Introduction to Corrections*, 5th Ed., Upper Saddle River, NJ, Prentice Hall, 1999.*

"Florida Attorney General Bob Butterworth's Top 10 Frivolous Prison Inmate Lawsuits," http://www.mindspring.com/~1am392/lawsuit.htm.

Fugate, Larry, "New law cracks down on frivolous inmate lawsuits," *Columbus Daily Reporter*, 7/19/96, http://sddtsun.sddt.com/~columbus/files/9607193.

Hanson, Roger A. and Henry W.K. Daley, *Challenging the Conditions of Prisons and Jails: A Report on § 1983 Litigation, Discussion Paper*, Bureau of Justice Statistics, NCJ - 151652, Jan. 1995.

Hopper, Columbus B., "The Impact of Litigation on Mississippi's Prison System," *Prison Journal*, 1985, 65: 54-63.

Inciardi, James A., *Criminal Justice*, 2nd Ed., N.Y., Hartcourt, Brace and Jovanovich, 1987 [appears in Champion].

"Inmate Rights and Privileges," Course 3502, Texas Dept. Of Corrections, Dr. Lynn J. Lund, et al., 1995.

James J. Gilmore, III, Virginia Attorney General New Release: Attorney General Gilmore Seeks Limits on Frivolous Inmate Lawsuits; Releases "Top 10" List, 1/29/97, http:/www.state.va.us/~oag/press/frivsuit.htm.

Murton, Thomas O. and Joe Hyams, *Accomplices to Crime: The Arkansas Prison Scandal*, N.Y., Grove Press, 1976 [appears in Champion].

Murton, Tom and Joe Hyams, *Inside Prison USA*, N.Y., Grove Press, 1969.

Schroeder, Kathleen, "A Recommendation to the FDA Concerning Drug Research on Prisoners," *Southern California Law Review*, 56: 969-1000 [appears in Champion].

Stevens, Dennis J., "Correctional Officer Attitudes: Job Satisfaction Levels Linked to Length of Employment," *The Keeper's Voice*, Fall, 1998.

Sutty, Thomas, et al., *Legal Issues for Correctional Staff Correspondence Course*, Lanham, MD, ACA, 1994.

Thomas, Fate, "The Crisis in our Jails: Overcrowded Beds or Underused Resources," *American Jails*; 2:60-62.

"Vicarious Liability: Inmate Awarded $37,500; says [Guard] He Wounded Tormented Him," *The Keeper's Voice*, IACO, Fall, 1998, p. 30.

See also:

Collins, William, *Correctional Law for the Correctional Officer*, Laurel, MD, American Correctional Association, 1990.

Maguire, Kathleen, and Ann L. Pastore (Eds.), *Sourcebook of Criminal Justice Statistics, 1995*, Bureau of Justice Statistics, NCJ 158900, 1996.

Chapter 15

Synopsis of Inmates' Rights

While Chapter 14 introduced the reader to an overall picture of inmate civil rights, this chapter will give an overview of specific inmate rights, discussing critical cases.

Many inmate rights have been created by the United States Supreme Court, whose decisions based on cases on appeal to it are binding and sets the direction in inmate rights that corrections has to follow.

The decisions of federal courts are only binding within their areas of jurisdiction and circuit courts are binding within that particular circuit. State supreme court decisions are only binding within that state. Courts look at other courts for guidance in making decisions. This concept is known as *precedent*. Precedent helps courts to be consistent and fair. [ACA, 1994]

Rulings by the U.S. Supreme Court in cases that are binding to everyone creates law. For example, the case of *Estelle v. Gamble* created standards that must be followed concerning inmate medical care. This concept is called *case law* where judicial precedent has been created by earlier court decisions and is different from legal statutes, administrative rules and regulations and constitutional law. [ACA, 1998] For example, the Supreme Court, when ruling about inmate health care, may refer to the *Estelle v. Gamble* case. Thus case law and precedent are very closely related.

In the past twenty years, several legislative actions by Congress have influenced greatly the direction and theme of dealing with inmate litigation. To understand the current state of inmate rights, one must be familiar with the Americans With Disabilities Act (ADA), the Prison Litigation Reform Act of 1996 (PLRA) and Civil Rights of Institutionalized Persons Act (CRIPA).

These acts were passed by the U.S. Congress, who now has taken a major role in the area of inmate rights by creating rights by legislation whereas these rights were normally defined by the courts. [Collins and Hagar, 1995]

Americans With Disabilities Act

The ADA is a federal law passed by Congress in 1990 and has been called the "Bill of Rights" for the disabled. Under the ADA, disability is generally defined as "a physical or mental impairment that substantially limits one or more of the major life activities of the individual." Also under the ADA definition of disability is a record of

247

such impairment or being regarded as suffering from such an impairment.

The ADA has an impact on corrections. Not only do correctional administrators have to make the physical plant accessible to disabled inmates, but disabled persons have to be given access to programs and services and these may have to be modified.

Early cases concerning ADA and inmates made assumptions that inmates were recipients of "government services, programs or activities." Later cases questioned whether inmates should have limitation protection by ADA or if they have the right to ADA protection at all.

This controversy over the amount of ADA protection for inmates is evident in several cases. In *Gates v. Rowland*, 39 F.3d 1439 (9th Cir. 1994), HIV-positive inmates protested a prison regulation prohibiting them from working in prison food service. The officials' position was that they were more concerned with possible disturbances by inmates rather than HIV transmission. The District Court ruled for the inmates, the Court of Appeals reversed the ruling. The Appeals Court stated that the regulation was justified due to the legitimate security needs of the prison. According to legal experts, ADA does not recognize such security concerns as a basis for discriminating against a person and, thus, a new exception to the law was created.

Purcell v. Pennsylvania Department of Corrections, Horn, E.D., No. 95-6720, 12/29/97, ruled that an inmate suffering from Tourette's Syndrome and a joint disease was entitled to reasonable accommodations in prison policy and be allowed to have access to his cell and a chair so he can release his tics in private and sit due to his inability to stand for long periods.

In *Yeskey v. Pennsylvania Department of Corrections*, 3d Cir., No. 96-7292, 7/10/97, a Circuit Court ruled an inmate suffering from hypertension did not have to obey a sentencing order requiring participation in a boot camp program. The Court ruled that ADA protection did apply.

As a result of the Yeskey case, the U.S. Supreme Court ruled unanimously that inmates in state and local prisons are entitled to ADA protection, stating that correctional facilities provide inmates with many activities, programs and services similar to the "public entity" provisions to the law, thus, rejecting Pennsylvania's Department of Corrections' claim that boot camps do not provide inmates with such services.

In April, 1998, the California Department of Corrections received $6.5 million in appropriations due to an injunction by the 9th Circuit Court in the case of *Armstrong v. Wilson*. The court found for the inmates who challenged Department of Corrections' lack of physical and program accommodations for disabled inmates, including the sight impaired and hearing impaired. Modifications include evacuation plans for disabled inmates, access to programs and work assignments and devices to assist sight and hearing impaired inmates.

Sources: *The Corrections Professional*: 8/8/97 — "Inmate's ADA Claim for Exclusion from Boot Camp Valid;" 12/12/97 — "Inmate with Tourettes May Have a Case Under ADA, Court Rules;" 7/10/98 — "ADA Clearly Applies to Prisons, Supreme Court Rules;" Collins, William, J.D., *Correctional Law for the Correctional Officer*, 2nd Ed., Lanham, MD, ACA, 1997.

Some lawmakers are taking steps to exclude inmates from ADA protections. In 1998, two U.S. Senators introduced legislation establishing the State and Local Prison Relief Act, which amends the ADA to exclude state and local prisons from ADA provisions relating to public service. The exclusion includes "any department, agency, district or instrumentality of a state and local government that operates a prison . . . with respect to the services, programs or activities relating to the prison." [*Corrections Professional*, 9/4/98]

The second major Act by Congress is the *Prison Litigation Reform Act* or *PLRA*, enacted in 1996. This has been viewed as an aggressive move to thwart frivolous litigation. The law has two major goals: to reduce federal court involvement in prison and jail matters and to reduce the number of lawsuits that are filed by inmates. The PRLA does not change or modify any substantive constitutional rights for inmates. It does set forth some obstacles that make it harder for an inmate to get a case to court; it dictates more sensible procedures for courts. [Collins and Grant, 1998]

The PRLA changes some procedural aspects of inmate litigation. In any civil rights action under § 1983, administrative remedies (grievances, inquiries to staff, etc.) must be exhausted. A full filing fee payment from the inmate is required unless an inmate has no income or assets. The court can order partial payment and monthly installments. The PRLA also has a "three strikes and you're out" section that says if an inmate has filed three lawsuits that are dismissed as frivolous, he/she cannot file future litigation unless the inmate is in imminent danger of serious physical harm. Other PRLA provisions address settlements, injunctions and prospective relief. [Erickson, 1996 in Stajkovic & Lovell, 1997]

The third law enacted by Congress that has had a major effect on inmate litigation is the *Civil Rights of Institutionalized Persons Act* or *CRIPA*.

Enacted by Congress in 1980, CRIPA gives the Department of Justice the power to bring court actions against state and local governments for violating the civil rights of persons in their care in public facilities, including prisons and jails. Like PRLA, CRIPA does not create new rights, but it gives power to the Attorney General to bring litigation based on constitutional or statutory rights of people in these facilities. As of June 1998, 325 institutions were investigated by the Civil Rights Division of the Department of Justice. [Puritz and Scali, 1998]

Other provisions of CRIPA say that a federal court can delay or postpone action on an inmate civil rights suit until the inmate has exhausted all available remedies under a grievance procedure approved by the U.S. Department of Justice and/or the federal court. [Collins, 1997] Like PLRA, the courts want inmates to file grievances and work with the facility staff in getting problems solved instead of filing lawsuits.

Grievance Procedures

Grievances are the best way for an inmate to complain. Correctional staff encourage inmates to file grievances instead of complaining by yelling at staff or showing anger and defiance.

The American Correctional Association defines a grievance or grievance process as "a circumstance or action considered [by the inmate] to be unjust and grounds for complaint or resentment and/or a response to the circumstance in the form of a written complaint filed with the appropriate body."

In other words, an action by staff or an existing situation in the facility that the inmate feels is injurious to his/her welfare qualifies for the filing of a grievance.

Grievance procedures usually consist of a form where the inmate states the complaint. The matter is handled by a staff member and the inmate receives a written response and a specific amount of time to appeal to a higher authority.

One grievance procedure that works well is in the Alexandria Detention Center in Alexandria, Virginia. Inmates receive a handbook that tells them that a grievance "is a way for you to make a written complaint concerning your health or welfare or about the operations and services in the Detention Center."

The handbook further states that disciplinary sanctions, housing assignment and your classification are not grievable.

Inmates are urged to use administrative means at their disposal, such as talking to the staff member or person involved—before filing a grievance.

There is a timetable—staff have four working days to respond in writing and the inmate may appeal to a supervisor who has five working days to respond.

Some facilities in their grievance procedures only permit grievances filed by individual inmates. In Alexandria, an inmate may file a grievance on behalf of a group of inmates and all involved inmates must sign the form.

> Sources: *Dictionary of Criminal Justice Terms,* Lanham, MD, ACA, 1997; Inmate Handbook, Office of Sheriff, Alexandria, Virginia, 1995.

Synopsis of Inmate Rights

As previously stated, the study of constitutional law as it applies to inmates is vast and detailed. For the correctional staff who are "on the line" daily, it is important to know the basic rights that inmates have. If a staff member encounters a problem or is uncertain, he/she should ask the supervisory staff for guidance. Ongoing training in these legal issues should be regular and mandatory. The material in the remainder of this chapter is not meant to give legal advice, but is meant to serve as a guide.

The material in Chapter 14 was intended to be an introduction to the subject of inmate rights, the U.S. Constitution, particularly the Bill of Rights, which guarantees fundamental rights to each citizen and the federal courts back this up. As we have seen, the balancing test decides the limits of these rights in respect to inmates. This is best illustrated in the words of the late Supreme Court Justice Harry Blackmun who stated, "Fundamental rights follow the prisoner through the walls which incarcerate him, but always with appropriate limitations." [Fisher, O'Brien and Austern, 1987]

As corrections moved into the current one hand on/one hand off era, a question was raised as to whether offenders who are incarcerated in jail awaiting trial, but who have not yet been convicted (*pretrial detainees*) should have greater rights than those inmates who are convicted. After all, if pretrial detainees could pay bond, they would be out in the community. Until 1979, the courts did not make a distinction between jails housing pretrial detainees and prisons housing convicted inmates. [Fisher, O'Brien and Austern, 1987]

The case of *Bell v. Wolfish*, 441 U.S. 520, 543-44 (1979) changed that — the rights of pretrial detainees will be judged as to whether they meet constitutional guidelines under a "punishment" test which asks if the rules are excessive and designed only for punishment. [Fisher, O'Brien and Austern, 1987]

The *Bell* case clearly decided the problem saying that "... maintaining institutional order and discipline are essential goals that may require limitation or retraction of the retained constitutional rights of both convicted prisoners and pretrial detainees." [Lund, *et al.*, 1995]

Thus, the rights that we enjoy on the outside can, in the court's view, be reasonably restricted on the inside. For the purposes of this book, a concise examination of inmate's rights will follow, looking at the First, Fourth, Eighth and Fourteenth Amendments to the U.S. Constitution.

First Amendment

The *First Amendment* is probably the right most cherished by Americans. It says that the Congress "shall make no law respecting establishment of religion or prohibiting the free exercise thereof; or abridging the freedom of speech or of the press; or the right of the people to peaceably assemble and to petition the Government for a redress of grievances." This guarantees four freedoms: religion, speech, press and association.

Religion: Correctional authorities have a duty to maintain security and the courts have recognized this. Corrections officials have explained to the courts that some restrictions are justified due to the maintenance of discipline or security, proper exercise of authority by staff, official discretion, the reasonableness of the religion and economic considerations. Generally, courts have said that these reasons are acceptable. [Palmer, 1997]

As for inmates, an inmate must show *sincerity of belief* or simply how sincere he/she is concerning religious beliefs. In one case, the court found the inmate was insincere due to a failure to request religious services for twelve years, failure to submit when requested by staff information about the religion, failing to file an administrative appeal upon denial of religious services, and having a generally unclear nature concerning the religion in question. [Collins, 1997]

When examining the issue of inmates' rights concerning religion, courts had to wrestle with the specific definition of what a religion is. One court developed a "does it look like a religion?" test, saying that a practice is a religion that parallels in doctrines and practice those of a traditional religion. In one case, a court decided that witchcraft was similar to the Church of Wicca and prison officials won the case, justifying facility restrictions. In another case, a court ruled that the Universal Life Church is *not* a religion. For a fee, by mail, one can become a "Doctor of Divinity." [Collins, 1997]

Special diets for religious purposes are allowed, the courts have ruled, unless the demand for a religious diet is extreme and poses unnecessary financial and administrative hardships on staff. [Collins, 1997]

In 1993, Congress passed the Religious Freedom Restoration Act (RFRA) which stipulated that if a correctional facility restricted an inmate's religious practices, the government (facility) must show that the restriction supports a legitimate penological interest and the said restriction is the least restrictive means. [Collins, 1997] However, for many reasons, including the resulting avalanche of inmate litigation challenging facility religious restrictions, RFRA was struck down by the Supreme Court in 1997. The Court felt that RFRA had intruded on state' rights by creating a broader protection than the First Amendment. Advocates of RFRA have said they will come up with a new law. [*Corrections Professional*, 7/11/97]

Correctional staff should remember this—with certain restrictions that support security, courts have ruled that concerning religion, inmates have the following four rights.

- assemble for religious purposes;
- receive and read religious mail;
- wear certain religious emblems;
- consult and correspond with clergy.

[ACA, 1994]

Religion is a sensitive issue and inmates will still attempt through litigation to broaden their rights.

Speech: Concerning corrections, speech is defined as to what inmates say in the facility and the right to communicate with persons on the outside. Thus, verbal speech and mail are looked at under the First Amendment. [ACA, 1994]

In examining an inmate's lawsuit claiming denial of free speech or unlawful restrictions on mail, the Supreme Court has applied a *clear and present danger test*. Meeting this test under the Constitution means that a rule, restriction, policy, etc., will be upheld "if necessary to prevent grave and immediate danger to interests that the government may lawfully protect." [ACA, 1998]

For example, inmates may converse, which is normal, but if two inmates were both security risks, troublemakers or disciplinary problems, they could be prevented from communicating due to a danger of making escape plans, planning to break the rules or creating a riot or disturbance. Inmates send and receive mail—incoming mail may be inspected in order to thwart the "clear and present danger" of introducing contraband or to deter contact with a negative influence such as a racist hate group. Both of these examples show to government interest of security, order and rehabilitation. [Fisher, O'Brien and Astern, 1987]

Concerning speech or expression, courts have ruled that prison restrictions are proper when barring speech that could incite inmates to riot or be viewed as lewd or obscene. Courts have ruled that speech shall "not be threatening to the point of causing an immediate disruption [riot, disturbance, fight, etc.]" or what are known as *fighting words*. [Clark, O'Brien, Austern, 1987]

One question that is asked by inmates is if they can see the press. In *Pell v. Procunier*, 417 U.S. 817 (1974), the Supreme Court ruled that the media has no right protected by the Constitution to interview specific inmates. Inmates can use alternative means such as mail or information transmitted from visitors. However, the facility can place restrictions on access—times, rules, etc., including the monitoring of inmate/press interviews. [Lund, *et al.*, 1995]

Mail: The inspection of inmate mail prevents contraband from being smuggled in or out of a facility and it enables the staff to detect plans for illegal activities, such as escape, gang activity, etc. Under the current approach by the courts, if corrections staff place restrictions on inmates sending and receiving mail, they must justify it. In the case of *McNamara v. Moody*, 606 F.2d 621 (5th Cir. 1979), an inmate's constitutional rights were violated by staff refusing to mail a letter to his girlfriend. The court said that censorship is limited to three things: escape plans, plans to disrupt prison operations or plans to introduce contraband. [Palmer, 1997]

With the stipulation that the regulation restricting mail meets case law guidelines, the courts have ruled that the restriction not be excessive. Also, if an inmate's mail is rejected, the inmate *and* the sender (letter's author, for example) must be notified and the sender can protest or appeal to authorities, who must decide the matter impartially by a neutral staff member. [Collins, 1997]

Staff can open inmate mail and inspect it for contraband. Legal mail—from attorneys and courts—should be opened with the inmate present, inspected, but not read as it enjoys a legal client privilege. Media mail is not privileged and can be treated as any other type of normal mail. [Collins, 1997]

Inmates can subscribe to and receive publications, such as newspapers, magazines, etc. Inflammatory materials may be restricted under the clear and present danger test. Also, courts have upheld *publishers only rules* which requires an inmate to receive books, magazines, etc., only from the publisher. [Collins, 1997]

Inmates may try to write to other inmates who are in other correctional facilities. Courts have felt that inmate-to-inmate communications were of a legitimate concern to staff, saying that such actions may foster inappropriate relations, such as gangs, communicate illegal acts (escapes, etc.), or to arrange violent acts. Such restrictions do not violate the First Amendment. [Palmer, 1997] Some institutions have adopted the practice of stamping outgoing mail with the name of the facility from where the mail is being sent, thus alerting another institution that the mail is coming from an inmate. Inmates do not, all the time, put the facility's name on the return address.

As correctional officers are aware, correctional facilities, for the most part, are same sex environments—men and women do not interact with each other except under controlled conditions. As one veteran jail officer said, "the hormones do not stop raging just because a man or woman comes to jail." [Cornelius, 1999]

Are sexually oriented materials that contain articles and pictures a threat to security? This is a gray area. Corrections officials can keep such material from inmates on the reasons that the material can lead to deviate behavior and is detrimental to rehabilitation. From the courts, however, there is a variety of definitions of what obscene material is. Staff who censor such material should have guidelines from their supervisors and the agency's legal advisor, a process of review and due process, and a chance to appeal the censor's decision should be included in agency policy. [Palmer, 1997]

In one case, *Harper v. Wallingford*, 877 F.2d 728 (9th Cir. 1989), a court upheld a ban on material from NAMBLA, the North American Man/Boy Love Association, after officials showed that it was detrimental to the pedophile to whom it was sent. The material advocated consensual sexual relations between adult and juvenile males. The court agreed also that it could lead to violence in the facility. [Collins, 1997]

Communications with the outside: visiting and phone: Besides mail, inmates communicate in two other frequent and convenient ways: visitors and the telephone.

While correctional facilities recognize the importance of attorney visits and respect their confidentiality, personal visiting is subject to more restrictions, based on the legitimate penological interest of security. There should be visiting for inmates; they need to maintain ties to family and friends. Visiting gives the inmate something positive to look forward to and this helps keep a positive climate.

Generally, the courts have said that a total ban on visiting violates the First Amendment, but regulation of visiting is crucial to the maintenance of security. The rights of inmates *and* security must be balanced. Officials can deny a personal visit. In one case, a sister was denied because she was suspected of bringing a firearm. A visitor who is unruly, disorderly or intoxicated can be denied access. Privacy is not required for inmates and facilities can approve visiting lists. Inmates have no rights to contact visits or conjugal visits. [Palmer, 1997]

Some facilities do allow *contact visits* — visits in which the inmate and visitor are in the same room with no physical barriers. The idea here is to provide an incentive, something that the inmate can earn for good behavior. The same holds true for *conjugal visits* in which the inmate can have a private visit with a spouse or significant other in which sexual relations are permitted. [Fisher, O'Brien, and Austern, 1987]

Access to Courts: Inmates having access to courts and the judicial system are covered by the First Amendment and the Sixth Amendment. Usually we think of the First Amendment part — the petitioning of the government for a redress of grievances. The Sixth Amendment guarantees such rights as a speedy and public trial, being able to confront witnesses and call witnesses and have the assistance of counsel.

The due process clause of the Fourteenth Amendment reinforces the right of access to the courts. [Palmer, 1997] In the hands off era, scant attention was paid to such issues as prison law libraries, aid from "jailhouse lawyers," etc. Many law libraries in the past were nothing more than a few law books thrown together on a bookcase which were of little help to the inmate. Our judicial system guarantees the accused representation by counsel, but the courts have stated that inmates have the right to adequate law libraries and assistance.

Several key cases have shaped the course of prison law libraries and the role of jailhouse lawyers:

> *Ex Parte Hull*, 312 U.S. 546 (1941): In this 1940 case, the Supreme Court found a state prison rule invalid requiring that all legal documents in an inmate's court proceeding be examined and censored by authorities before filing with the court.
>
> *Bounds v. Smith*, 430 U.S. 817 (1977): The Supreme Court supported the supplying of legal resources to inmates, either in an adequate law library or by other alternatives. These alternatives included paralegal training for inmates, volunteer law students, volunteer attorneys, etc. Subsequent decisions have stated the necessity and critical nature of having adequate materials in law libraries — namely, state codes, court reports, law dictionaries and legal reference materials. This does not mean that prison and jails have to supply every imaginable legal resource in the law library. In *U.S. v. Garza*, 664 F.2d 135 (7th Cir. 1981), inmates' rights *are not*

violated if a law library's resources are limited and he/she could get materials from his/her attorney.

Johnson v. Avery, 393 U.S. 483 (1969): This case dealt with the "jailhouse lawyer" and the right of an inmate to receive assistance from another inmate. The Supreme Court said that the activities of jailhouse lawyers can be restricted—certain times, certain places, etc., and no fees are to be paid. The jailhouse lawyer can "practice" if no other reasonable alternatives to legal services are available.

[Palmer, 1997]

Correctional officers should follow these common sense rules: inmates have a right of access to legal materials so that they can practice their right of access to the courts. Other inmates can assist them. Finally, if an inmate needs to go to the law library and he/she is not abusing it by socializing or vandalism, allow him/her to go. If the inmate requests the assistance of another inmate in preparing legal papers or conducting research, allow it if it is within security guidelines.

Recently, a Tennessee Appeals Court found in favor of an inmate who sued a correctional officer for harassment, verbal abuse and unwarranted disciplinary actions for allegedly possessing too many legal papers in his cell. The inmate was the prison's law library clerk and a jailhouse lawyer. The inmate complained that the officer read the legal papers and told the inmate that he did not have the right to assist other inmates or to have their legal paperwork. Even though the lower court found for the officer, the Appeals Court reversed that, saying that restrictions on papers in cells is a legitimate security concern, that was not the issue in this case. [*Sanders v. Jones*, Tenn. Ct. App., No. 02A01-9610-CV-00261, 3/6/97, in the *Corrections Professional*, 4/4/97]

A point is made clear with this case: the courts take a supportive view of inmates and their legal work and it implies that this right of access to the courts and all of its ramifications must be respected.

One recent case involving inmate law libraries is *Lewis v. Casey*, 116 S. Ct. 2174 (1996). In this case, the Supreme Court stood by its *Bounds v. Smith* decision, saying that correctional facilities have a duty to assist inmates by providing law libraries or persons trained in the law. In *Lewis*, the court said that an inmate must show actual harm to win a denial of access claim. More simply, if an inmate shows that he actually lost a case in court due directly to an inadequate law library, he could win a lawsuit. [Collins, 1997]

Fourth Amendment

The *Fourth Amendment* deals with unlawful searches and seizures. It says that "the right of the people to be secure in their persons, houses, papers and effects, against unreasonable searches and seizures, shall not be violated and no warrants shall issue, but upon probable cause, supported by oath or affirmation, and particularly describing the place to be searched and the persons or things to be seized." Basically, the Fourth Amendment means that citizens and their dwellings, work places, etc., cannot be searched without reason; there are protections such as police having probable cause and obtaining a search warrant, etc.

In a corrections facility, inmates do not have the same protections as people on the outside. To maintain the legitimate penological interest of security, inmates, visitors, cellblocks, common areas, work areas, etc., must be randomly and regularly searched without warrants and without probable cause. The balancing test leans towards the institution. Corrections personnel must not harass the inmate (such as searching the inmate every thirty minutes for eight hours) or act unprofessionally. The dignity of the inmate must be respected.

Strip searches and body cavity searches are outside the norm of pat downs or frisks. These types of searches are unique and could undermine the dignity of the inmates. Policies and procedures should be in place that state the reasons for these types of searches and guidelines that are used. In inmate suits concerning searches, courts have recommended these practices.

Eighth Amendment

Another way to describe the *Eighth Amendment* is to think of the words *cruel and unusual punishment*. Although short in text, the Eighth Amendment has had a significant impact on corrections and inmate litigation. It says that "excessive bail shall not be required, nor excessive fines imposed, nor cruel and unusual punishment inflicted." Short, but to the point. The phrase "cruel and unusual punishment" has been interpreted by inmates to mean overcrowding to excessive disciplinary actions set by prison disciplinary boards to claims that staff used excessive and unnecessary force.

Staff must remember that a cruel and unusual punishment accusation accuses the staff of causing the inmate undue pain and/or suffering or anguish. The most noteworthy cases have involved conditions of confinement, such as deficiencies in housing, food, medical care and sanitation. [Stojkovic and Lovell, 1997]

Though the phrase "cruel and unusual punishment" may mean a lot of things, the Supreme Court has developed a test to clarify "cruel and unusual punishment."

- situation shocks the conscience of the Court;
- situation violates civilized society's evolving standards of decency;
- punishment to the inmate[s] is disproportionate to the offense (i.e., minor offense, excessive punishment);
- involves the wanton (deliberate) and unnecessary infliction of pain.

[Collins, 1997]

A summary of the following areas clarifies courts' involvement with the Eighth Amendment:

Conditions of confinement: litigation that claims that one or more conditions in a correctional facility amount to cruel and unusual punishment. The conditions relate to "basic human needs." [ACA, 1998]

In *Wilson v. Seiter*, 111 S. Ct. 2321 (1991), the Supreme Court clarified conditions of confinement as they apply to the Eighth Amendment. The Court said that for conditions to be considered cruel and unusual punishment, they have to be very bad where inmates *are not* provided with one or more basic human needs. Secondly, the staff (defendants) knew of serious problems and deficiencies and failed to take corrective actions. This failure to act is called *deliberate indifference*. [Collins, 1997]

Courts prior to *Wilson* used the *totality of conditions test* when looking at conditions saying that *all* of the conditions had to be bad. *Wilson* changed that saying that conditions can be examined separately. [Collins and Hagar, 1995]

Basic Human Needs of Inmates

When looking at whether conditions meet the basic human needs test, correctional staff should objectively ask themselves — "would I, if incarcerated, wish to live in this facility?" The basic human needs, according to the Supreme Court in *Wilson v. Seiter* are:

1. *Food*: that is nutritious, adequate, and is served in a sanitary manner.

2. *Clothing*: that is protective from the climate and provides privacy and is in good repair.

3. *Shelter*: concerns the overall environment—noise, heating, cooling, ventilation, maintenance, cell sizes, etc. Shelter cases concern mainly the physical plant.

4. *Sanitation*: deals with cleanliness, leaking plumbing, vermin, etc.

5. *Medical care*: lawsuits are popular, focusing on how medical services are delivered, both medical and dental care.

6. *Personal safety*: asks "are the inmates reasonably safe?" Do procedures such as classification, patrol, etc., promote safety or cause deficiencies? Overcrowded cases generally cite personal safety, but the Court said in *Bell v. Wolfish* and *Rhodes v. Chapman*, 101 S.Ct. 2392 (1981) that crowding of inmates (i.e., double celling) is all right if inmates' basic human needs are met. Inmates must be protected from harm by other inmates. Staff are liable if they know of a situation of possible harm to an inmate and do nothing.

7. *Exercise*: can be an issue if the lack of it amounts to cruel and unusual punishment, such as not being provided for a long period of time. Inmates in lockdown such as in maximum security units without exercise could result in a suit.

> Source: Collins, William, J.D., *Correctional Law for the Correctional Officer, 2nd Ed.,* 1997, Lanham, MD, ACA.

Medical care: Suits involving medical care vary in scope due to each case, like each medical situation, has a different set of facts that are open to opinions, which can determine if the medical care in question is adequate. [Palmer, 1998]

Courts ask these basic questions in determining adequate medical and dental care:

- Are inmates getting timely, prompt access to medical professionals who are qualified and properly trained?
- Are inmates receiving generally appropriate diagnosis of medical problems?
- Are inmates receiving timely and appropriate treatment for, at a minimum, serious medical needs?

[Collins, 1997]

Inmates are entitled to good, quality, basic medical care. The benchmark case of *Estelle v. Gamble*, 429 U.S. 97, 97 S. Ct. 285 (1976), set the standard for inmate medical care, saying that medical care was inadequate when staff showed a "deliberate indifference to serious medical needs."

Both pre-trial detainees *and* convicted inmates have the same rights to medical care. [Fisher, O'Brien, and Austern, 1987]

Staff must be careful when dealing with inmates' medical issues. If an inmate complains of a possible medical problem, it is best to refer him/her to the medical staff immediately or, if necessary, notify the medical staff. Staff should put themselves in the inmate's place—if the inmate is in discomfort, notify the medics.

According to the courts, staff can establish deliberate indifference in any of the following three ways. First, an essential part of a medical/health care delivery system is missing. Secondly, there is no response to a serious medical need. Finally, there is an *extremely* inadequate response to a serious medical need or problem. Staff may wonder what serious medical needs are. They are needs ordered by the facility medical staff or obvious to non-medical staff. [Fisher, O'Brien, Austern, 1987]

Two cases illustrate what the courts viewed as a inadequate and adequate medical systems:

In *Gates v. Collier*, 501 F.2d 1291 (5th Cir. 1974), a federal court found that the Mississippi State Penitentiary medical system was inadequate. Over 1,800 inmates were served by only one full-time physician, several in-mate assistants and a hospital that was substandard.

In *Miller v. Carson*, 401 F. Supp. 835 (M.D., Fla. 1975), a Florida county prison with a maximum capacity of 432 inmates had an adequate medical system of one full-time physician, a licensed physician's assistant, thirteen nurses, twenty-four hour crisis intervention and close proximity to a hospital for emergencies. Both the doctor and physician's assistant were on twenty-four hour call. [Palmer, 1997]

Over the years, courts have had ample time to define and fine tune the concept of health care delivery systems. Generally, a good correctional health care delivery system has:

- an initial intake interview by qualified staff to include screening and a medical history;
- a physical exam within a few days;
- a system that allows inmates frequent access to health care personnel, including sick call;
- visits to inmates by dental, mental health and medical professionals;
- transportation services for unusual or emergency medical problems, such as to a hospital;
- a classification system that looks at inmate medical needs;
- procedures to handle substance abuse, medical and psychological problems;
- medical records that are accurate, complete *and* confidential;

- staff training in basic first aid and emergency procedures, such as CPR training (cardiac pulmonary resuscitation).

[Fisher, O'Brien and Austern, 1987]

Correctional staff must be aware of the medical needs of inmates. In the case of *Bradley v. Puckett,* et al. *v. U.S. Court of Appeals,* 5th Cir., No. 98-60102, a handicapped inmate was placed in segregation due to having a homemade knife. The inmate wore a leg brace and had to take a shower with a chair. He claimed that he was segregated without items to properly bathe and resorted to toilet water after he could not bathe. As a result, he incurred a fungal infection. A district court found for staff, saying that the condition was eventually corrected, but the appeals court reversed that decision and remanded the case for further action. [*The Corrections Professional,* 12/11/98]

Another recent case illustrates this. In *Noland v. Wheatley,* 835 F. Supp. 476 (N.D. Ind. 1993), a court found unconstitutional the conditions under which a semi-quadriplegic inmate without a colon or bladder was confined: housed in a safety cell because his wheelchair would not fit in a regular cell doorway; the cell had no bed, no toilet and no running water; the inmate had to empty body waste from his urostomy and colostomy bags in a floor drain. Due to no running water, he had to wait until "bath day" to wash his soiled hands. [Collins and Hager, 1995]

To summarize, there are, according to attorney William Rold, three basic rights of inmates concerning health care:

1. The right to access care—to get to see the health care practitioner.
2. The right to care that is offered—if a doctor says that an inmate needs an x-ray, dialysis or tests, he receives them.
3. The right to professional judgment—doctors are to treat inmates like patients.

[*Corrections Professional,* 11/20/98]

Use of Force: The basic rule for correctional officers and the use of force is that correctional officers can use force to protect themselves, other staff and inmates (including from themselves, such as in an overt suicidal act) from serious bodily harm or death. Force can also be used to enforce compliance with rules and regulations. The courts, in inmate rights cases, look at whether the force was reasonable, justified and excessive.

The amount of force being used may escalate to the point that the inmate's resistance is overcome, but beyond that it may be excessive. For example, an unruly inmate refuses to leave his cell for a disciplinary hearing. He backs up to a far wall screaming at officers to come in and get him. Attempts to talk him down are fruitless. Obviously, this cannot continue. Discipline and order in the institution must be restored. Officers go in and grab the inmate who punches and kicks. The officers defend themselves, striking the inmate. The inmate is placed on the floor and handcuffs are applied. He is led to a segregation unit. He goes limp, the officers end up dragging him. At the segregation unit, before the restraints are removed, several officers punch and kick the inmate severely, causing internal injuries.

Are those last punches excessive force? Yes. After reasonable attempts to calm the inmate fail, officers were justified in physically moving the inmate, defending themselves against his blows, restraining him and even dragging him. The inmate's resistance was overcome and the situation was resolved. The "extra blows" at the end were not justified and the officers may be liable.

Courts in recent years have supported legitimate security-related polices and procedures that are deemed necessary to control violent and disruptive inmates or inmates who are "out of control." The courts may use a *malicious and sadistic test* to see if restrictions placed on disruptive inmates are excessive. This test can also be used to determine if the force used on an inmate was excessive and unnecessary. Five factors are considered:

1. The need for the use of force: the situation, events leading to it, etc.
2. The amount of force used: too much?
3. Extent of any injuries sustained by the inmate.
4. The threat perceived by a reasonable correctional officer.
5. The efforts by officers to temper the use of force.

[Collins and Hagar, 1995]

Point five is critical. In a use of force situation, the ideal way to resolve it is to "talk the inmate down" or use persuasion or a show of force in order to *avoid* the usage of force, whenever possible. Sadly, sometimes force has to be used.

Fourteenth Amendment

The *Fourteenth Amendment* is quite lengthy. For the study of inmate rights, a part of Section I applies: "...nor shall any State deprive any person of life, liberty, or property, without due process of law; nor deny to any person within its jurisdiction the equal protection of the laws." This clause has come to mean having due process or procedures in disciplinary proceedings, where the inmate possibly will be subjected to a loss, moving to disciplinary segregation, loss of good time, privileges, etc.

Simply, institutional discipline can place an additional burden on an inmate and procedures should be fair—balancing the security needs of the institution and the need of the inmate to be treated fairly. For example, in *Howard v. Smyth*, 365 F.2d 428 (4th Cir. 1966), a court found unconstitutional the action of one facility of placing an inmate in solitary confinement without a hearing because of the inmate's activities in requesting Black Muslim services. [Palmer, 1997]

A good rule for officers to follow is that inmates are due a hearing (or a form of a "trial") if they are facing a disciplinary charge. In 1974, the landmark case of *Wolff v. McDonnell*, 418 U.S. 539 (1974), put forth the procedural requirements that are required in inmate disciplinary cases. They are:

1. *A hearing*: the inmate has the right to be present, but he/she can waive this by words or behavior. The hearing personnel must be impartial.
2. *Advanced written notice of the charges*: staff must give this to the inmate at least twenty-four hours prior to the hearing so that the inmate can prepare a defense.
3. *An opportunity to call witnesses and present evidence in a defense*: there is an exception, where the witnesses could be hazardous to safety—such as if a witness is an enemy, informant, etc. The facility must justify the denial if the accused inmate litigates. There is no right to cross-examine or confront witnesses. The hearing board or officer controls witness proceedings.
4. *Assistance*: legal references say sometimes. Inmates have no right to an attorney in disciplinary cases. Some institutions allow them only to observe that due process is being followed. Usually inmates may have the assistance of another inmate or staff member, at the discretion of the facility. If an inmate is illiterate or it is apparent that he/she has difficulty understanding the proceedings, the role of an assistant is critical.
5. *Written decision*: a written decision must be given to the inmate as to the decision and the evidence used for the reasoning of the decision. This serves two purposes—the inmate can better understand what has transpired and the entire proceedings are better understood when reviewed by a higher authority, such as the facility command staff—or even court. This document should be detailed, not just stating something like "guilty based on officer's report" or "guilty due to evidence."

[Collins, 1997]

Although not required by the Constitution, it is best to have a practice of *administrative review*, a practice whereby the proceedings and related evidence (and *only* these) are reviewed by a higher authority over the hearing board/officer. The Fourteenth Amendment concerns uniform treatment so inmates *must* be notified of their right to appeal. [Palmer, 1997] However, the inmate should appeal in writing within a certain time frame and state the reasons for his/her appeal. The written answer to the appeal is then delivered to the inmate.

Another way that needs mention is procedural due process when placing inmates in administrative segregation (AS). The inmate may not have broken a rule, but he/she may be unsuitable for living with other inmates due to mental instability, poor hygiene, argumentative personality, etc. In these cases, where an inmate does not request administrative segregation, some sort of due process is required.

The hearing should be less formal than a disciplinary hearing. It is basically a review of the facts recommending administrative segregation. Its nature is non-adversarial, but inmate must receive prior notice and be offered an opportunity to respond in writing. [Palmer, 1997] Generally, the Institutional Classification Committee (ICC) holds the hearing. Periodic checks on the welfare of the inmate are necessary.

Inmates can be placed in administrative segregation pending disciplinary actions without a hearing for the safety and security of the facility. For example, if an inmate refuses to obey an officer's order or commits a serious rule violation, he/she can be placed in segregation pending further action, such as a disciplinary hearing. Such moves are necessary and often immediate. Some inmates cannot, for the security and smooth operation of the institution, remain in population.

Legal scholars have stated that the above situation is the most important exception to the due process rule: an emergency situation where the inmate presents a clear and present danger to himself/herself or others [inmates and staff]. The administrator may take reasonable action under the circumstances to quell or defuse the emergency. The subsequent due process hearing [administration segregation or disciplinary segregation] is "after the fact" and should justify the action that was taken. [Lund, et al., 1995]

The courts have looked very carefully at placing inmates into solitary confinement, either for administrative segregation or for disciplinary reasons. The conditions should be clean, sanitary and humane. Periodic review is required in a meaningful manner, not just a cursory conversation. Inmates must have a due process hearing before being placed in segregation and it must be justified on one or a combination of these reasons:

1. Personal or facility security;
2. Protection of inmate population;

3. Health/medical reasons;
4. To prevent escapes;
5. For punishment.

[Lund, et al., 1995]

Correctional officers should remember that *any* time the inmate has "something to lose," such as being in general population, good time, etc., a hearing has to be held. Not only does it guarantee equal treatment of all inmates in terms of due process, it serves as a written record in case the inmate sues.

The concept of losses to the inmate by being placed in segregation created what the courts called a *liberty interest*. These interests (custody level, housing, programs, etc.) require due process protection such as through hearings, etc. Concerning regulations, language has to be specific and mandatory as to what conditions, rules, etc., subject an inmate to segregation. [ACA, 1998]

The focus for many years was on the language of the regulations. Correctional facilities had to be very careful in writing procedures placing inmates in segregation or taking away a liberty interest. Lawsuits were filed over trivial things, such as an inmate claiming he did not receive due process when he got a tray lunch, instead of a sack lunch. The Supreme Court, in *Sanders v. Connor*, 45 S. Ct. 2293 (1995), changed the traditional view of due process, saying that a liberty interest will not be created by procedural language, but a decision by authorities results in a significant deprivation in relation to normal incidents of prison life. These deprivations were also described as "atypical." The impact on corrections is still unclear. Most facilities continue to have specific policies and procedures. [Collins, 1997]

Apparently, this is the Court's "common sense" approach to the due process issue. How the inmate is actually deprived is viewed as more important than if procedures are followed precisely to the letter. It will be interesting to see how this affects corrections in the next few years.

Correctional staff must develop ways to protect themselves from inmate litigation. Anyone can sue, but winning is a different story.

Staff Protectors Against Inmate Litigation

1. *Recognition/awareness*: staff should recognize that civil liability is a potential problem and should be aware of conditions or situation that could lead to an inmate lawsuit. Anticipate areas of liability; be proactive rather than reactive.

2. *Education/training*: classes, seminars, etc., that provide education and training concerning constitutional rights of inmates should be mandatory at the entry and in-service levels.

3. *Selection*: personnel who handle agency hiring should not hire staff who are unfit for handling inmates and ensuring equal treatment.

4. *Correct policies and procedures*: policies and procedures should be in place that guarantee compliance with case law, government standards and standards from organizations such as the American Correctional Association, if accredited. Policies must be regularly reviewed, staff should act within the scope of their authority, as set forth in procedures.

5. *Supervision*: supervisors must correct problems and are responsible for what is going on in the facility. Courts do not want to hear "I didn't know."

6. *Discipline*: administrators must take action against staff exhibiting unacceptable conduct. These actions include termination, suspension, demotion, oral/written reprimand, etc. Problem staff cannot be ignored.

7. *Communication*: Communications should be clear between supervisors, line/support staff, inmates and the public. The more people can communicate, the easier problems can be solved. Public concerns that are addressed enhances the agency's image and perhaps litigation can be avoided. Line staff should ask their supervisors if uncertainty exists.

8. *Document*: write it down. Enough cannot be said about this. Detailed, accurate records must be kept, including logs, incident reports, memoranda about inmate behavior, due process hearings, medical records, etc. This documentation may prove invaluable in court.

Sources: American Correctional Association, *Legal Issues for Correctional Staff Correspondence Courts, Book I, The Legal System*, ACA, Lanham, MD, 1994, author: William C. Collins; "Civil Liberty: The War Goes On," by Charles E. Friend, *Sheriff*, Vol. 44, No. 5, Sep-Oct. 1992.

Summary

This chapter, and the preceding one, are meant to be a guide to inmate rights and not to serve as legal advice. Ongoing training in inmate rights should be given to every correctional worker, as it is a vast area.

Concerning the Constitution, the courts have said that restrictions on its freedoms in correctional facilities are allowed for good reason. However, the courts have supported inmates in matters of obtaining decent medical care, religious freedom, no cruel and unusual punishment and due process.

Inmates are also allowed access to the courts through adequate law libraries and for the most part, persons training in the law, including "jailhouse lawyers." If these allowances are restricted, correctional administrators must have good reason.

Finally, through training and good administrative practices, staff can defend themselves against inmate lawsuits.

Review Questions

1. Define these Acts by Congress: ADA, PLRA and CRIPA.

2. What are grievance procedures and why are they important in the study of inmate litigation?

3. What are the rights that inmates have concerning religion?

4. What are allowed restrictions on inmate mail, speech and visiting?

5. What are the components of the cruel and unusual punishment test?

6. What are the seven basic human needs of inmates?

7. What due process rights do inmates have in cases of disciplinary segregation and administrative segregation?

Terms/Concepts

Precedent

Prison Litigation Reform
Act (PLRA)

Grievances

Pre-trial detainees

First Amendment

Sincerity of belief

Clear and present danger test

Fighting words

Publishers only rules

Conjugal visits

Americans with Disabilities
Act (ADA)

Eighth Amendment

Civil Rights of Institutionalized
Persons Act (CRIPA)

Deliberate indifference

Totality of conditions test

Malicious and sadistic test

Fourteenth Amendment

Administrative review

Liberty interest

Contact visits

Fourth Amendment

Cruel and unusual punishment

References

"ADA Clearly Applies to Prisons, Supreme Court Rules," *The Corrections Professional*, 7/10/98.

Collins, William J.D., *Correctional Law for the Correctional Officer*, 2nd Ed., Lanham, MD, ACA, 1997.

Collins, William C. and John Hagar, "Jails and the Courts: Issues for Today, Issues for Tomorrow," *American Jails*, May/June, 1995.

Dictionary of Criminal Justice Terms, American Correctional Association, Lanham, MD, 1998.

Erickson, A., "Prison Litigation Reform Act," *The Prison Law Page*, 1996. http://www.wco.com@aerick/

"Inmate With Tourette's May Have a Case Under ADA, Court Rules," *The Corrections Professional*, 12/12/97.

"Inmates' ADA Claim for Exclusion from Boot Camp Valid," *The Corrections Professional*, 8/8/97.

Legal Issues for Correctional Staff Correspondence Course, Book I, The Legal System; Book II, Inmate Rights, 1994, Laurel, MD, ACA, consultant: William Collins.

"Senators Introduce Bill to Exclude Prisoners from ADA Services," *The Corrections Professional*, 9/4/98.

Appendix A

Maintaining Safety and Security by Managing Contraband

by Edward W. Szostak

American Jails, July/August 1998, pp. 62-64

Contraband is any item that is prohibited in a correctional facility. Contraband in a correctional facility is a very serious matter. It requires diligent attention by correctional staff daily to combat the creativity of inmates in their efforts to create or acquire these forbidden items. Contraband may be a pen, paper clip, currency, gum, powdered coffee creamers, cigarettes, matches, lighters, or even certain types of shoes or sneakers. Contraband varies at each facility depending on the level of security and classification of inmates. Some form of contraband exists in most correctional environments.

The Albany County Correctional Facility is currently a 1,005-bed facility (megajail) that has experienced many phases of construction since 1982. The original facility was built in 1931 and had a 350-bed capacity.

The facility has an average daily population of 739 and currently employs a staff of 325. The 1998 budget has allocated the hiring of 32 new corrections positions and 7 registered nurses. We are in the process of filling these positions.

The Albany County Correctional Facility is proud to state that as of January 27, 1997, we became an accredited facility by the New York State Sheriffs' Association and the New York State Commission of Correction.

The Albany County Correctional Facility has experienced a variety of contraband items, i.e., homemade knives (shanks), homemade alcohol (home brew), and in order to create contraband hiding places inmates have hollowed out books and bars of soap. We have found bars of soap carved into various shapes including the shape of a small handgun. The gun appears quite genuine once colored with a black magic marker or pen. Broom and mop handles can be fashioned into spears, shanks or clubs; bedsheets braided like rope; broken plexiglas mirrors and pens can be sharpened and made into shanks. Even harmless powdered coffee creamers can be dangerous. When the powdered creamer is blown through a hollow pen or straw-like device onto a flame, it becomes a crude flame thrower.

Construction Projects

Correctional staff working in facilities that have experienced construction projects, whether major or minor, need to be attentive. We all recognize our business is somewhat unique; therefore, we must look at and handle things differently than businesses not concerned with the security issues
we encounter. Common equipment or items used by contractors must not
be left abandoned or improperly disposed of because inmates can acquire
them and use them for entirely different purposes. Account for everything.
All construction workers and managers will need to be informed of security requirements long before the job begins and reminded throughout the
project. Prebid conferences, preconstruction meetings, and all construc-
tion-related documents must clearly state the requirements that will be enforced. Security staff must constantly review deficiencies, address them,
and notify supervisors immediately.

Contractors must be prohibited from bringing in glass soda bottles,
pocket knives, money, and medications. The contractors should also be
instructed not to have any contact with inmates. They need to be advised
to properly inventory all materials such as screws, nails, and spent shell
casings (unused ammunition for nail guns). Vehicle security procedures
also need to be addressed, requiring that all vehicles and keys be secured
at all times. Tools and heavy equipment must be secured and ladders are
to be removed at the end of each day and properly secured.

Contraband Type & Methods of Obtaining

Some items once allowed, but now forbidden, introduce a whole new
array of security problems. For example, the Albany County Correctional
Facility is now a smoke free facility and has been for over three years. This
has generated some interest by inmates who illegally obtain smokes of any
kind and something to ignite them. Smuggling tobacco products by mail
and/or packages, visitors, and even bribing staff are current methods used
to introduce contraband. Other methods include inserting drugs or weapons
into a rubber handball, sealing it, then throwing it over perimeter fences
or walls into recreation areas for the intended recipient. Obviously, correction officers need to be diligent in their efforts to search for and detect
such methods. Contraband has also been introduced by the inmates' family members, even going so far as to placing contraband in an infant's di-
aper. Shoes, boots, and sneakers are also sources of contraband. Most foot
apparel contains a metal arch support that reinforces the firmness of the

footwear. This metal arch has been removed by inmates and then sharpened into homemade shanks or shivs.

Major Facility Searches/Shakedowns

To minimize the amount of contraband over the years the staff of the Albany County Correctional Facility has conducted three major shakedowns, all following the 1991, 1993, and 1996 construction projects. The entire facility was shut down and searched from top to bottom. It was estimated to cost approximately $10,000.00 per search, each search taking between 8 to 12 hours to complete. Teams needed to be established. Our teams consisted of a K-9 unit and their handlers from local law enforcement agencies, identification officers for photographic evidence, property officers to account for confiscated items, maintenance staff to provide access to plumbing and electrical areas, additional correction officers, supervisors, and administrators.

An announcement was made to all inmates the night prior to lockdown time (22:00) of the shakedown at 07:00. Reports of toilets flushing continuously throughout the night were noted by correction officers working the midnight shifts. Officers also found items thrown into common areas during their routine rounds.

Contraband Control

Once a method of making a weapon or obtaining prohibited items has been identified, measures are taken to minimize future access and opportunity. Such measures include inmates found in possession of contraband being prosecuted to the fullest extent of the law; daily searches of individual housing units; portable metal detectors; and K-9 patrols being used during inmate visitations.

Additionally, changes have been made to equipment and supplies to reduce availability of articles that can be used as weapons. Such measures include stainless steel toilets and sinks replacing porcelain fixtures, plastic replacing metal mop handles, and mopheads that had metal frames and screws now having plastic frames and clips. We purchase our cleaning supplies in plastic containers instead of containers that use metal lids. Factory-sealed bakery products with plastic clips replace items that were once sealed with metal twist ties. These metal twist ties can be used as a conductor of ignition in electrical outlets. Heavy duty nonbreakable plastic footlockers replace metal footlockers and all-plastic chairs replace metal and wood office furniture. Only clear trash liners are used because they permit visual inspection of contents.

The most recent step we have taken is seeking and obtaining the funding for the purchase of orange-colored canvas foot wear for all inmates upon admission. Sheriff James L. Campbell persuaded the Albany County Legislature to provide the $20,000.00 needed to purchase the canvas sneakers. Fortunately, the Albany County Sheriff's Office has experienced a good working relationship with the legislative branch of our county government.

Once the canvas sneakers are purchased and received, all inmates' personal shoes, boots, and sneakers are confiscated and placed with their property and held until their release. They will then be issued a pair of bright orange facility-issued canvas sneakers. Surprisingly, during the budget hearings, the media took great interest in this topic. This resulted in positive public relations for the facility with state and local media groups.

Sheriff James L. Campbell and I are proud to say that we have a very dedicated and professional staff. Training plays an important role in ensuring that officers and civilian staff *always practice safe techniques* during their everyday routines. These factors and our conscious efforts greatly reduce contraband in the Albany County Correctional Facility.

* * *

Edward W. Szostak is the Superintendent of the Albany County Correctional Facility, located in Albany, New York. He began his career as a corrections officer in January 1975. He rose through the ranks of sergeant, lieutenant, captain, chief, and assistant superintendent, moving to acting superintendent in 1990 and earning the full-fledged title the following year. During his tenure the facility expanded from a 350-bed institution to its now 1,005-bed capacity, went smoke free, and was awarded a Certificate of Accreditation in January 1997 by the New York State Commission of Correction and the New York State Sheriffs' Association. He can be reached by writing to him in care of the Albany County Correctional Facility, 840 Albany Shaker Road, Albany, New York 12211, or calling (518) 869-2609.

Photos by Al Roland, Sr. Identification Officer.

Reprinted by permission of the American Jail Association.

Appendix B

Escape Plan

No matter how secure the institution, inmates will try to escape. During an escape attempt, officers must act quickly to stop the attempt and recapture the inmate(s). That is why a functional escape plan is vitally important for every institution. While the methods used by inmates in escape attempts vary, escape plans should contain the fundamental search and surveillance techniques that cover most situations.

A functional plan includes the following elements:

- *Defining an escape.* A clear definition is needed of what specifically constitutes an escape and the use of deadly force to stop escapees, in the particular jurisdiction involved, as opposed to an inmate being "off-limits," "out of bounds," or some other lesser infraction.
- *Reporting an escape.* Staff in the institution must know whom they should notify in the event they believe an inmate is missing. In most cases, this is the control center.
- *Alerting the perimeter and gateposts.* As soon as an inmate is believed to be missing, the perimeter and gatepost staff and any outlying patrol staff should be notified.
- *Securing the area.* The entire institution should be secured; inmates must return to their quarters/cells.
- *Providing a count.* The inmates in the institution should be counted immediately, to determine the identity of the missing inmates; in most cases, a picture card (identification) count will be needed to verify the identity of those missing.
- *Notifying top staff.* The plan should specify the order in which top staff should be notified, usually starting with the warden.
- *Stating hostage information.* The plan clearly should state that no inmate with a hostage is to be released, and that no hostage has any authority.
- *Identifying key posts to continue to staff.* Some areas can be secured and their staff assigned to the escape hunt; others, such as the powerhouse and food service, must continue to operate; these positions should be identified in advance so no confusion results from removing staff from a critical post.

275

- *Establishing a command center.* This area includes not only internal communications and command functions, but also communication with local and state law enforcement personnel assisting in the escape hunt.
- *Recalling staff.* Using a current list of all employees and preestablished call-up procedures, off-duty employees should be told to report.
- *Notifying local law enforcement.* This section of the plan should specify who is authorized to notify local law enforcement personnel of the escape, and by what means; it also may involve distribution of escape flyers.
- *Using internal searches to apprehend hideouts.* The plan should specify internal search procedures to apprehend inmates who may be hiding inside the facility, awaiting darkness, fog, or some other time when it may be more favorable to try to escape the secure compound.
- *Planning external searches.* Plans/procedures need to be in place that include the use of force regarding "fresh pursuit," and coordination with allied agencies.
- *Establishing outside escape posts.* The plan should establish fixed and roving escape posts, identify the equipment that should go on each post, and describe the other procedures necessary to staff these posts, including issuance of equipment.
- *Providing staff support on escape posts.* The plan should provide for the regular relief, feeding, and checking of staff on remote posts.
- *Offering strategies for apprehending and restraining escapees.* The plan should provide staff with clear guidance on actions they should and should not take when apprehending an escapee. At least two officers should be present to search any escapees after they are captured; if only one officer captures an inmate, the inmate should stay "spreadeagled" on the ground until backup assistance arrives.
- *Notifying of capture.* When inmates have been captured, the procedures must specify who will notify all law enforcement agencies, communities, and the media.
- *Interviewing escapees.* The plan must ensure that any interviews with escapees are done in a way that does not hamper the criminal prosecution of an escapee by compromising any constitutional rights.

[Reprinted with permission from the American Correctional Association: "Chapter 7: Emergency Plans and Procedures," *Correctional Officer Resource Guide*, 3rd Edition, edited by Dan Bales, 1997, pp. 66-67.

Appendix C

Ethics

Emanating from all debates on ethics and morality is a charge to all citizens directing us to reflect on our personal moral and ethical principles for the betterment of our society. We need to review both our professional and personal ethical postures. Leaders of public and private agencies, professional disciplines, associations and corporations have an additional responsibility to develop ethical and moral codes of conduct to guide the personal behaviors of the individuals affiliated with their organizations. Doing so will help the organization attain its goals.

Those of us in correction, in view of the public scrutiny we endure, must move hastily to ensure that we have sound ethical codes in place. Those codes, consistent with the mission of the agency, should embody the intent of the applicable positions of the U.S. Constitution and state laws. Once we have implemented such codes, our concerns about scrutiny from the public and the media should diminish.

Every correctional employee should have a personal and professional sense of duty to forward the interest of corrections. That means our behavior on and off the work site should strive to be beyond reproach. We must strive to be honest, upright, virtuous, decent and credible. We should be lawful people, because law, not chaos, is the dominating principle in the universe.

Correctional leaders need to be ethical people. As Robert Noyce, the inventor of the silicon chip said, "I don't believe unethical people get ahead in business. If ethics are poor at the top, that behavior is copied down through the organization." The "do as I say but not as I do" approach to management can be disastrous to any organization.

For corrections to attain and sustain a posture beyond reproach, we must engage in self-regulation; regulation beyond that which is imposed on us by other authorized entities. To be successful in this endeavor, all correctional employees have a duty to report violations committed by co-workers. Why should we engage in such reporting? Because the image of all correctional employees and the overall health of our profession are at stake. We must become whistle blowers. For corrections to be successful and respected as a profession, we must demonstrate deference, respect, allegiance, loyalty and dedication to our missions and objectives.

We should report all behavior engaged in by co-workers on or off the

277

work site that could potentially bring discredit on us. Examples of such behavior include alcohol and drug abuse, converting government property to one's own, trafficking, dereliction of duty (including abusing inmates), and inappropriate language in the workplace. We must police ourselves. If we ignore problems, we should not expect to see the violators change for the better. It was J.W. Sullivan who once said, "Some people are like dirty clothes—they only come clean when they are in hot water."

Reasonable people will adapt to change when they know the results will be good. Individuals who only seek marginal accomplishments need only to make small sacrifices, but those who are to achieve much must sacrifice much.

[Reprinted with permission. Excerpt from "Examining the Role of Ethics in Corrections," by Harold W. Clarke, Director, Department of Correctional Services, Lincoln, Nebraska, *The State of Corrections*, Proceedings, ACA Annual Conferences, 1992, pp. 68-69.

Code of Ethics

4. **Supervision and Management**

   a. Supervisory staff at all levels are responsible and will be held accountable for the performance of personnel under their command.

   b. Supervisory staff must provide instructions to subordinates in a clear understandable manner.

   c. Supervisory staff at all levels are responsible for the implementation of policy and command decisions. Supervisory staff shall ensure compliance with policy through direction, supervision and inspection of subordinates.

   d. Supervisory staff at all levels are responsible for identifying and reporting deficiencies in operational procedures.

5. **Use of Alcohol and Controlled Substance**

   a. All staff are prohibited from using alcohol, illegal drugs or controlled substance while on-duty. Any use of such substance will be grounds for disciplinary action and/or immediate termination.

   b. Staff who are taking prescription medication under the direction of a physician, must immediately notify their immediate supervisor.

   c. Staff is prohibited from consuming, selling, purchasing or transporting alcoholic beverages while in uniform either on or off duty.

d. Staff shall cooperate fully with internal affairs in investigations to include polygraph examination or other testing to determine use of alcohol or illegal drugs. Refusal to cooperate will be grounds for dismissal.

e. Disciplinary action for violations of Standard Operating Procedures and General Orders may range from verbal reprimand to dismissal.

6. **Relationship With Inmates**

a. In the event that an immediate family member or close associate of any employee is confined at the Clarke-Frederick-Winchester Regional Adult Detention Center, the employee shall immediately notify the Administrator in writing.

b. Employees shall always maintain a professional relationship with inmates. All communication between employees and inmates (both written and verbal) shall be on a professional level. Employees shall never fraternize with or develop personal relationships with inmates.

c. Employees shall not display favoritism or preferential treatment to one inmate or group of inmates, over another.

d. No employee may deal with any inmate except in a professional relationship that will support the approved goals of the Clarke-Frederick-Winchester Regional Adult Detention Center. Employees must never accept for themselves or any member of their family, and personal gift, favor or service from an inmate or from any inmate's family or close associate, no matter how trivial the favor, gift or service may seem. No employee shall give any gifts, favors or services to inmates, their families or close associates.

e. No employee shall enter into any business relationship with any inmate or inmate's family (e.g. selling, buying or trading personal property), or employ them in any capacity.

f. Other than incidentally, no employee shall have any outside contact with an inmate, inmate's family or close associate, except for those activities which are an approved, integral part of functions of the Clarke-Frederick-Winchester Regional Adult Detention Center and a part of the employee's job description.

7. **Public Relations — Release of Information — Freedom of Speech**

a. Staff shall not release to any person or organization outside the employ of the Detention Center any official report, orders, procedures or any official document without the written approval of the Administrator.

b. Staff shall not remove from the premises, alter or destroy any report or document which is the property of the Detention Center.

c. Staff are not prohibited from providing their personal views relating to the operation of the facility, other government agencies or political organizations, as long as said staff specifically identifies his or her expressions as personal and the person in no way represents him or her self as a spokesperson for the Detention Center or Regional Jail Board.

d. Staff shall not provide the home address or telephone number of current or former employees of the Detention Center to any individual or organization outside of the Detention Center without permission of the individual and the Administrator of the facility.

[Excerpt from General Order Number 1, *Code of Ethics*, Clarke-Frederick-Winchester (Virginia) Regional Adult Detention Center, used with their permission.]

Index